IMAGES
of America

SAND LAKE REVISITED

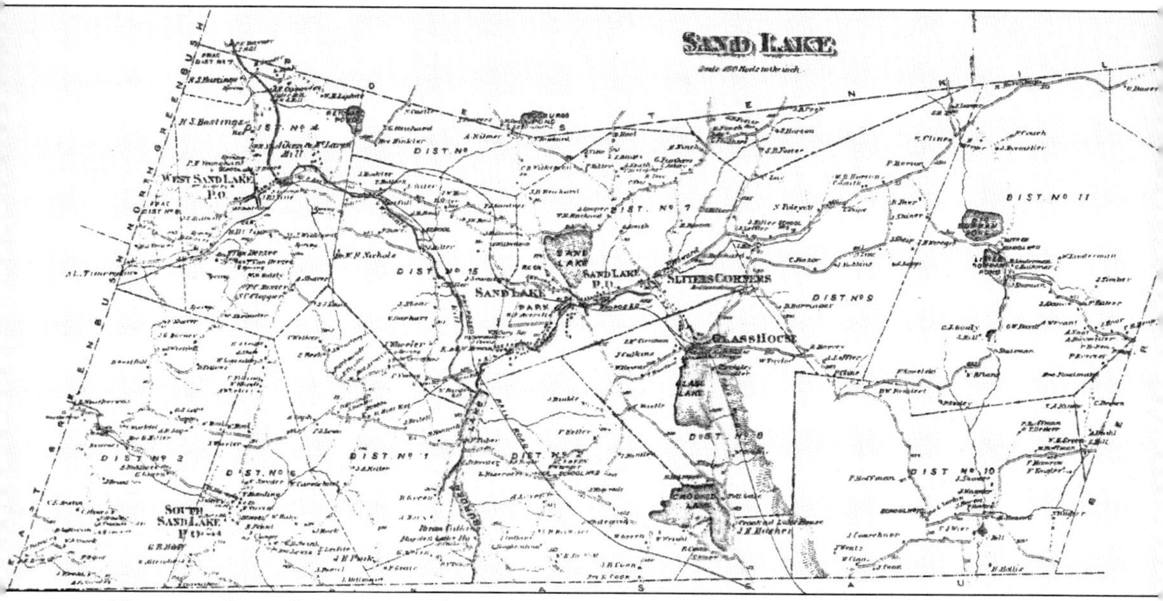

Town of Sand Lake Map. This map shows the town lines and school districts in 1876. It is from the *Rensselaer County Atlas*, by F. W. Beers, copyright 1876. (Sand Lake Historical Society Collection.)

On the cover: **Sharing the Road.** In the early days of the automobile, a horseless carriage and a horse-drawn carriage share the roadway in Sand Lake. (Alice Tifft.)

IMAGES
of America

SAND LAKE REVISITED

Mary D. French and Andrew St. J. Mace
for the Sand Lake Historical Society

ARCADIA
PUBLISHING

ISBN 978-0-7385-5475-4

Published by Arcadia Publishing
Charleston SC, Chicago IL, Portsmouth NH, San Francisco CA

Printed in the United States of America

Library of Congress Catalog Card Number: 2007925497

For all general information contact Arcadia Publishing at:
Telephone 843-853-2070
Fax 843-853-0044
E-mail sales@arcadiapublishing.com
For customer service and orders:
Toll-Free 1-888-313-2665

Visit us on the Internet at www.arcadiapublishing.com

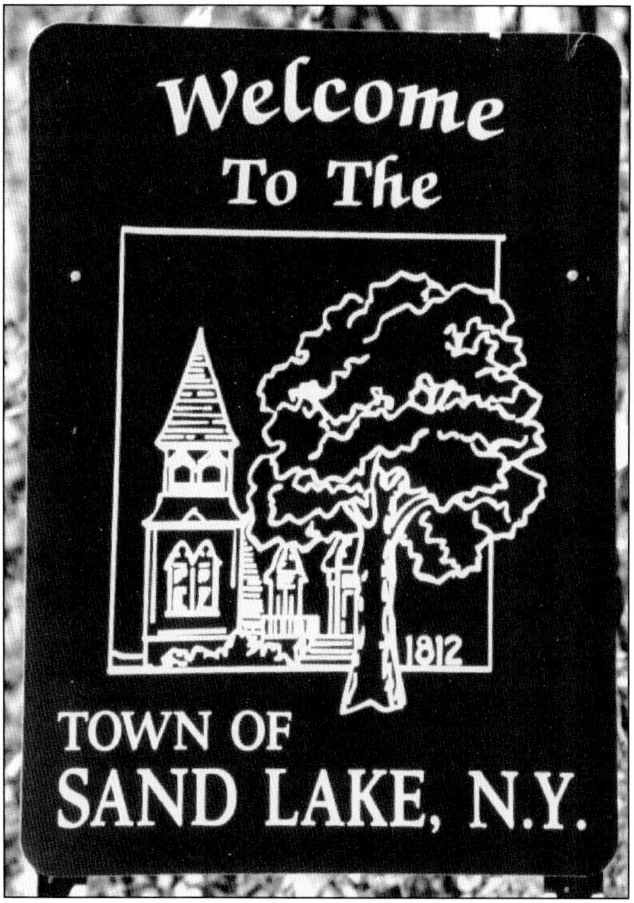

WELCOME TO THE TOWN OF SAND LAKE. This sign with the town hall and large oak tree, designated the Liberty Tree at the bicentennial celebration, bids a welcome to all at each major entry point to the town of Sand Lake (see *Sand Lake*, page 2). Since the sign's inception in 1985 the town hall location has changed. (Sand Lake Historical Society Collection.)

Contents

ACKNOWLEDGMENTS

Since *Sand Lake* was published in 2001, many persons have asked when the next book would be coming out. It took a request from Arcadia Publishing editor Pam O'Neil for previous coauthor Mary D. French to seek a coauthor for a new book. Andrew St. J. Mace agreed to be that person. The harmonious working relationship we had developed as editor and publisher of the Sand Lake Historical Society newsletter, *Historical Highlights*, carried over in the compiling of *Sand Lake Revisited*. Special gratitude is expressed to town historian Judy Rowe for her encouragement, guidance, and support in preparing *Sand Lake Revisited*. Thank you also goes to the Sand Lake Historical Society board of trustees for being our cheerleaders and sponsors.

We gratefully acknowledge the persons and organizations that made photographs and information available. They appear in parentheses at the end of captions and are listed in alphabetical order: aGatherin' (aG); Andrew Mace (AM); Aubrey Primeau (AP); Averill Park and Sand Lake Fire Company (APSLFC); Alice Tifft (AT); Ada and Wesley Miller (A&WM); Barbara Boughton, great-great-granddaughter of John Henry and Mary E. Meyers (BB); Beverly Duell-Moore (BD-M); Barbara Lerch Tourgee, Ph.D., daughter of Josephine Middleton Lerch (BLT); Barbara Stadtlander, granddaughter of Arthur and Alice Wilford (BS); Bruce V. Beck (BVB); Bonnie Wittmann (BW); Charles Viens (CV); Donald Carpentier (DC); Doris Gallant (DG); Daniel Holser (DH); Edith Gundrum (EG); Edna Pierce (EP); E. Richard Castle (ERC); Gordon French (GF); Gladys Larkin (GL); Helen Crape Guy (HCG); Irving Sewell (IS); John "Russ" Arekian Jr. (JA); Joan Bradley (JB); Joseph Connors Jr. (JC); Janet Oliver (JO); Judy Rowe (JR); Janine T. Budesheim (JTB); John Warren (JW); Kristine Zeronda (KZ); Larry Glander (LG); Lawrence Herzog (LH); Lawrence Malone (LM); M. Duane Wehnau (MDW); Martin Reid (MR); Michael St. Germain (MSt.G); Marjorie Werger (MW); Nancy Hilt Bonesteel (NHB); Nancy Soule Brown, daughter of Marjorie Roberts Soule and great-grandniece of Charles and Marcus Peck (NSB); Rensselaer County Historical Society, Troy, New York (RCHS); Robert I. Moore (RIM); Robert Shuey (RS); Robert Wagner (RW); Sand Lake Center for the Arts/Circle Theatre Players (SLCA/CTP); Sand Lake Historical Society Collection (SLHSC); Sgt. Walter A. Adams American Legion Post Unit 1021 (SWAAALPU); Town of Sand Lake Collection (TSLC); Virginia Bailey (VB); and William Mixter Green Jr. (WMG).

Sources are acknowledged within the caption or within the parentheses at the end of the caption.

INTRODUCTION

As with our first book, *Sand Lake*, the generous support of persons with postcards, pictures, ephemera, suggestions, and leads to sources of information have made working on *Sand Lake Revisited* an exciting excursion. Our challenge has been to design the book to stand on its own merit but to also assist any reader using both copies with an easy cross-reference. This was done by inserting a parenthetical reference to the earlier book: (see Sand Lake, page number). For those interested in additional sources, Sylvester's History of Rensselaer County relates a detailed and in-depth account of Sand Lake's earliest beginnings. Perhaps you have also seen the Sand Lake Historical Society's house tour booklets that are now out of print; *Sand Lake History*, begun by Madolyn Carpenter and Charles Viens in 1979; and *Pictorial History of Ulinesville 1776 to West Sand Lake 1976*, by Sanford Young and Charles Viens. Some of the pictures in those booklets are included in the chapters of this book.

About equidistant from Troy and Albany, Sand Lake is a flourishing township within Rensselaer County in New York State. Prior to 1791, Sand Lake was part of Albany County, within the Manor of Rensselaerwyck, which extended east and west from the Hudson River. It became part of Rensselaer County in 1791, and by 1812, Sand Lake had been formed from the towns of Greenbush and Berlin. When sections were removed to Greenbush in 1843 and to the town of Poestenkill in 1848, the present boundaries of Sand Lake were finally established. The hamlet of Sand Lake also lies within the township.

The receipt of many photographs of farming gave impetus to going back to Sand Lake's agricultural beginnings. This also included ice harvesting, which was necessary to keep food fresh, especially in the summer. The Wynantskill Creek's waterpower completed the industry emphasis of the first chapter with a saga of how a pair of long johns made it through Faith Mills from the start of raw wool to being tucked in a box and sent to the customer. The myriad of businesses needed for running the mills, maintaining the mill workers and their families, and providing goods and produce to the neighboring cities is captured in the second chapter, along with the Troy and New England Railway, which made transportation so accessible. Many merchants advertised in the Rensselaer County Agricultural and Horticultural Society brochure for the fair in 1904 on the present West Sand Lake School grounds. The third chapter reveals the reasons for the nickname "Upstate Coney Island." The attraction of seven lakes, country hospitality, and many recreational activities swelled the town's population during the summer months. We visit the carousel and its hand-carved animal rides close up. For a faster ride, we also visit a homemade iceboat known to go up to 80 miles per hour on the Hudson River but slowing to a less rapid speed on the Burden Lakes. Hotels and inns that have catered to their clients' recreational pursuits have been included here. Next we revisited and updated how the town's community services of fire, medical and ambulance services, armed services, and schools have been provided for over the years.

Contrast the first horse-drawn, hand-pumped fire apparatus with the now state-of-the-art facilities of the Averill Park and Sand Lake Fire Company, complete with an airboat for lake rescues. The town can be proud of the excellent quality and up-to-date services it has rendered to its citizens throughout the years.

Churches and visits to cemeteries speak to the spiritual needs and fellowship activities of the town's people. In 2006, 137 years after his death, Willard Griggs, the sheriff who lost his life in the line of duty, was honored at his monument in Sand Lake Union Cemetery. The Anti-Rent War had become violent.

In the last chapter, we make the acquaintance of persons, places, and residences we did not meet in our first book, or we meet them with a new focus. The first New York State botanist, Charles Peck, was a Sand Lake resident. For 30 years, Mary Hilt reported on Sand Lake happenings and gave a humorous twist to everyday life in her column in the *Troy Record*. On April 14, 2007, the naming of the Averill Park Post Office in honor of Maj. George Quamo, recipient of at least 26 medals, whose bravery saved the lives of 14 of his men, was celebrated.

With the passage of time, the area has changed. The many water-powered mills so prevalent along the Wynantskill Creek became obsolete or were ravaged by fire. The advent of the automobile brought freedom for travel to new places and for the commute to work. Several of the hotels, no longer a mecca for tourists, were either razed or burned down. Summer camps were winterized for year-round use. Gradually, Sand Lake has become a residential community, with most merchants in business for the maintenance of the local population. Reuse of buildings is encouraged. The former Sand Lake Presbyterian Church reused as the town hall now has had another rebirth as the Center for the Arts, home of the Circle Theatre Players, offering many venues of drama, concerts, art, theater, and music workshops.

As you read *Sand Lake Revisited*, we invite you to enjoy the collective efforts of all who contributed toward its coming to fruition and again have carried out the motto of the Sand Lake Historical Society: Preserving the Past—Enriching the Future.

—Mary D. French and Andrew St. J. Mace

Sand Lake Historical Society Logo. The Sand Lake Historical Society combined its motto and the image of a glassblower to create this logo. (SLHSC.)

One

Farming and Industry

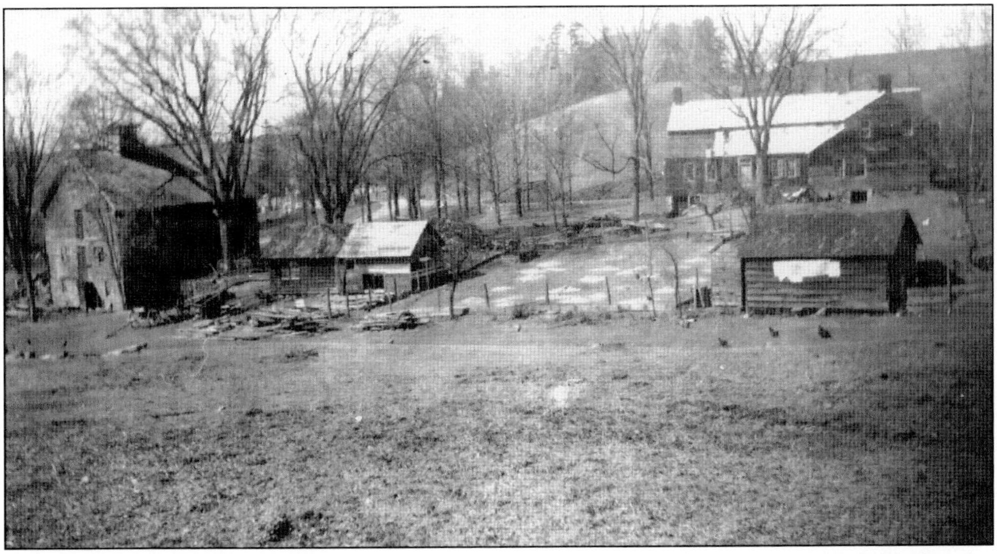

Middleton Farm Buildings. Farming was a major industry in the town of Sand Lake. On a 1788–1790 map of the hamlet of West Sand Lake (see page 118), the property consisting of 325 acres on lots 4 and 5 was the largest parcel and the home of Barent Uline. It was owned by the Middleton family from 1915 to the 1930s. Carl and Emma Wicks owned the house from 1953 to 1984. It is currently the home of Gary Ashley. The smallest of the other farm parcels on the map was 67 acres for the church lot on the current Parker Road. Several photographs that follow give a glimpse of farming when horsepower preceded motorized equipment. With the Wynantskill Creek so pronounced on the map, other industry centered around the water, which was harnessed to power the machinery for woolen, grist, paper, and hosiery mills. As the Wynantskill Creek joined the Hudson River in Troy, it furnished waterpower for the largest waterwheel in North America at the Burden Iron Company (see *Sand Lake*, page 78). (BLT.)

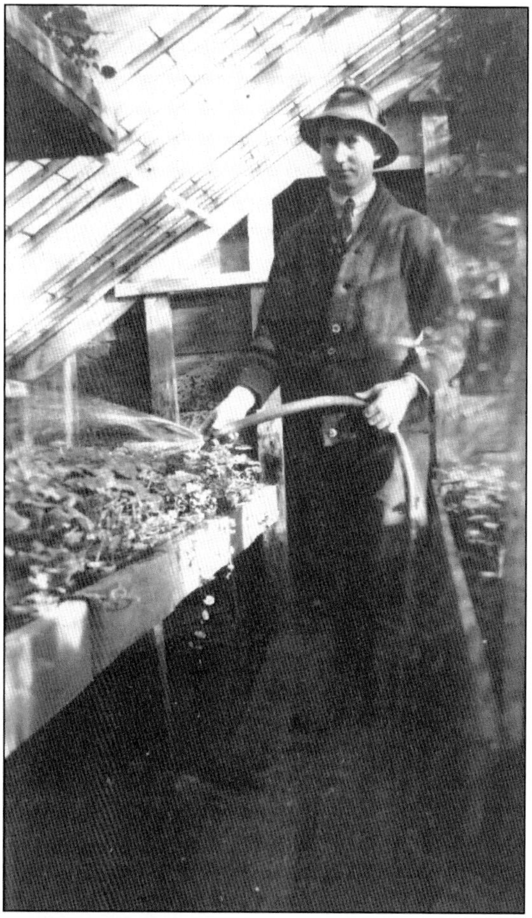

Middleton Greenhouse. Alfred Middleton had a greenhouse from the 1920s to the 1950s near Sherwin's Laundry on Route 150. (BLT.)

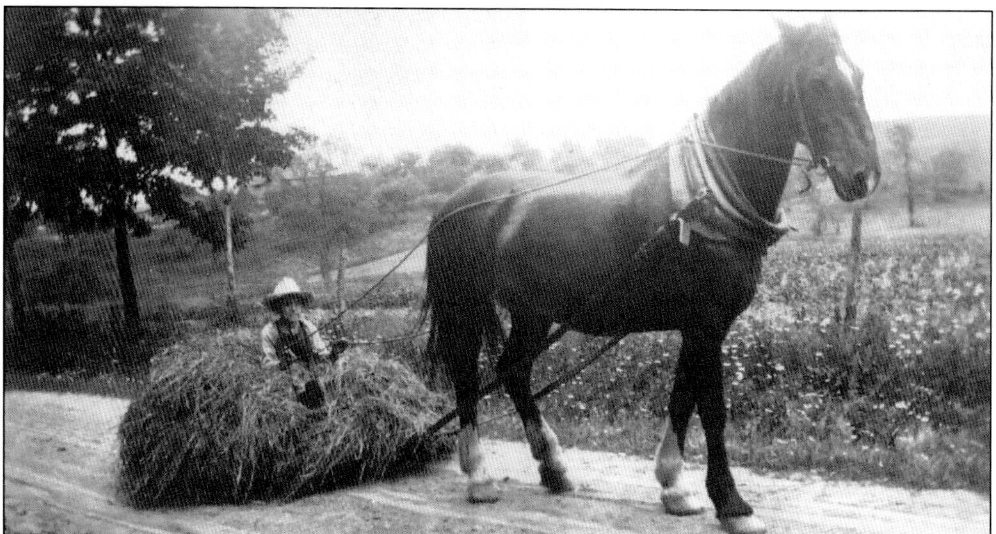

Hayride. Taking hay from the loft to where it was needed to feed cattle or horses was a good time for a fun ride. (BLT.)

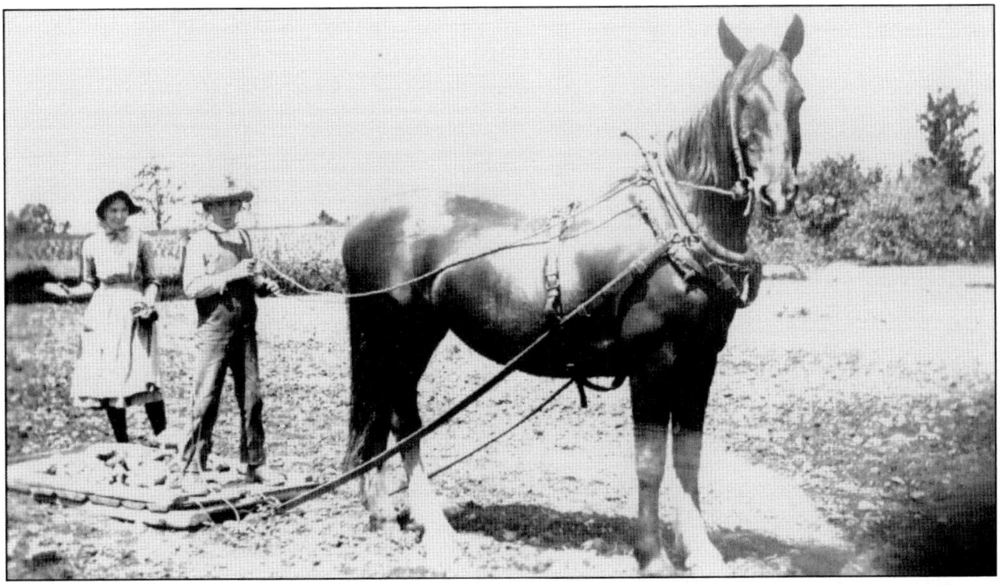

STONE BOAT. Stones in a field prohibited a good yield of crops. Emmor and Josephine Middleton use their horse-drawn stone boat to move the load, which gets heavier as they clear stones and rocks from the field. (BLT.)

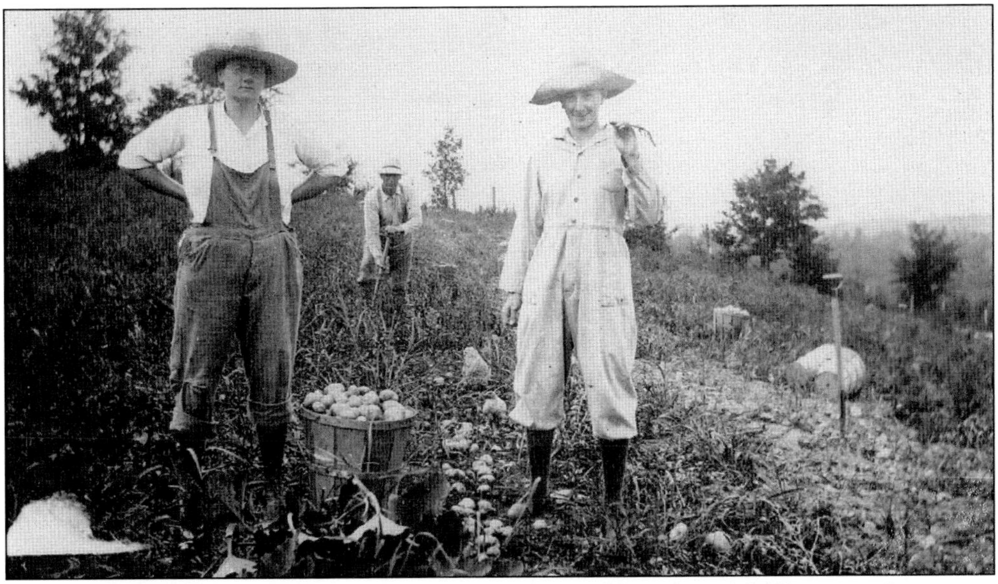

POTATO HARVEST. From left to right, Maggie, John, and Josephine Middleton are harvesting potatoes around 1912 at Sliter's Corners in the area of Route 150 and County Routes 50 and 55. In the 1800s, the hamlet of Sand Lake used to be known as Sliter's Corners. (BLT.)

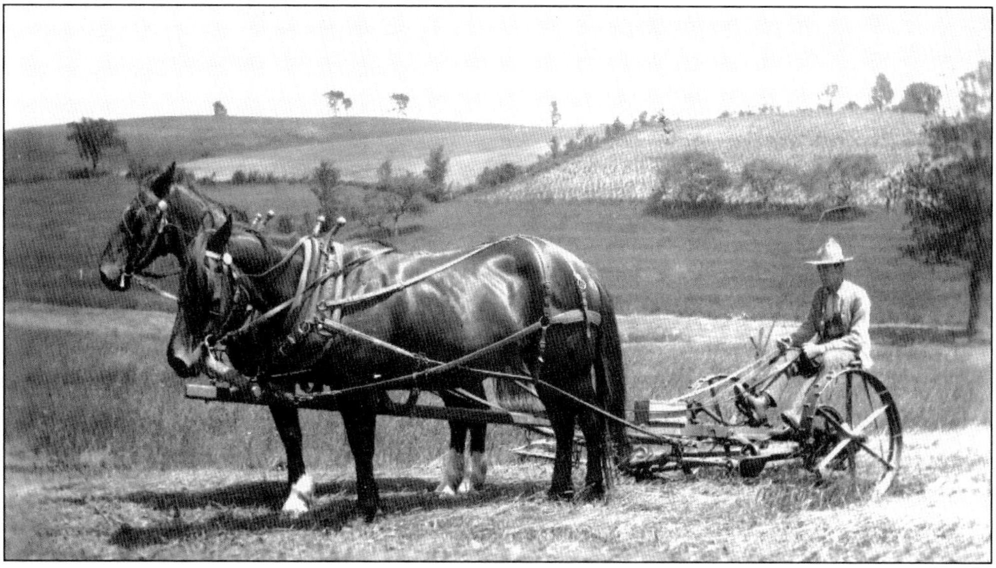

CUTTING HAY. Sitting on a mower pulled by horses to cut hay may have been hard on the seat but much easier on the back compared to a man wielding a scythe. (BLT.)

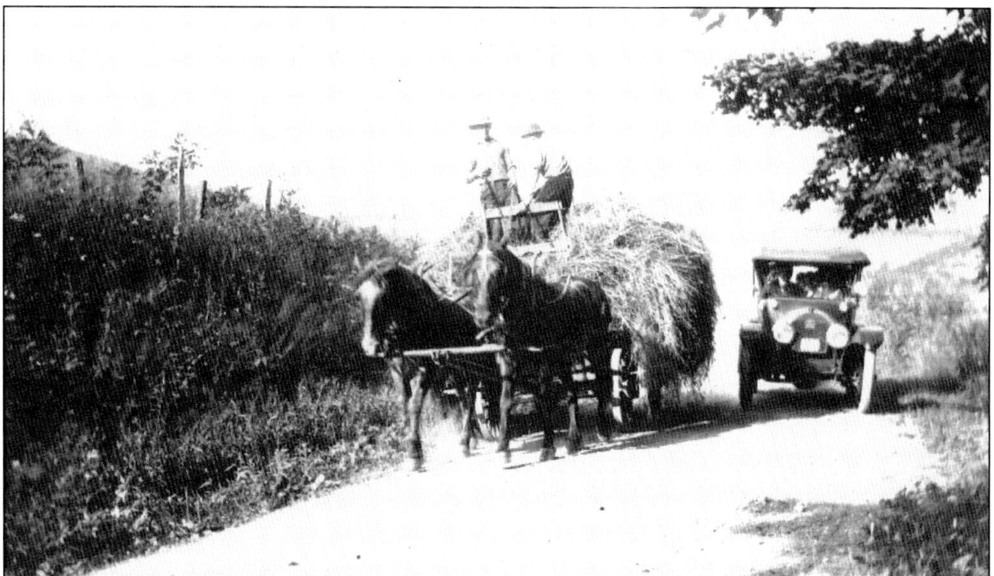

LOAD OF HAY. The hay is loaded and on its way to the barn and hayloft. The car is passing to reach its destination. The farmhands riding have hot work ahead unloading the hay into the loft. They may envy the passengers in the car who seemingly have an easier life. (BLT.)

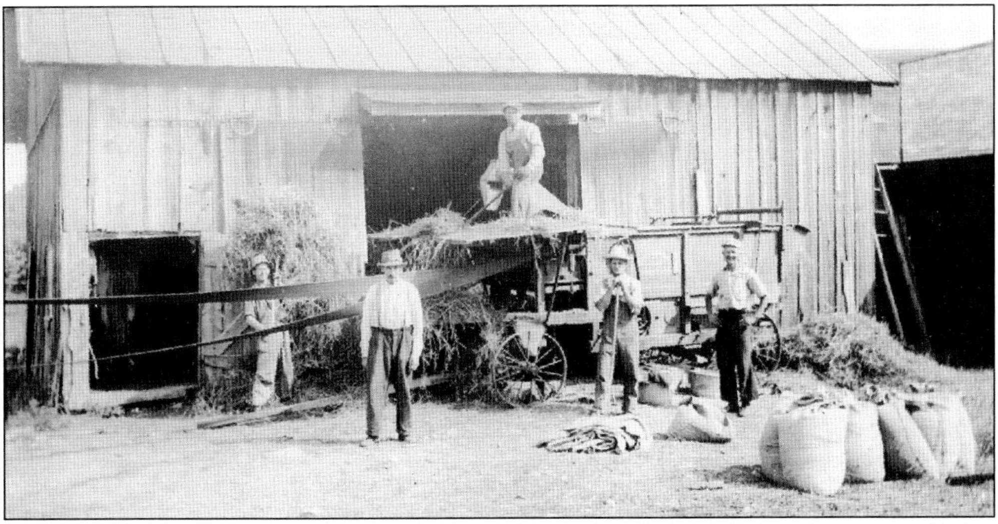

THRESHING OATS. Seen here are, from left to right, unidentified, Edith Gundrum's grandfather John Teal, her father, Walter Teal, on top of the load of oats, William Deckett, and unidentified. Walter Teal owned the threshing machine and would go from farm to farm during the harvesting season. (EG.)

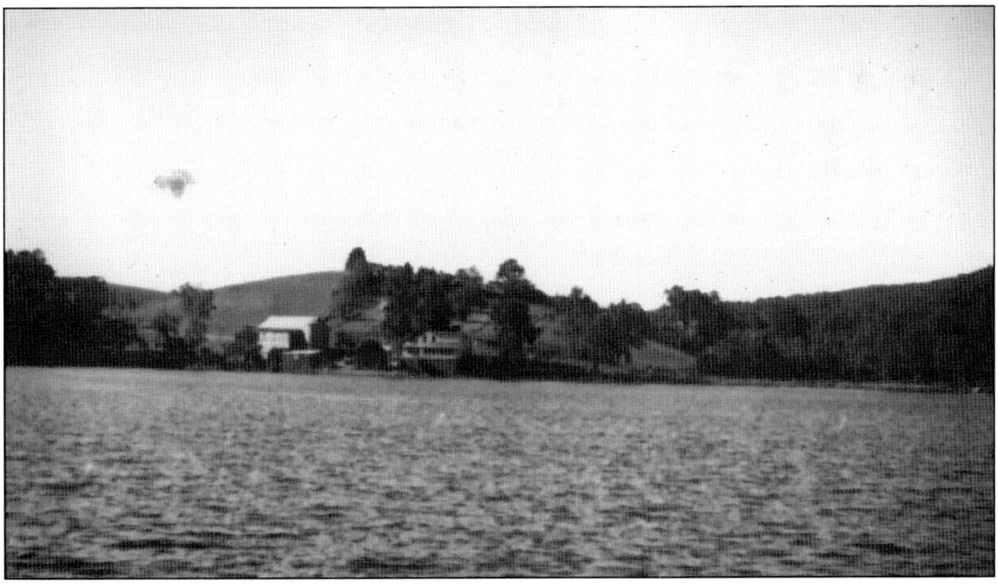

SMITH FARM. Beginning his farm with 45 acres, Elmer C. Smith Sr. expanded it to 140 acres from Crooked Lake on both sides of Eastern Union Turnpike to the shoreline of Glass Lake. It was a self-supporting farm. Milking cows provided an income, as did the ice he cut on Crooked Lake. Several Smith sons received acreage from the farm. The house is now the residence of Richard Rusin. (JA.)

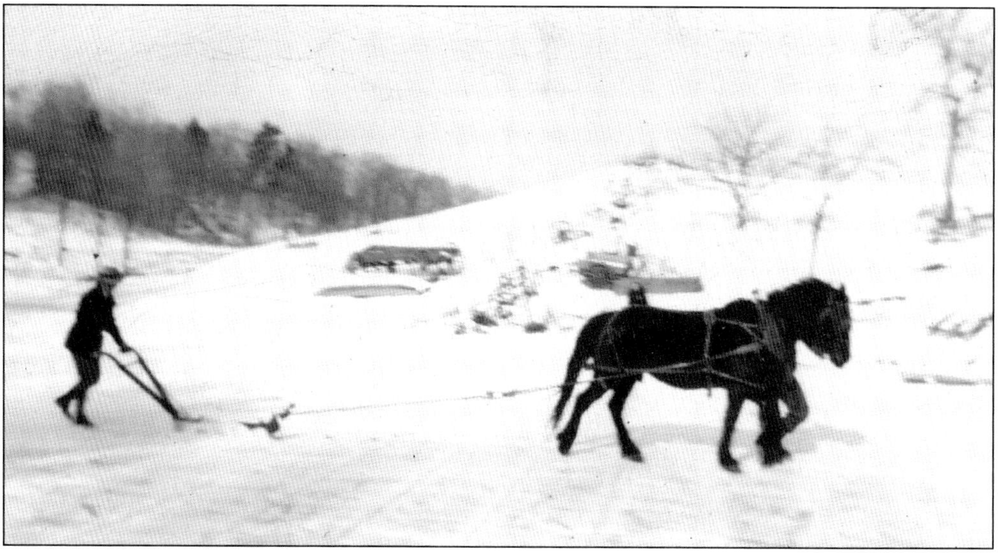

PLOWING THE LAKE FOR ICE HARVESTING. William Mixter Green Jr. is removing snow from Burden Lake to score the surface of the ice for cutting. (WMG.)

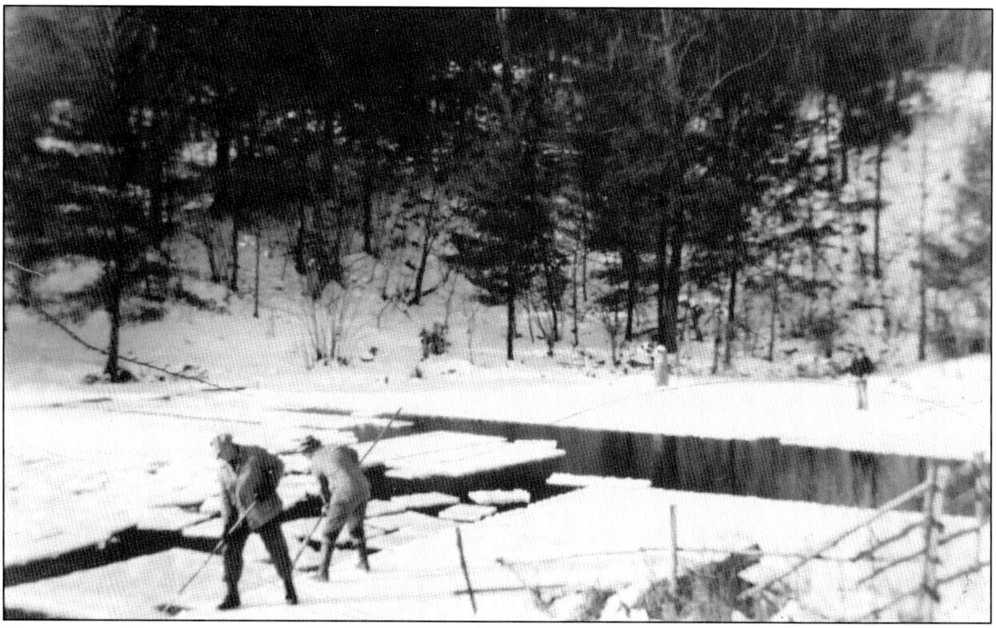

BREAKING CAKES FROM THE ICE FLOE. This distance picture shows more of the lake, which has been cut for the ice harvesting. The harvesters are breaking cakes from the large ice floe to fit on the runway to be sent to the icehouse. (WMG.)

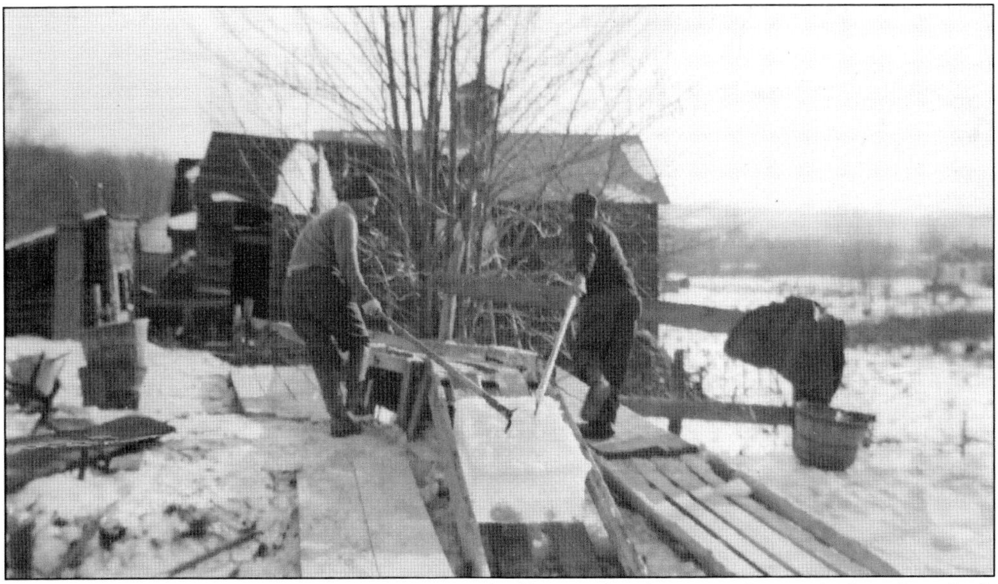

Pulling Ice up the Runway. Blocks scored off 32 inches by 22 inches and 12 inches thick weighed 300 pounds. Two men are needed to pull these cakes of ice up the ramp to go into the icehouse. (WMG.)

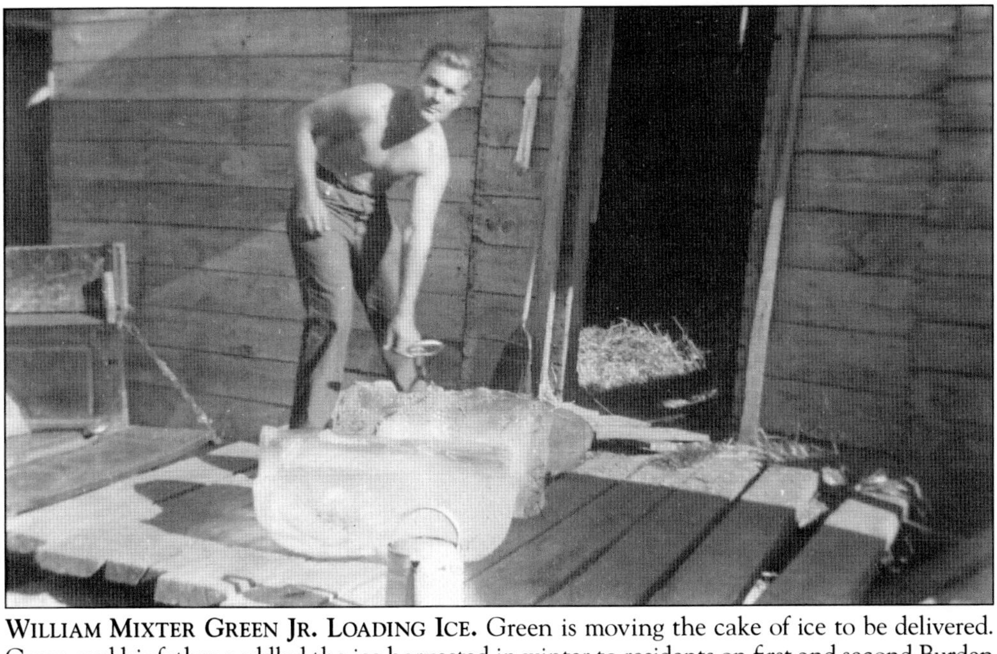

William Mixter Green Jr. Loading Ice. Green is moving the cake of ice to be delivered. Green and his father peddled the ice harvested in winter to residents on first and second Burden Lakes. The 300-pound blocks were subdivided into six 50-pound blocks. Blocks cost 15¢ for 25 pounds and 25¢ for 50 pounds. Before electric refrigerators, ice for iceboxes was an everyday necessity. (WMG.)

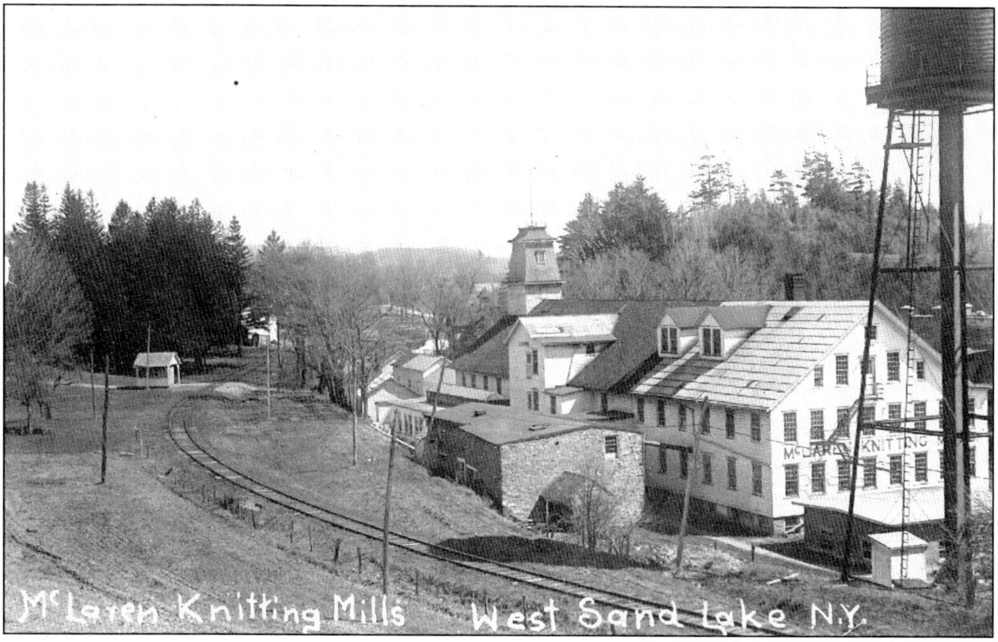

McLaren Knitting Mill. The Troy and New England Railway tracks can be seen behind the McLaren Knitting Mill (see *Sand Lake*, pages 24 and 25). Cedarhurst would be on the other side of the tracks. (RS.)

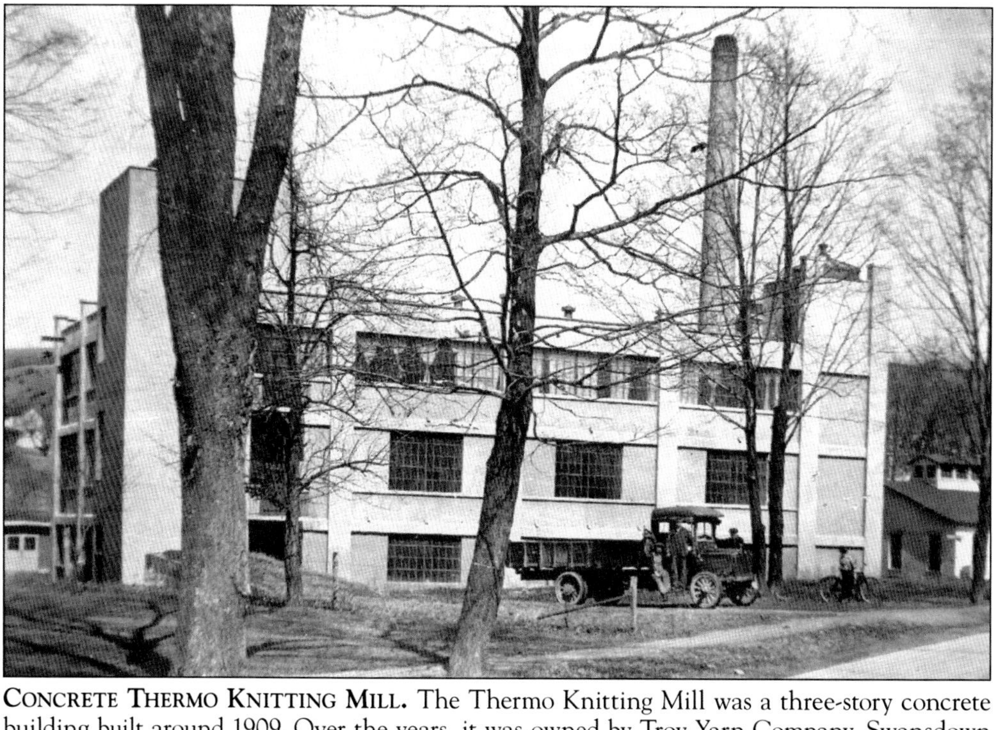

Concrete Thermo Knitting Mill. The Thermo Knitting Mill was a three-story concrete building built around 1909. Over the years, it was owned by Troy Yarn Company, Swansdown Knitting Company, Faith Mills, and again by Troy Yarn Company. It is now owned by Bonded Concrete. (CV.)

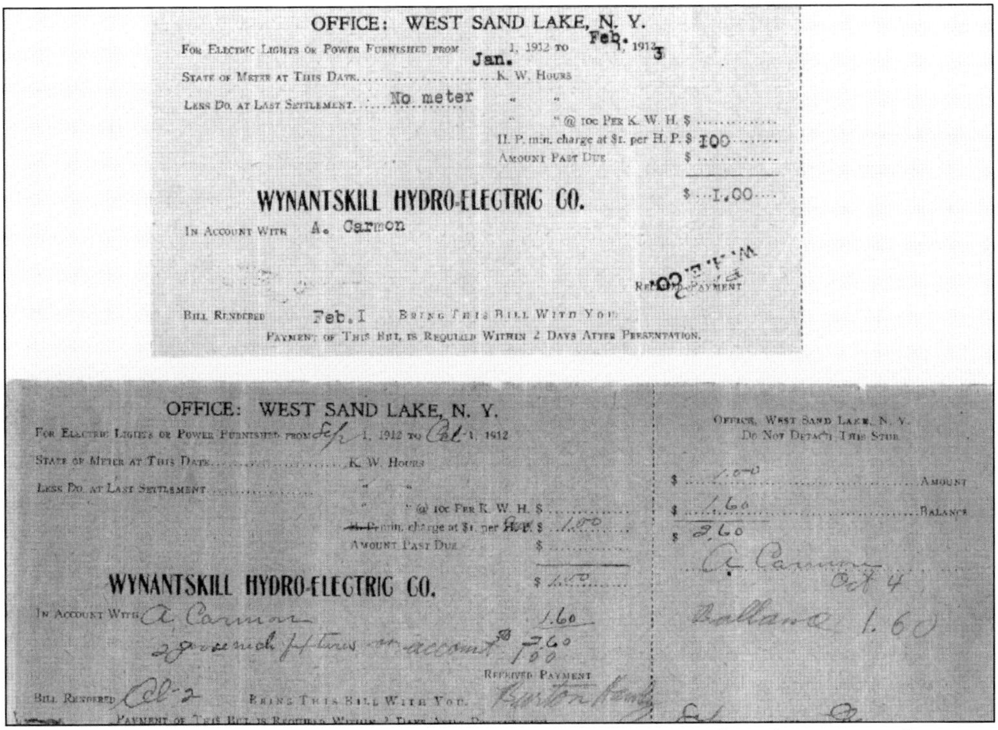

OFFICE: WEST SAND LAKE, N. Y.

For Electric Lights or Power Furnished from Jan. 1, 1912 to Feb. 1, 1913

State of Meter at This Date.......................K. W. Hours

Less Do. at Last Settlement.......No meter

" @ 10c Per K. W. H. $ ....

H. P. min. charge at $1. per H. P. $ 100

Amount Past Due $ ....

WYNANTSKILL HYDRO-ELECTRIC CO. $ 1.00

In Account With A. Carmon

Received Payment

Bill Rendered Feb. 1 Bring This Bill With You.

Payment of This Bill is Required Within 2 Days After Presentation.

OFFICE: WEST SAND LAKE, N. Y.

For Electric Lights or Power Furnished from Sep 1, 1912 to Oct 1, 1912

State of Meter at This Date.......................K. W. Hours

Less Do. at Last Settlement

" @ 10c Per K. W. H. $

H. P. min. charge at $1. per H. P. $ 1.00

Amount Past Due $

WYNANTSKILL HYDRO-ELECTRIC CO. $ 1.00

In Account With A. Carmon 1.60

2 gooseneck fixtures on account 2.60

1.00

Received Payment

Bill Rendered Oct 2 Bring This Bill With You.

Office, West Sand Lake, N. Y.

Do Not Detach This Stub

$ 1.00 Amount

$ 1.60 Balance

$ 2.60

A. Carmon

Oct 4

Balance 1.60

WYNANTSKILL HYDRO-ELECTRIC COMPANY BILLS. A. Carmon purchased minimum electricity for $1 and two gooseneck fixtures for $1.60 in September 1912 and minimum electricity for $1 in January 1913. (aG.)

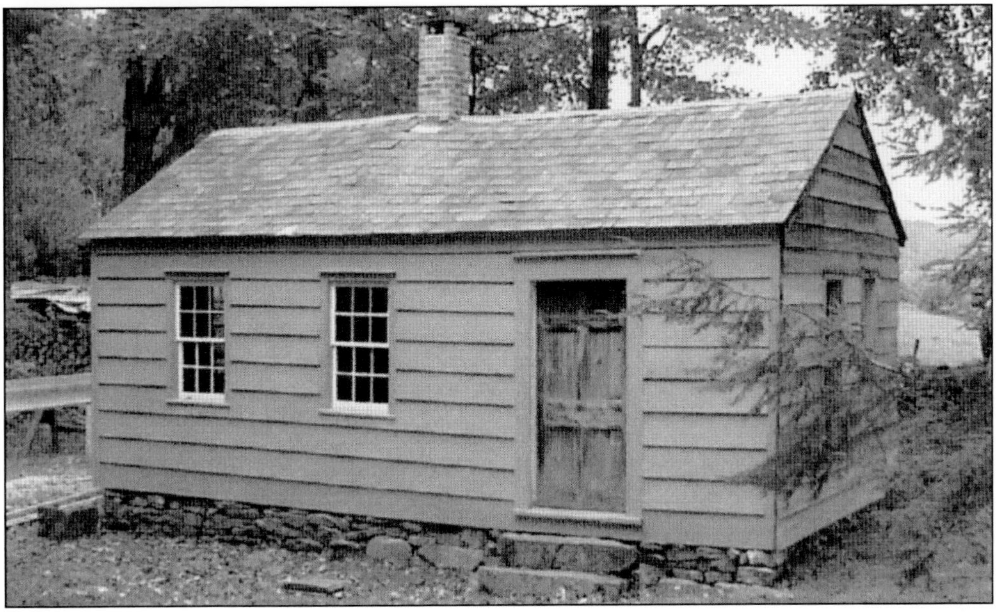

TINSMITH SHOP. Clarence Bame's tinsmith shop and property had been sold to Miller's Market for its parking lot and was about to be demolished. Donald Carpentier requested and received time to remove the building, numbered board by numbered board. He reassembled it in his reconstructed 19th-century, early-American, Eastfield Village in East Nassau. (TSLC.)

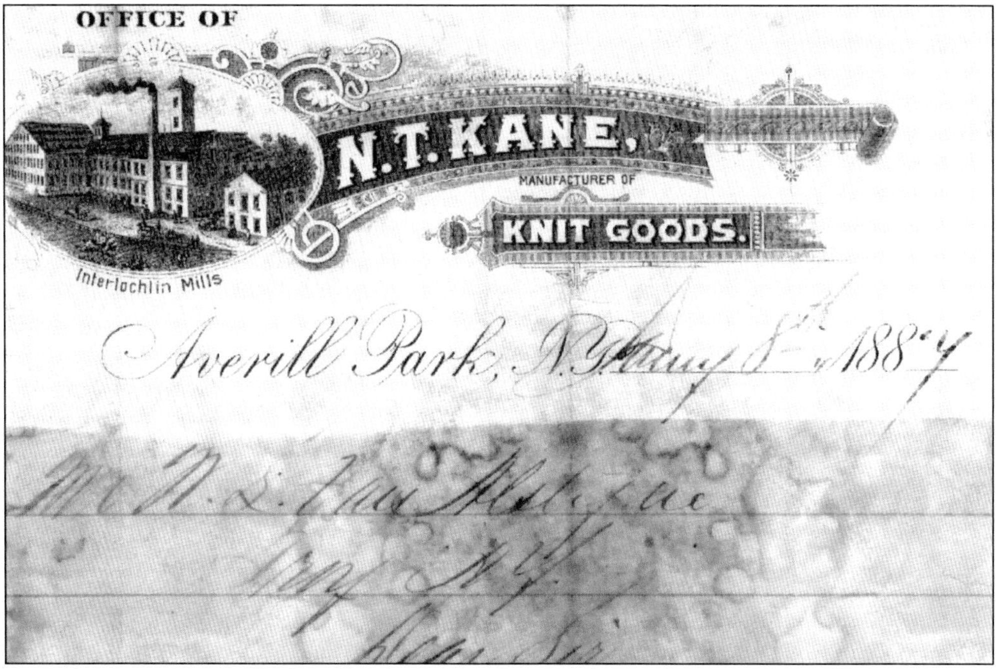
OFFICE OF

N. T. KANE,

MANUFACTURER OF

KNIT GOODS.

Interlochlin Mills

Averill Park, N.Y. Aug 8th 1884

Mr N. L. Van Alstyne

Troy N.Y.

N. T. KANE LETTER. The letterhead on this correspondence illustrates the mill of N. T. Kane Knit Goods. In this August 8, 1884, letter, Kane wrote to N. L. Van Alstyne about a policy and asked for a rebate on his cancelled policy. (aG.)

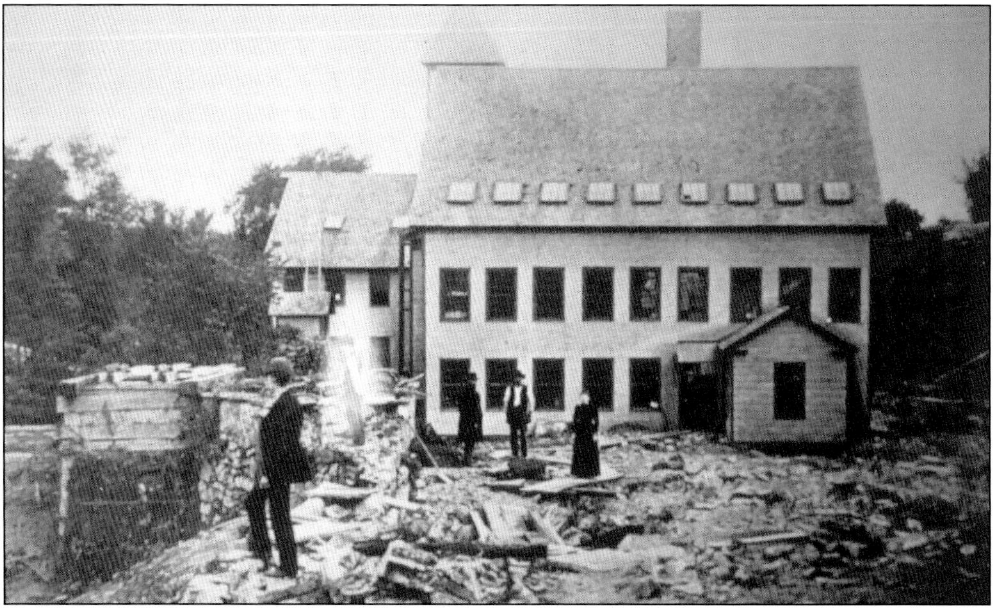

THE FLOOD AT KANE'S MILL, AVERILL PARK. As recounted in the *Troy Record* on January 8, 1946, "Kane's Mill on Burden Lake Road lost the two bridges on Kane's pond during the flood of 1891. Dams at Knowlson's Mill, McLaren's Mill, and McConihe's factory were also destroyed. At West Sand Lake, near the gristmill on the main highway, a gully 100 feet wide and 30–50 feet deep was gouged out, and the bridge below Milo Hastings' gristmill went down the Wynantskill Creek" (SLHSC.)

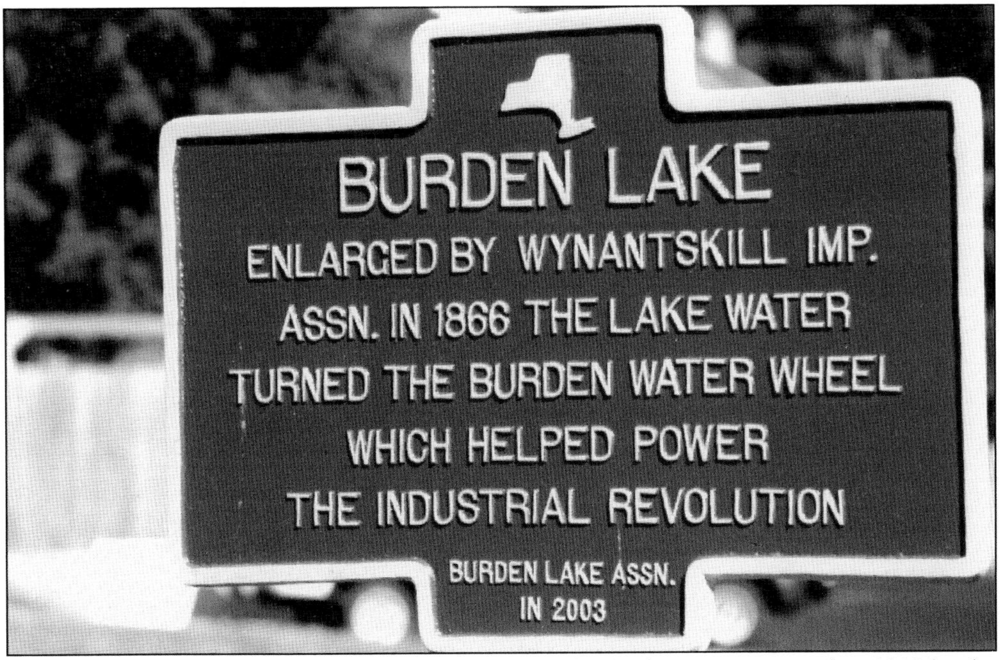

BURDEN LAKE HISTORICAL MARKER. As stated on the marker, it was erected in 2003 by the Burden Lake Improvement Association. It has been missing since 2005. (SLHSC.)

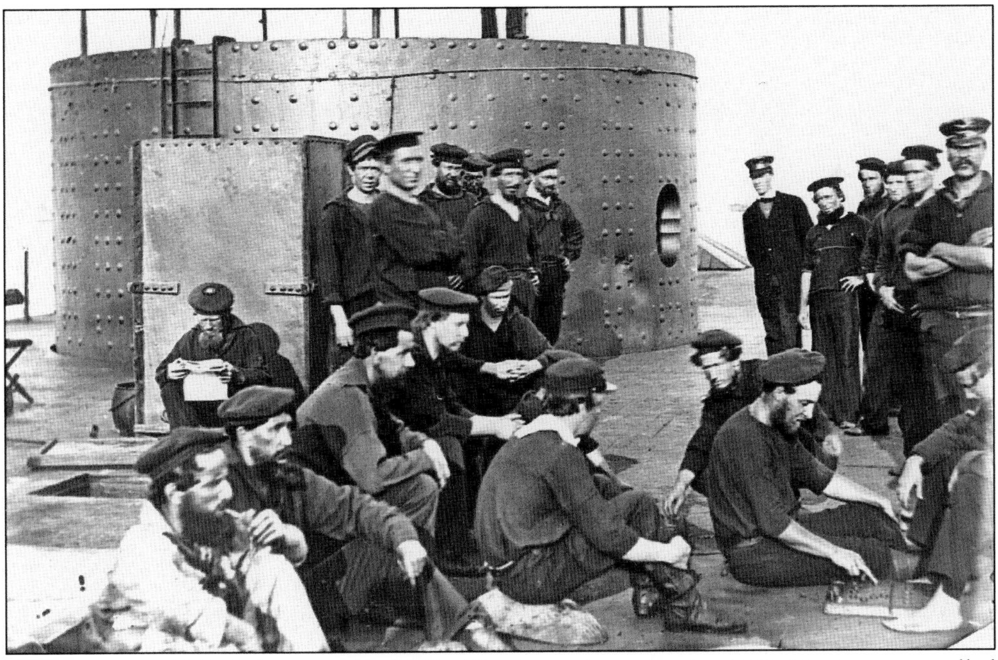

CREW OF THE USS MONITOR, C. 1862. The iron plates for the USS *Monitor* were rolled in 100 days from scrap iron at the Albany Iron Works of Troy. Waterpower to run the mill originated in the town of Sand Lake, with the headwaters of the Wynantskill Creek at Crooked Lake and Glass Lake. The water flow was controlled at Glass Lake and the Burden Lakes. Here the USS *Monitor*'s crew is taking a break on the deck with the ship's famous turret clearly in view. (RCHS.)

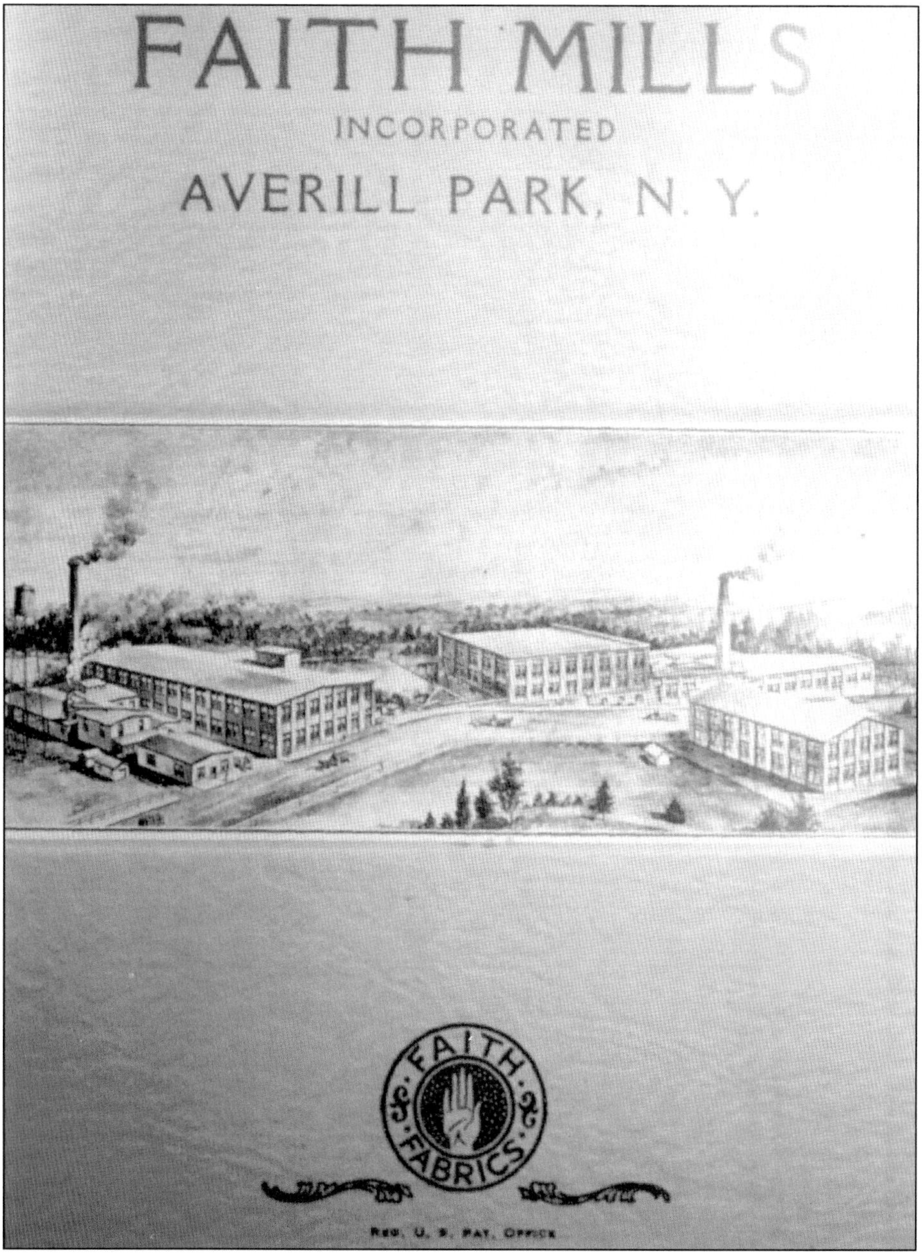

Faith Mills Complex. Cotton or wool from the warehouse (right in foreground) went to the storage building across the road and downstairs to the mixing room. Wool or cotton/wool blend was pulled into fine pieces, picked apart by many needles, and blown through pipes up to main mill (left). Fed into carding machines, it came out as yarn and was spun onto long rollers. Upstairs the mule spinners fed the ends from the rolls through the machine, and the yarn segments were spun onto bobbins. On the same floor, bobbins were fed into the knitting machines to knit the material, which was washed, dyed, and dried in the basement, before it went up one floor to the cutting room. Underwear sections were cut, tied into bundles, and sent up one more floor to the sewing room. The number of pieces sewn determined a person's pay. Completed garments were inspected for flaws and sent down one floor to be shipped. (SLHSC.)

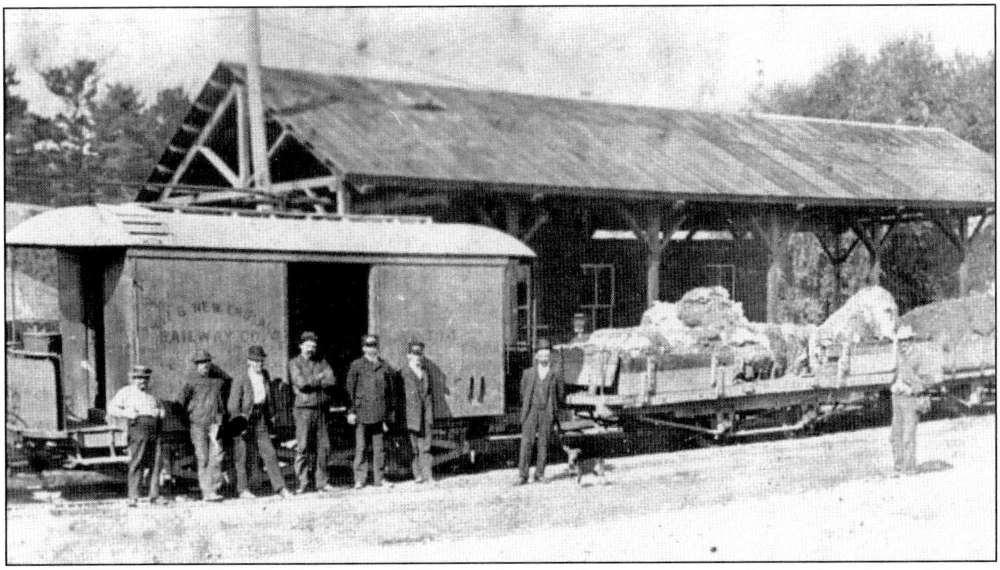

Troy and New England Railway Freight Cars. These cars, loaded with shoddy (reclaimed wool), are on their way to mills in Sand Lake. This is the beginning of the set of long johns shown as the finished product in the next picture. (CV.)

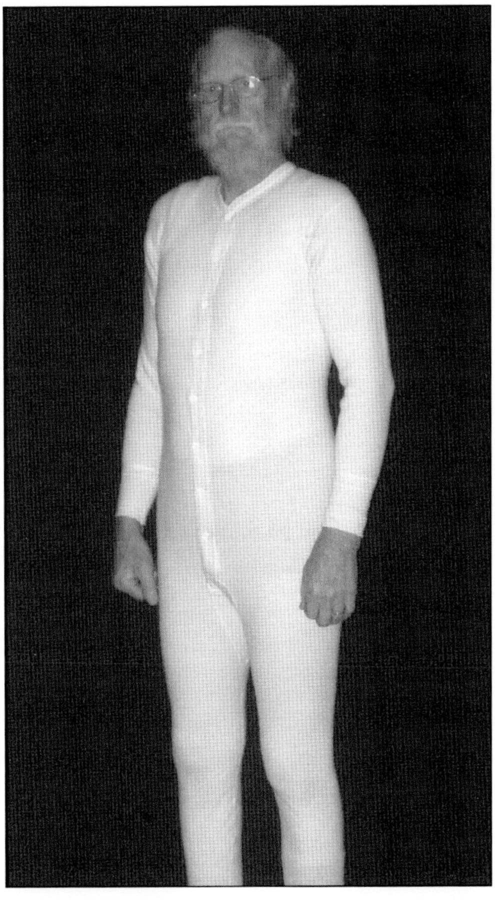

Faith Mills Long Johns. Eugene Langley is wearing 100 percent wool long johns; the entire manufacturing process was completed at Faith Mills (see *Sand Lake*, pages 66–70). As a fully integrated mill complex, every family knew persons who worked in receiving, picking, carding, spinning, knitting, washing, dyeing, drying, cutting, sewing, labeling, packaging, shipping, or office work. (TSLC.)

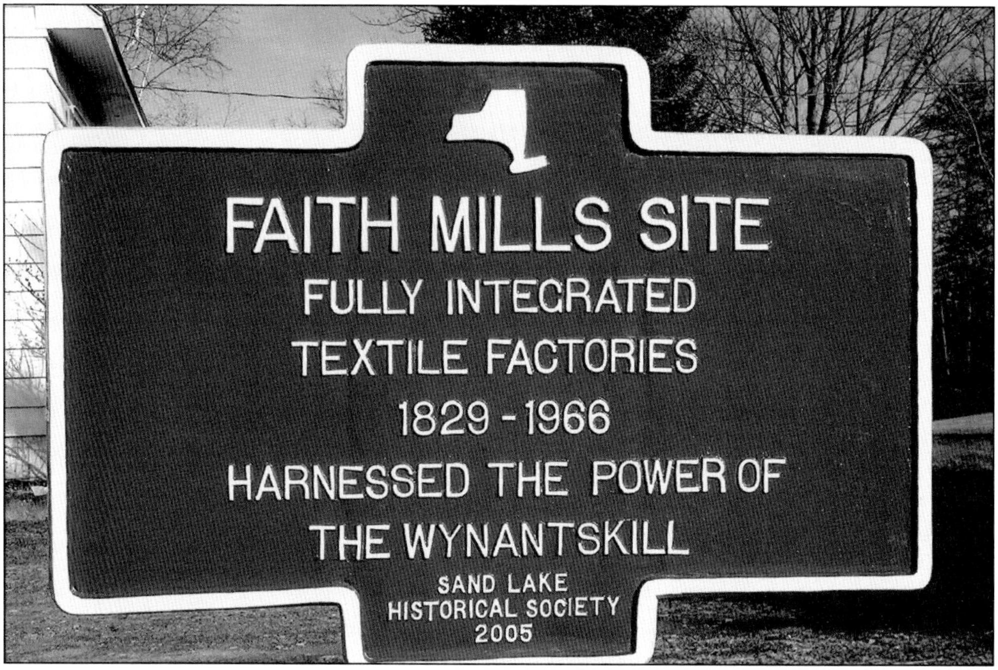

FAITH MILLS MARKER. This historical marker now reminds everyone of the complex industry at the Faith Mills site, made possible with the harnessed power of the Wynantskill Creek. (SLHSC.)

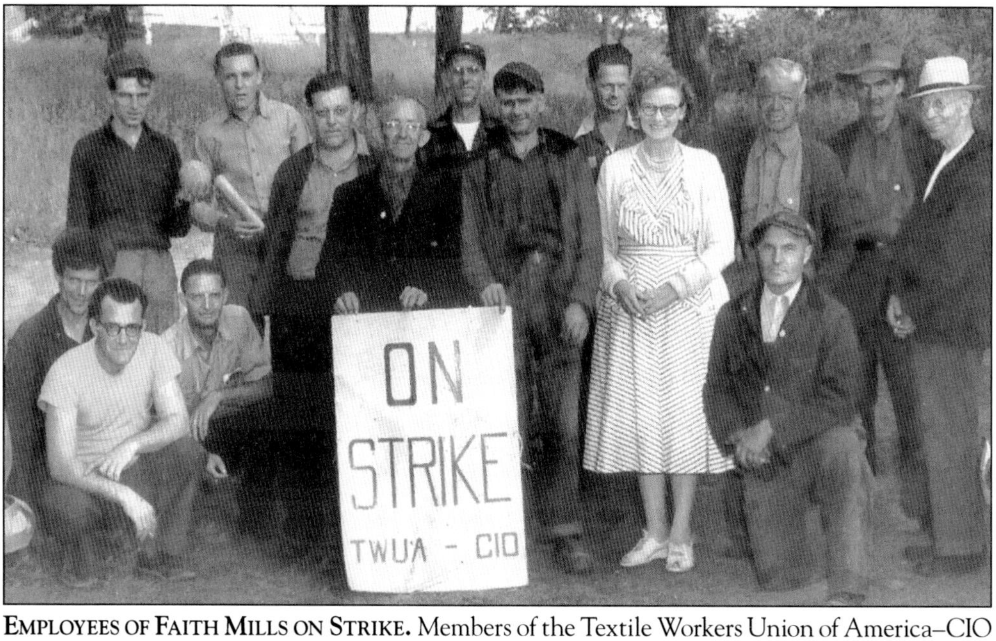

EMPLOYEES OF FAITH MILLS ON STRIKE. Members of the Textile Workers Union of America–CIO (Congress of Industrial Organizations) seen here are, from left to right, (kneeling) two unidentified, William Williams, and Edward Ernst; (standing) unidentified, Joseph Biittig Jr. (holding a ball of yarn and a shuttle), Edward Warren, Fred Fields, two unidentified, William Miller, two unidentified, Robert Berry Sr., and Arthur Butler. The employees went on strike in 1962; true to their word, the owners closed Faith Mills. (JW.)

Two

BUSINESS

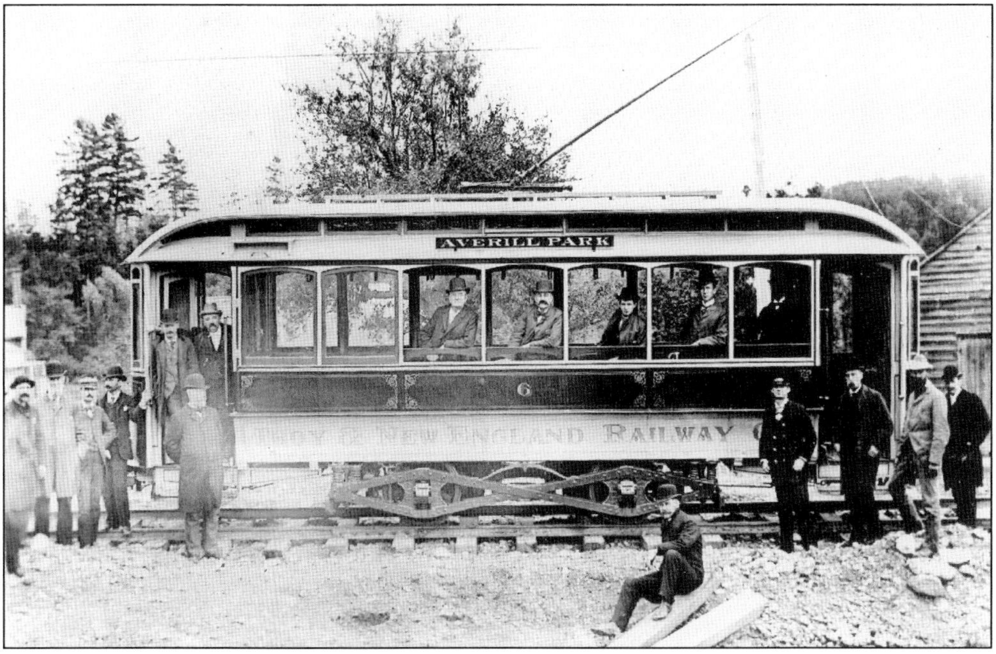

FIRST TROY AND NEW ENGLAND TROLLEY CAR RUN. The first run of the Troy and New England Railway was on September 30, 1895, with car No. 6. It also had the honor of being the last car to run on March 31, 1925. During those years, the trolley had a major impact on the business community of Sand Lake. In the summer, there could be up to five cars bringing passengers from Troy at the Albia station to tourist attractions in Sand Lake. Younger folks wanted the seat behind the motorman for the best view and the strongest breeze. When the trolley arrived at the hill into the Averill Park station, it would be going very slowly. Then the youngsters would often jump off the trolley and run alongside. Freight was also transported by the trolley. Passenger services, hotels, markets, pharmacies, and funeral homes were all businesses in Sand Lake. (MSt.G.)

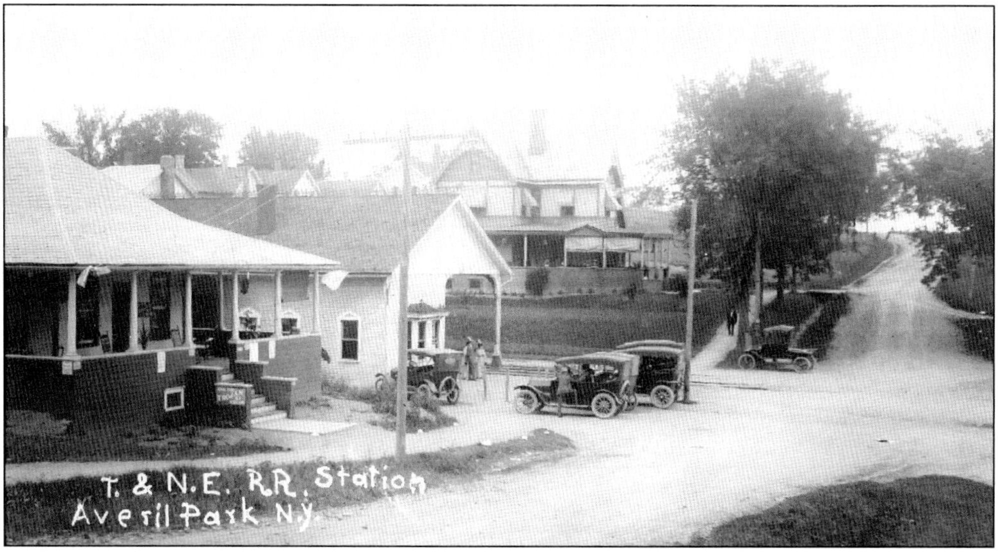

TROY AND NEW ENGLAND RAILWAY. Here one sees that cars have taken over the horse-and-buggy livery for taxi service. (A&WM.)

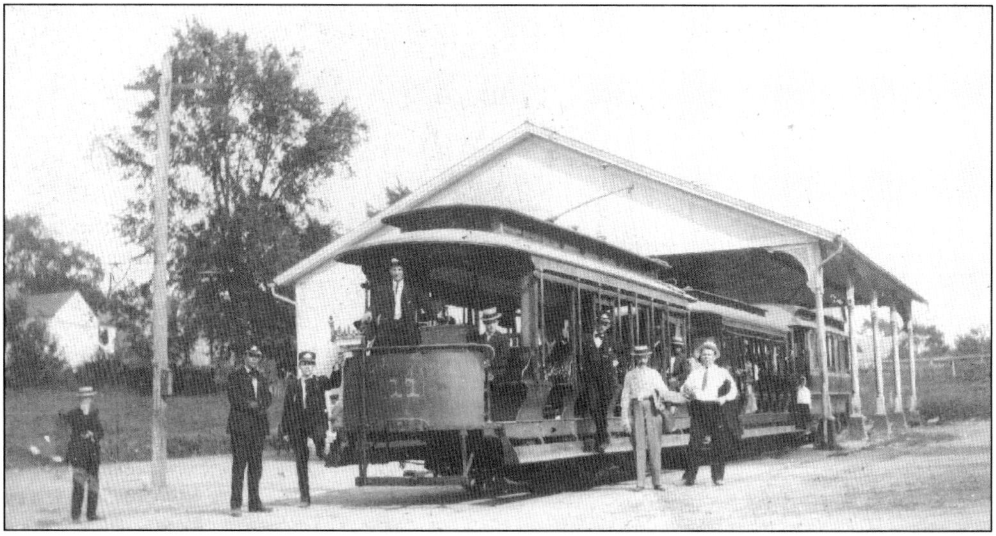

THREE CARS AT AVERILL PARK STATION. Three cars of the Troy and New England Railway are at the Averill Park station. These open cars had seven bench seats across the width of car and would hold six passengers, who boarded from either side. There was room on the front and back platforms for additional passengers to stand. The claim of the 1904 advertisement on the next page for 150 passengers on a trip could be met. (JC.)

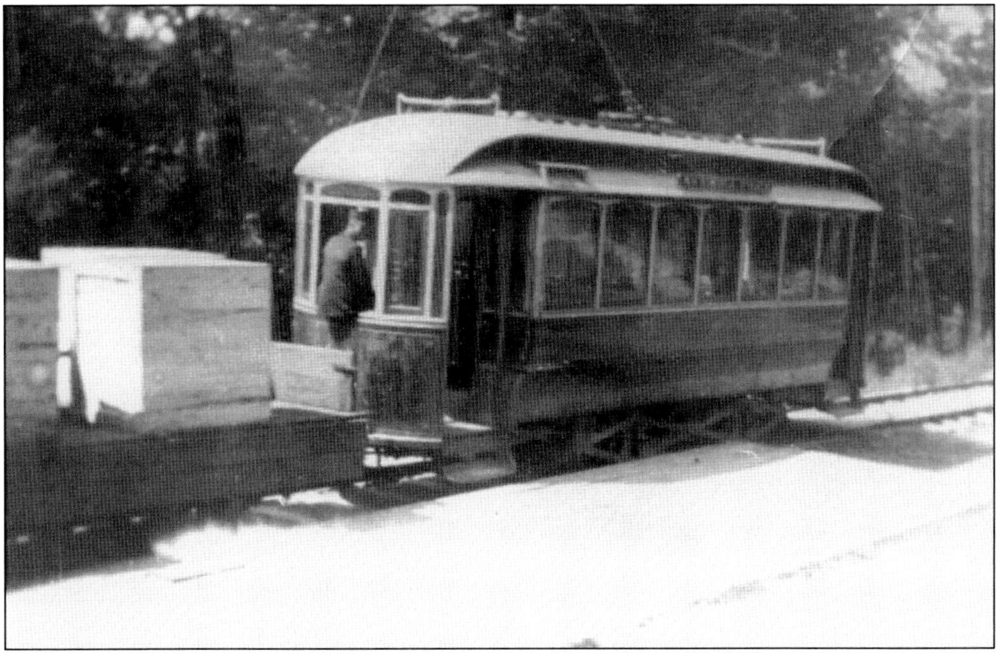

TROY AND NEW ENGLAND RAILWAY FREIGHT TRAILER. This car and freight trailer, with a very large load on its way to Averill Park, made a stop at the Brookside Park station. (CV.)

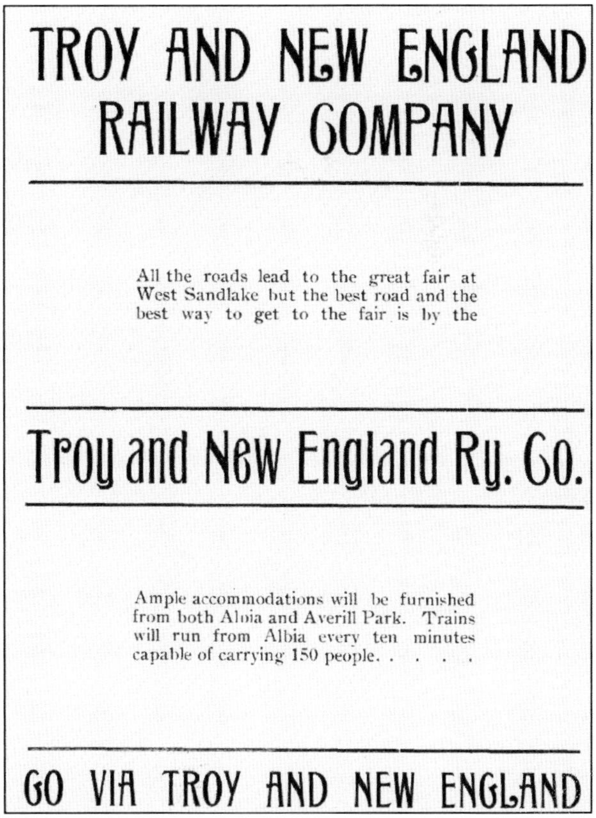

TROY AND NEW ENGLAND RAILWAY COMPANY

All the roads lead to the great fair at West Sandlake but the best road and the best way to get to the fair is by the

Troy and New England Ry. Co.

Ample accommodations will be furnished from both Albia and Averill Park. Trains will run from Albia every ten minutes capable of carrying 150 people. . . . .

GO VIA TROY AND NEW ENGLAND

TROY AND NEW ENGLAND RAILWAY ADVERTISEMENT. In the brochure for the 1904 Rensselaer County Agricultural and Horticultural Society Fair, Troy and New England Railway touted a frequency of every 10 minutes and the capacity of 150 passengers. (SLHSC.)

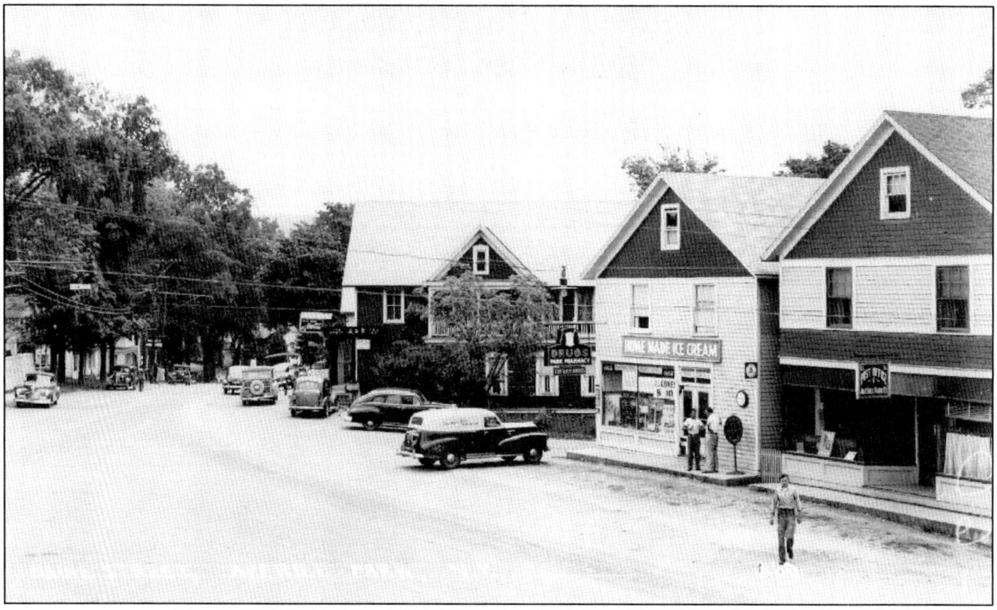

AVERILL PARK VILLAGE. On right side of the road are the Great Atlantic and Pacific Tea Company (A&P), Park Pharmacy, and Averill Park Post Office. (EG.)

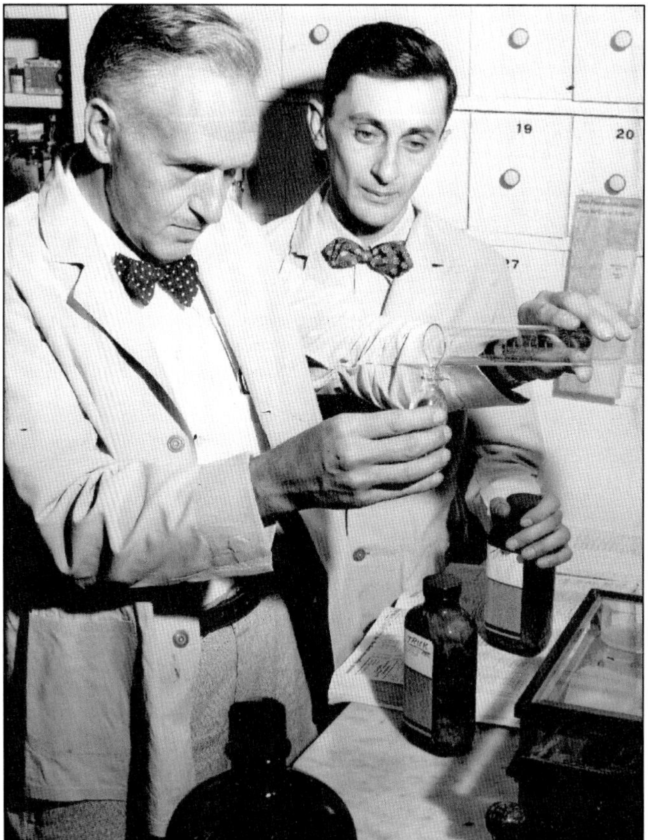

BENJAMIN SILBERG. Shown here are Benjamin Silberg (left), owner of the Park Pharmacy in Averill Park, and his assistant pharmacist Martin Toomajian. Silberg helped develop a new antiarthritic hormone compound in 1950. When Jerry Lewis was a high school pupil in 1942, he was hired as a soda jerk (see *Sand Lake*, page 48). (MSt.G, *Times Union* photograph.)

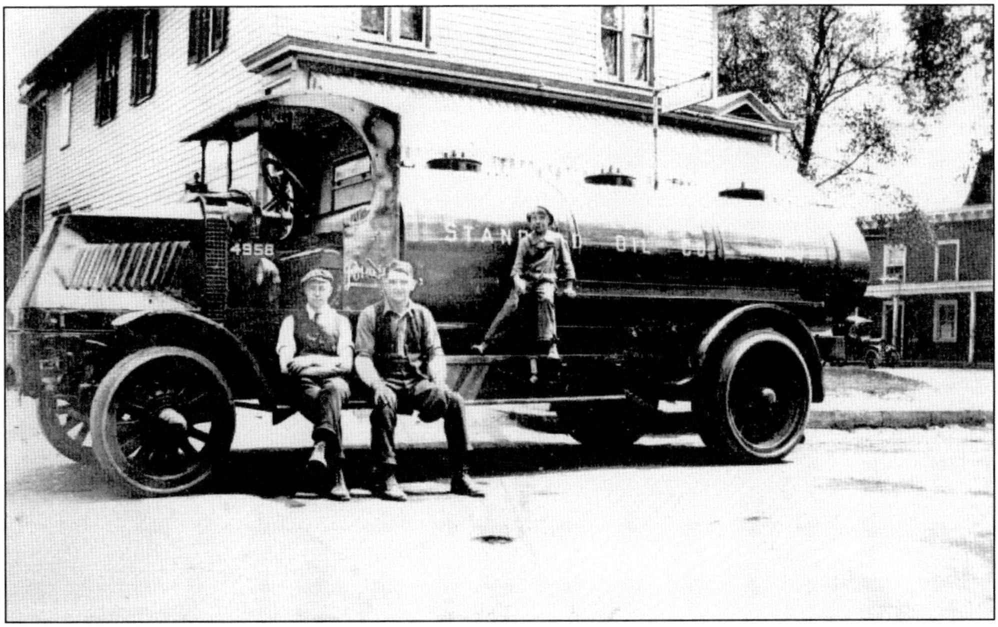

Legenbauer Gas and Oil Company. Adam "Mindy" Legenbauer is seated, without a cap, on the running board of the Standard Oil Company truck in front of Stout's Hardware Store around 1920. In 1966, this building became Legenbauer Gas and Oil Company and was operated by Mindy's sons Charles and Paul. Mindy's grandson James Legenbauer has been operating the business since 1997. (TSLC.)

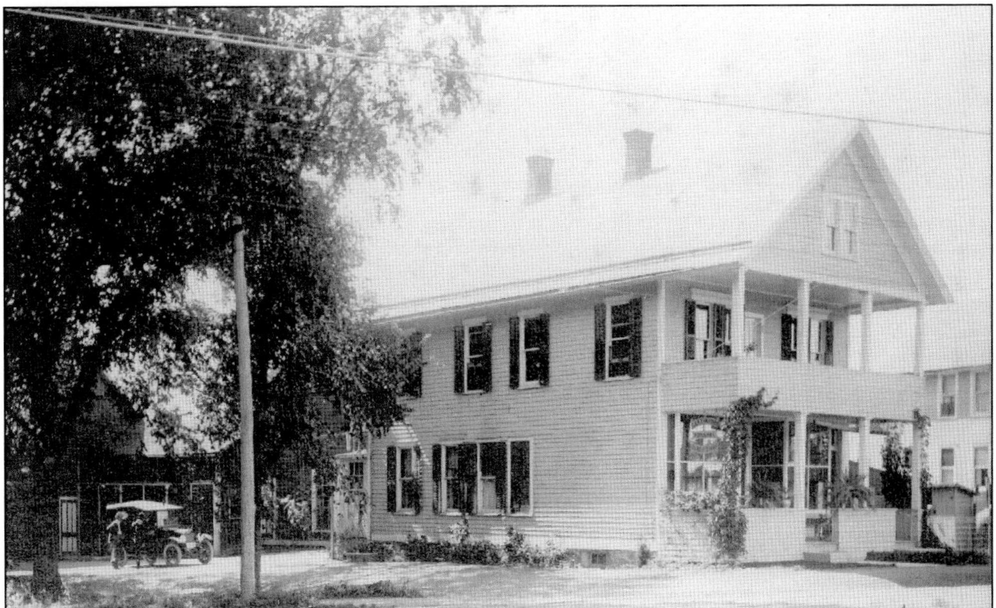

First Larkin Funeral Home. Willis Larkin Sr. and his wife, Alice, had their first funeral home in the first house behind the Jiffy Mart on Old Route 66. Both were funeral directors and embalmers. Willis also had a stable and ran a horse-and-buggy livery business from the large barn behind the house (see page 71). (GL.)

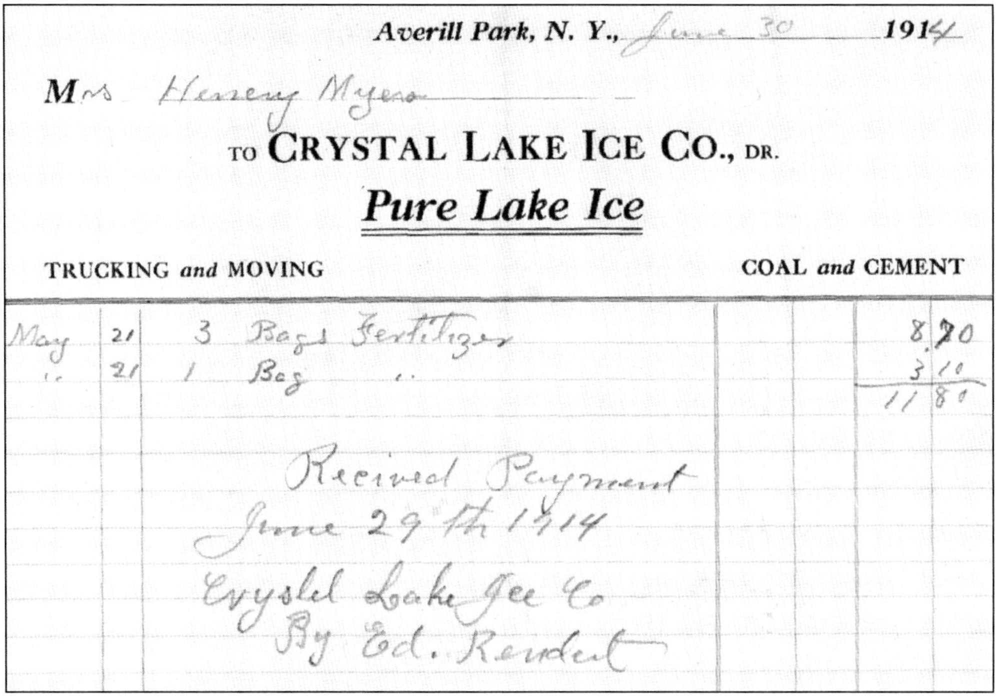

Averill Park, N. Y., June 30 1914

Mrs Henry Myers

TO CRYSTAL LAKE ICE CO., DR.

Pure Lake Ice

TRUCKING *and* MOVING

COAL *and* CEMENT

May	21	3 Bags Fertilizer	8.70
"	21	1 Bag "	3.10
			11.80

Recived Payment
June 29th 1914
Crystal Lake Ice Co
By Ed. Rendert

CRYSTAL LAKE ICE COMPANY. Edward Rendert diversified his company to sell coal, cement, and fertilizer as well as ice. As the letterhead indicates, he would also do trucking and moving. (BB.)

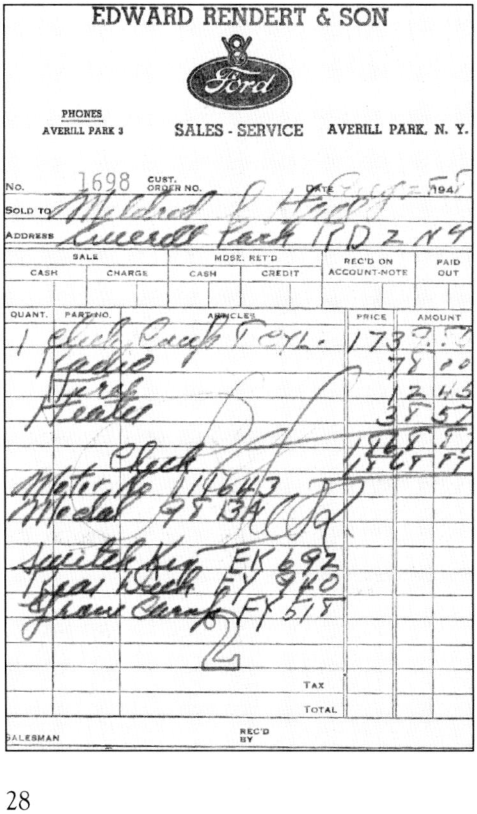

EDWARD RENDERT & SON

PHONES
AVERILL PARK 3

SALES - SERVICE

AVERILL PARK, N. Y.

NO. 1698 CUST. ORDER NO. DATE 194

SOLD TO Mildred

ADDRESS Averill Park RD 2 NY

SALE CASH CHARGE | MDSE. RET'D CASH CREDIT | REC'D ON ACCOUNT-NOTE | PAID OUT

QUANT.	PART NO.	ARTICLES	PRICE	AMOUNT
1		Coupe 8 CYL.		
		Radio	78	00
			12	45
		Heater	38	57
			1868	87
		Check	1868	87
		Motor No		
		Switch Key EK 692		
		EY 940		
		FX 518		

TAX

TOTAL

SALESMAN

REC'D BY

EDWARD RENDERT AND SON CAR RECEIPT. In August 1948, a new eight-cylinder coupe with a radio and heater cost $1,868.87, and the sale was completed with one payment. (MSt.G.)

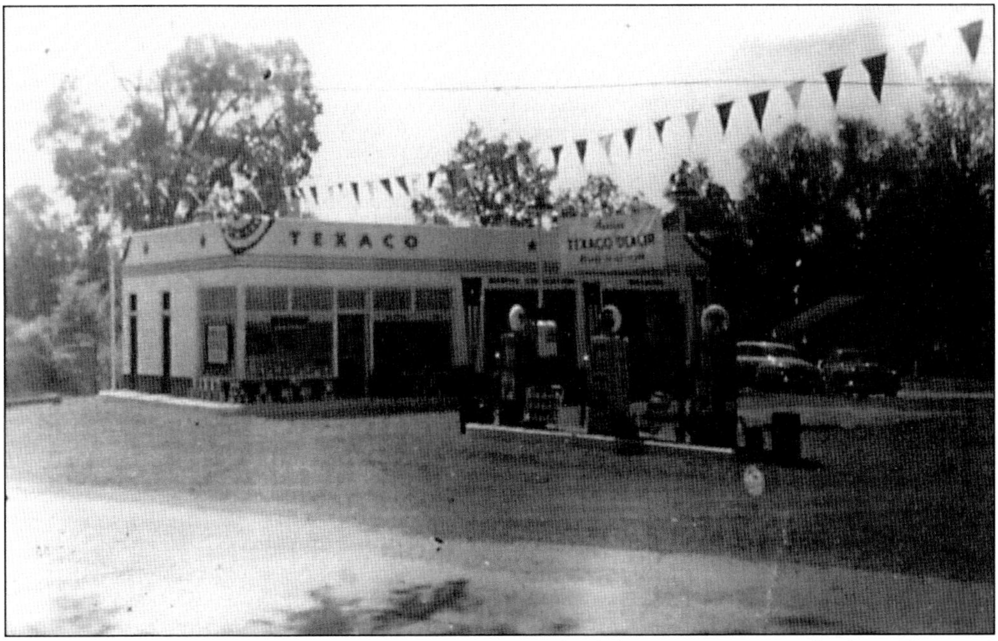

TEXACO STATION. In the late 1940s, Fred Kainer Sr. had this Texaco station built on Route 43 at Eastern Union Turnpike. Miller's Automotive now occupies the building. (MSt.G.)

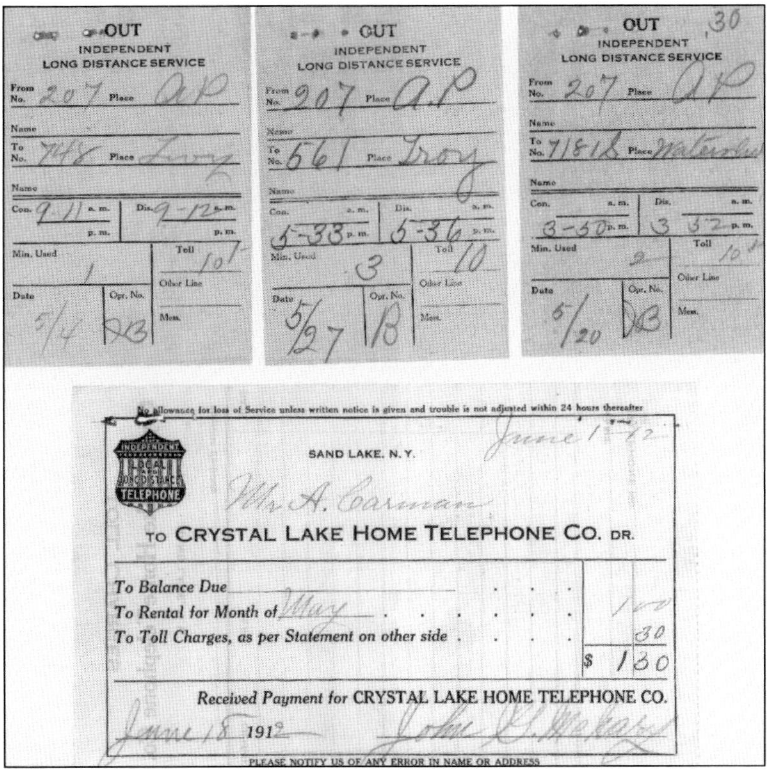

OUT
INDEPENDENT
LONG DISTANCE SERVICE
From No. 207 Place A.P
Name
To No. 748 Place Troy
Name
Con. 9.11 a.m. Dis. 9.12 a.m.
Min. Used 1 Toll 10
Date 5/4 Opr. No.

OUT
INDEPENDENT
LONG DISTANCE SERVICE
From No. 207 Place A.P
Name
To No. 561 Place Troy
Name
Con. 5-33 p.m. Dis. 5-36 p.m.
Min. Used 3 Toll 10
Date 5/27 Opr. No.

OUT 30
INDEPENDENT
LONG DISTANCE SERVICE
From No. 207 Place A.P
Name
To No. Place
Name
Con. 3-50 p.m. Dis. 3 52 p.m.
Min. Used 2 Toll 10
Date 5/20 Opr. No.

No allowance for loss of Service unless written notice is given and trouble is not adjusted within 24 hours thereafter

INDEPENDENT LOCAL LONG DISTANCE TELEPHONE

SAND LAKE, N. Y.

Mr A. Carman

TO CRYSTAL LAKE HOME TELEPHONE CO. DR.

To Balance Due	
To Rental for Month of May	1 00
To Toll Charges, as per Statement on other side	30
	$ 1 30

Received Payment for CRYSTAL LAKE HOME TELEPHONE CO.

June 18 1912

PLEASE NOTIFY US OF ANY ERROR IN NAME OR ADDRESS

THE CRYSTAL LAKE HOME TELEPHONE COMPANY. A. Carman's telephone bill was $1 for local telephone number 207 for May 1912 plus additional charges for three long-distance calls. Most persons shared party lines and placed all calls through a local operator. (aG.)

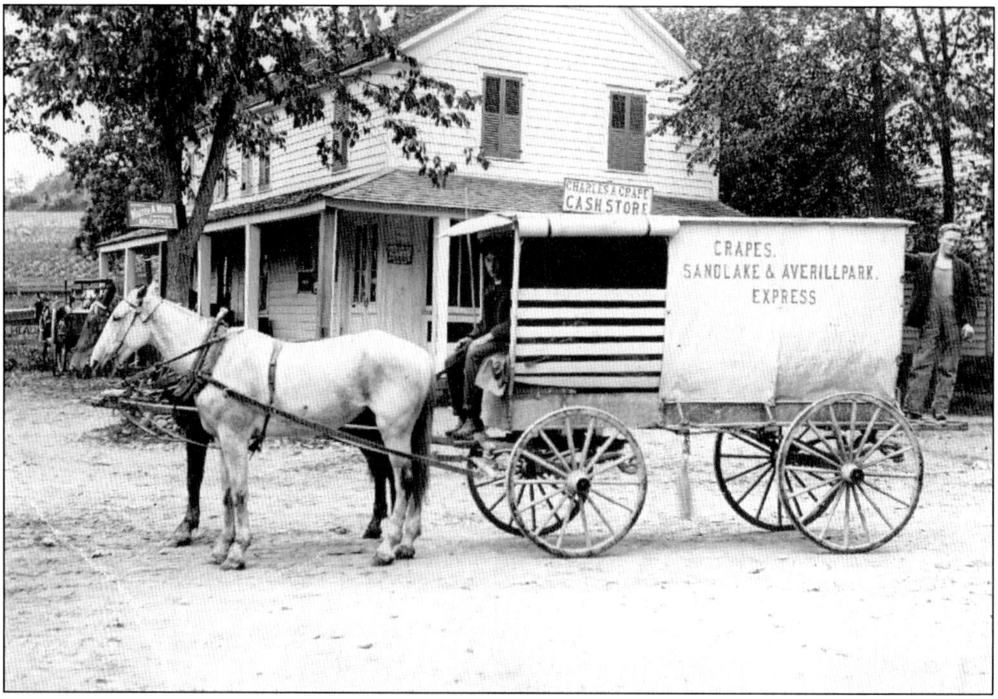

CRAPE'S STORE. Charles Crape ran a store as well as a delivery service across the road from Crist Crape's Central Hotel, on the northeast corner of Routes 43 and 66 and County Route 42, Taborton Road. (TSLC.)

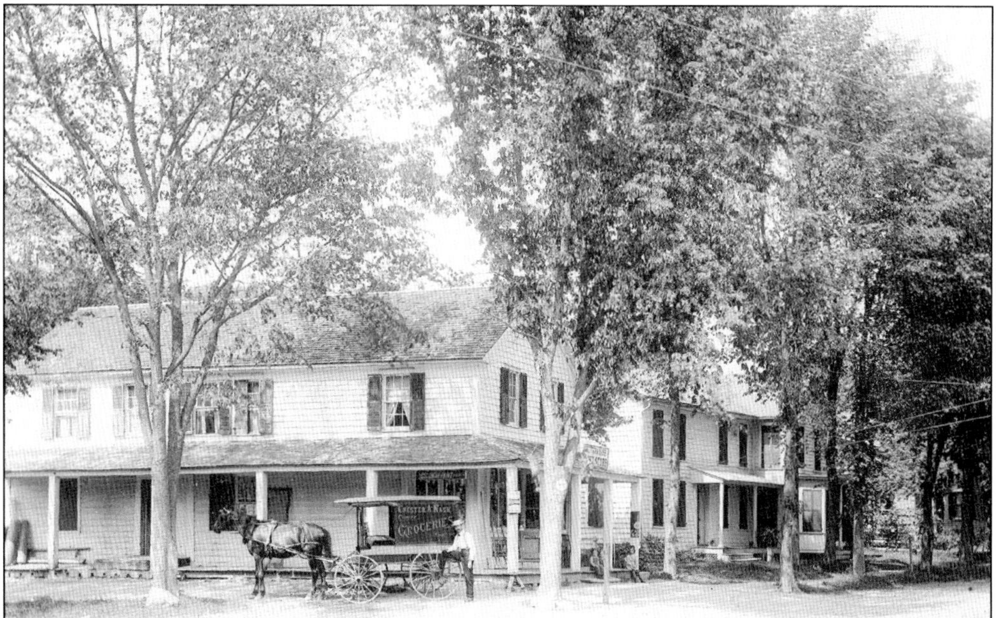

CHESTER A. NASH STORE. Prior to locating at the A. E. Horton store (see *Sand Lake*, page 80), Chester A. Nash had a grocery store at the same location as seen in the photograph above. (AT.)

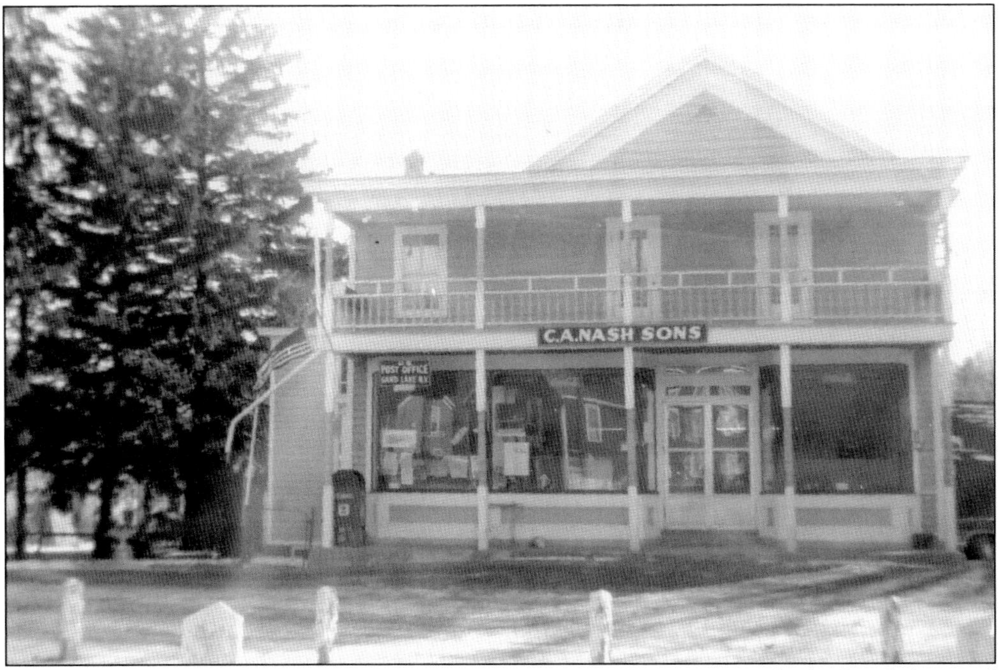

C. A. NASH STORE. In the early 1970s, the C. A. Nash Store prominently displayed the Sand Lake Post Office sign, which can also be viewed in the next photograph. The post office was located here from 1907 to 1978 (see *Sand Lake*, page 80). (SLHSC.)

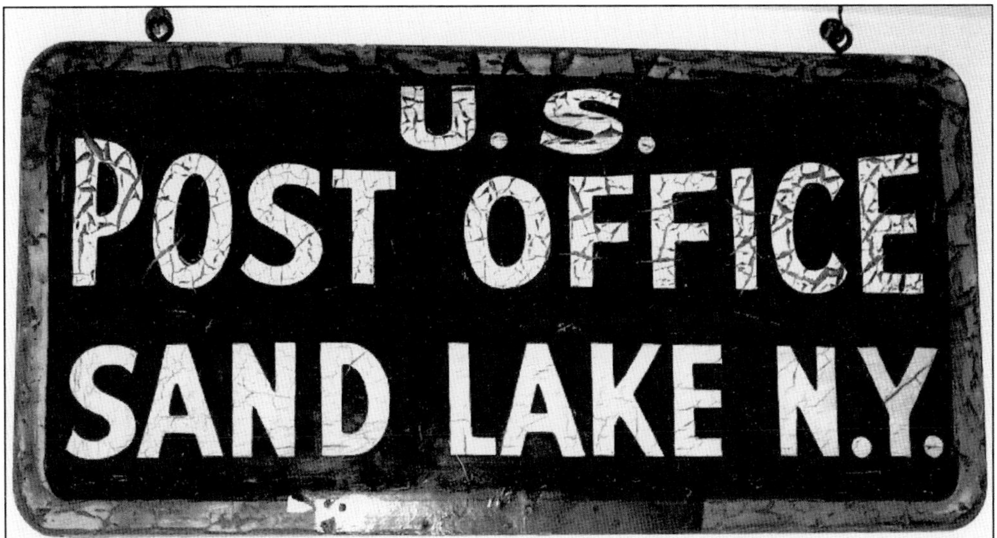

POST OFFICE SIGN. The Sand Lake Post Office sign, which told the building's function over the years, was rescued by Bruce Beck when the post office moved across the road. It reminds him of his Sand Lake roots as it hangs proudly in his home. (BVB.)

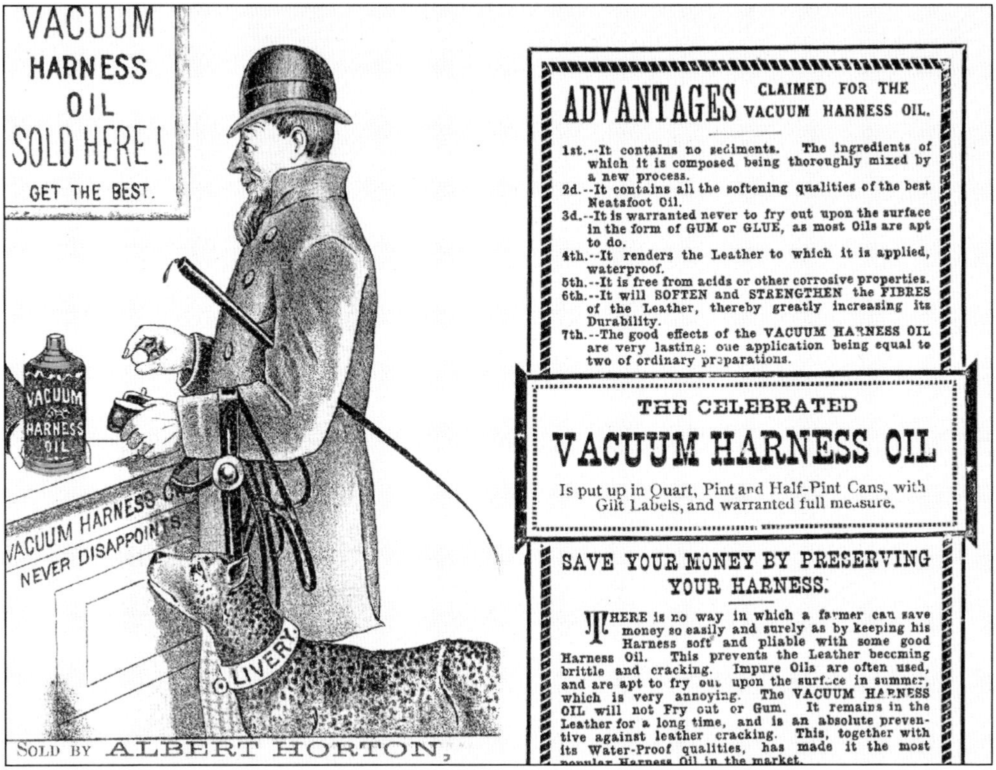

VACUUM HARNESS OIL. This flyer tells the many advantages of Vacuum Harness Oil. The dog with the word *livery* on its collar may be in need of Vacuum Harness Oil sold at Albert Horton's store. (A&WM.)

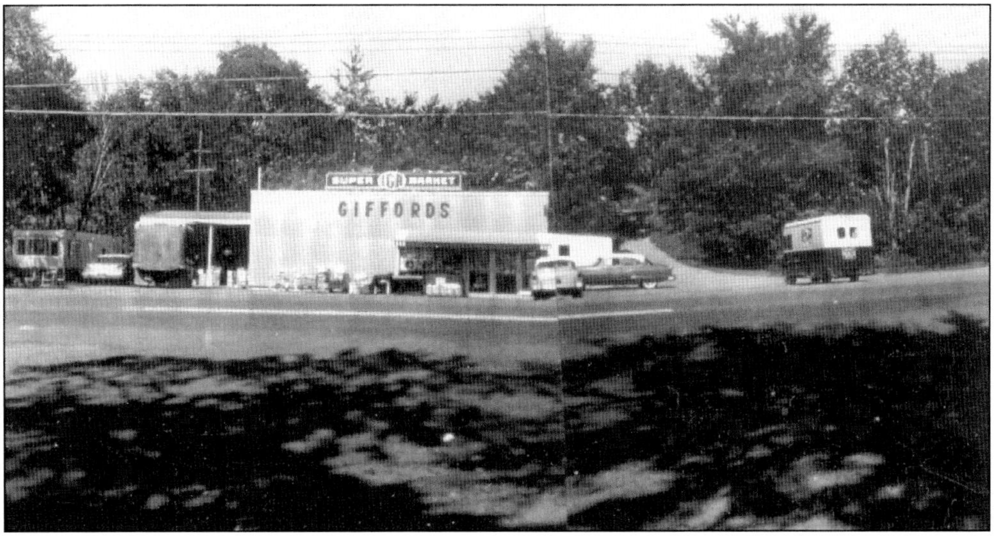

GIFFORD'S IGA MARKET. Gifford's Market was located on lots 8 and 9 of the glass factory site. It was begun as a convenience store. Albert and Phoebe Gifford purchased it in the 1940s and upgraded it to an Independent Grocers Alliance (IGA) supermarket. Albert Goodwin Jr. bought it in 1964. Henry and Judy Rowe were its owners from 1969 to 1985, when it was sold to John and Sophie Butwell. It burned in 1997 and was never reopened. (TSLC.)

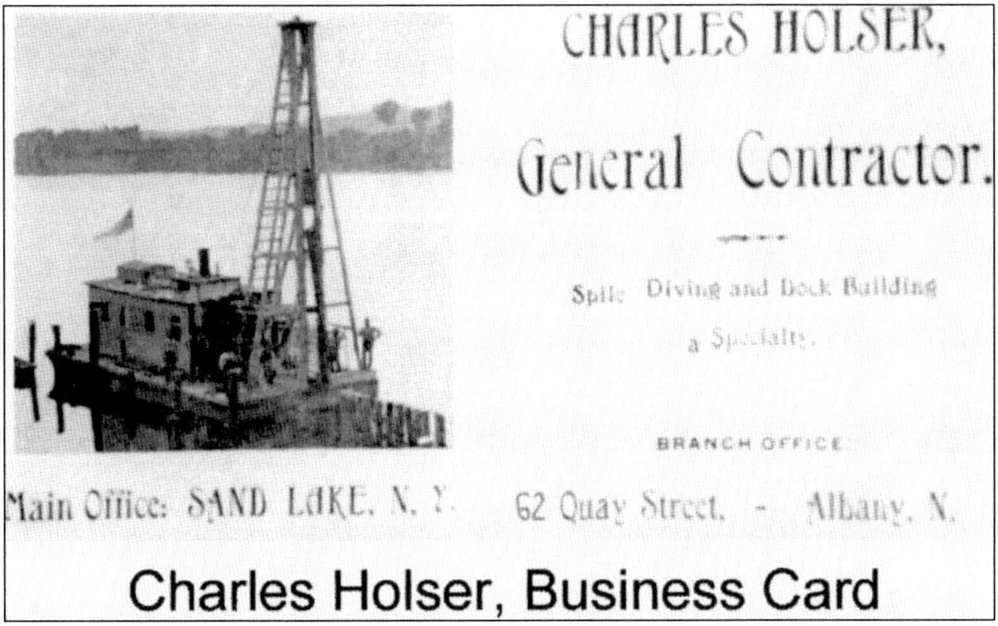

CHARLES HOLSER'S BUSINESS CARD. Shown on this business card is the machine that Charles Holser used to drive spiles, the large wooden stakes used in waterfront dock construction. Holser was Sand Lake town supervisor from 1892 to 1895. After moving to Poestenkill, he was elected town supervisor there in 1906. (DH.)

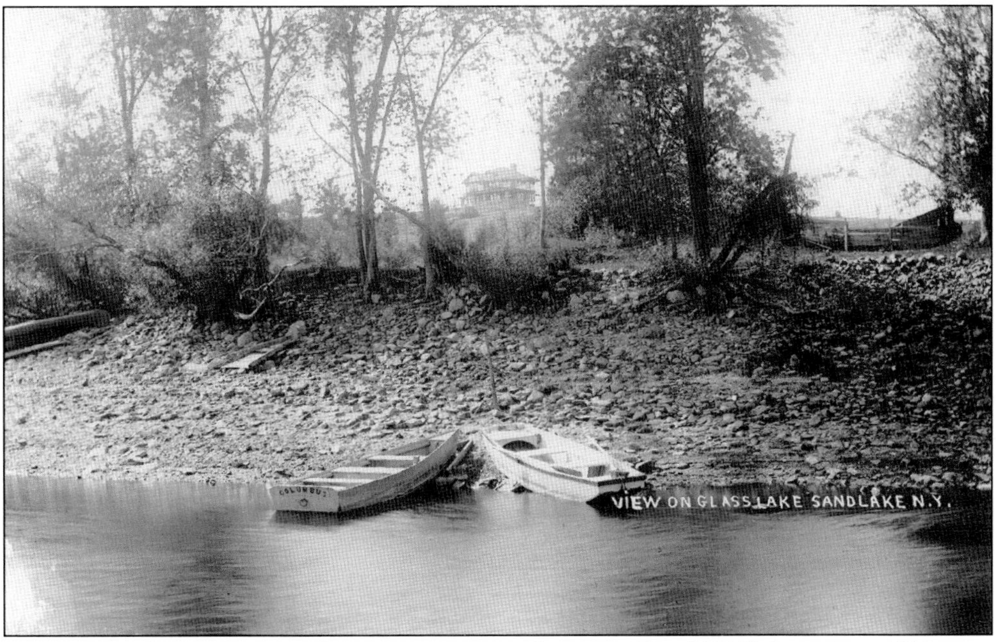

GLASS LAKE GLASS FACTORY SITE. To quote town historian Harold Tifft from the *c.* 1958 script of his postcard narration, "The top of this bank was the site of the famous glass factory. Around 1900 this whole shore was filled with chunks of glass of all colors. They have all been picked up although occasionally one is found." (AT.)

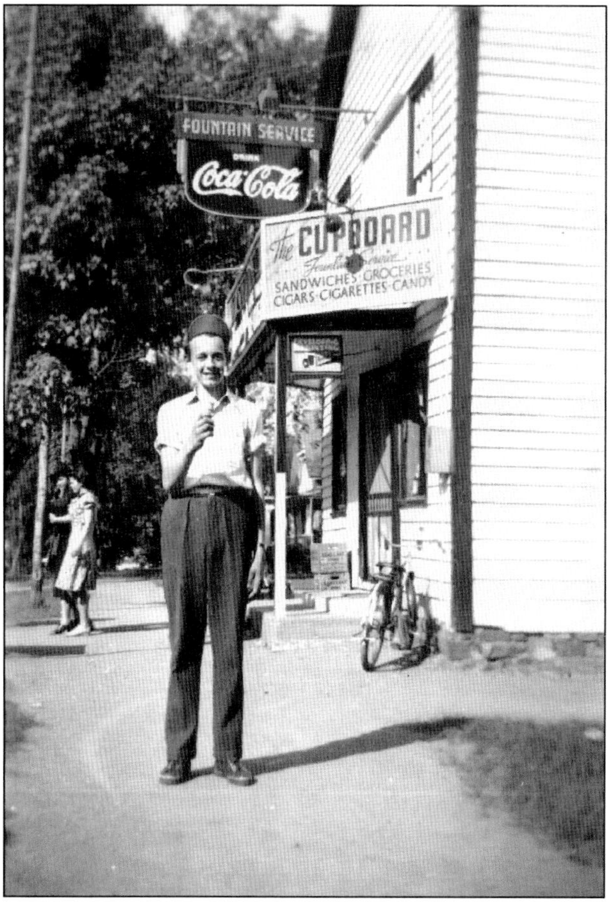

ELDON SNYDER AT THE CUPBOARD. The Cupboard had fountain service, groceries, candy, Sand Lake Springs soda, film developing, and fireworks. Eldon Snyder is enjoying an ice-cream cone. He later became a Lutheran pastor. (IS.)

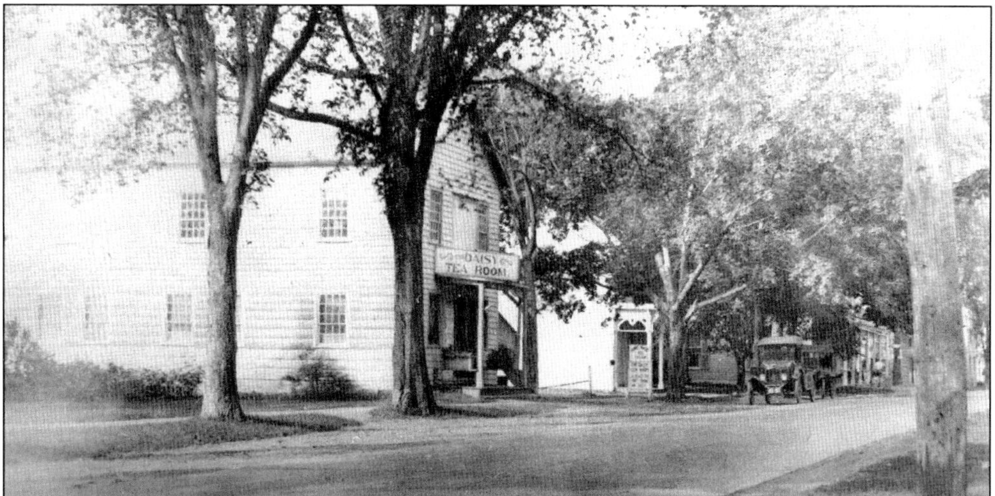

DAISY TEA ROOM. This store was built around 1835 and housed a grocery store, a carriage shop, the Daisy Tea Room, and the Cupboard. Its last occupant was the Lake Pharmacy before the pharmacy moved across Route 43 in West Sand Lake and the property became the Miller's Market parking lot. (CV.)

PATRICIA SEWELL. Irving Sewell's sister Patricia, around 1941, is standing in front of her father's barbershop, which was located just east of Miller's Market on Route 43. (IS.)

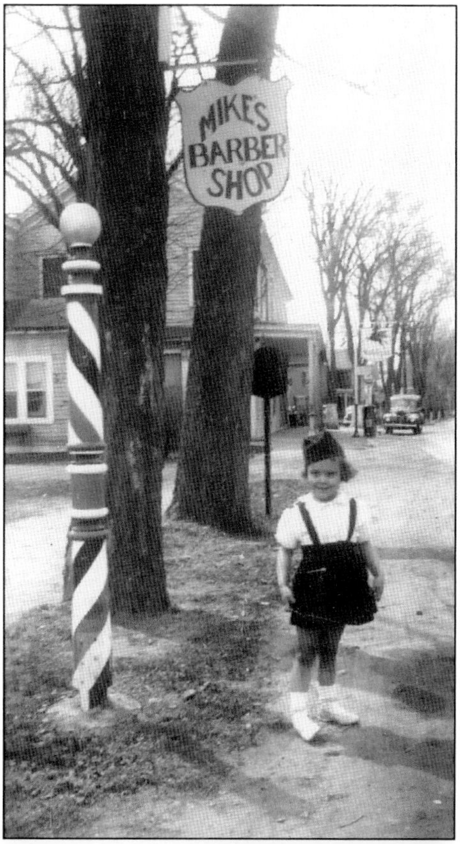

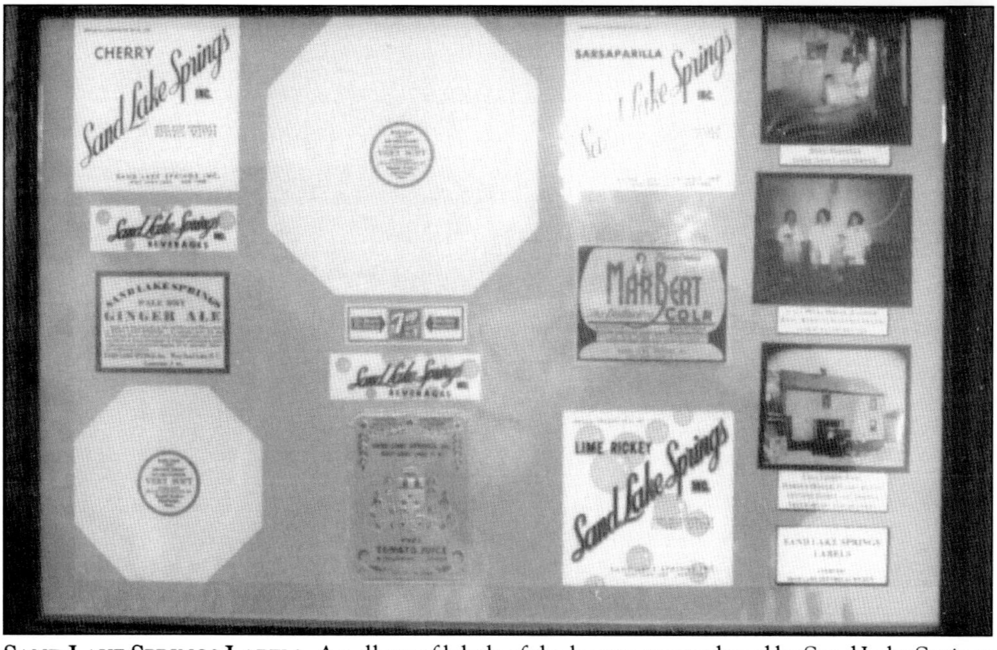

SAND LAKE SPRINGS LABELS. A collage of labels of the beverages produced by Sand Lake Springs (see *Sand Lake*, page 23) was framed and is on display in the Sand Lake Town Hall. (SLHSC.)

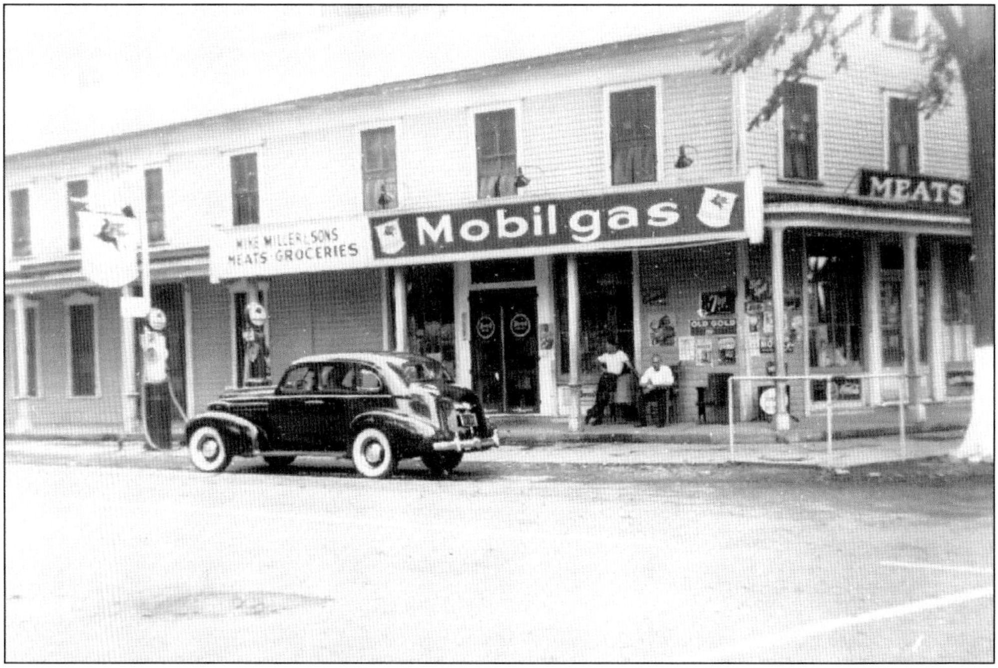

MIKE MILLER AND SONS MEATS-GROCERIES. From the Buick parked near the Mobil gas pumps, this view is from around 1939. The building was built in 1878 (see *Sand Lake,* page 34). (AM.)

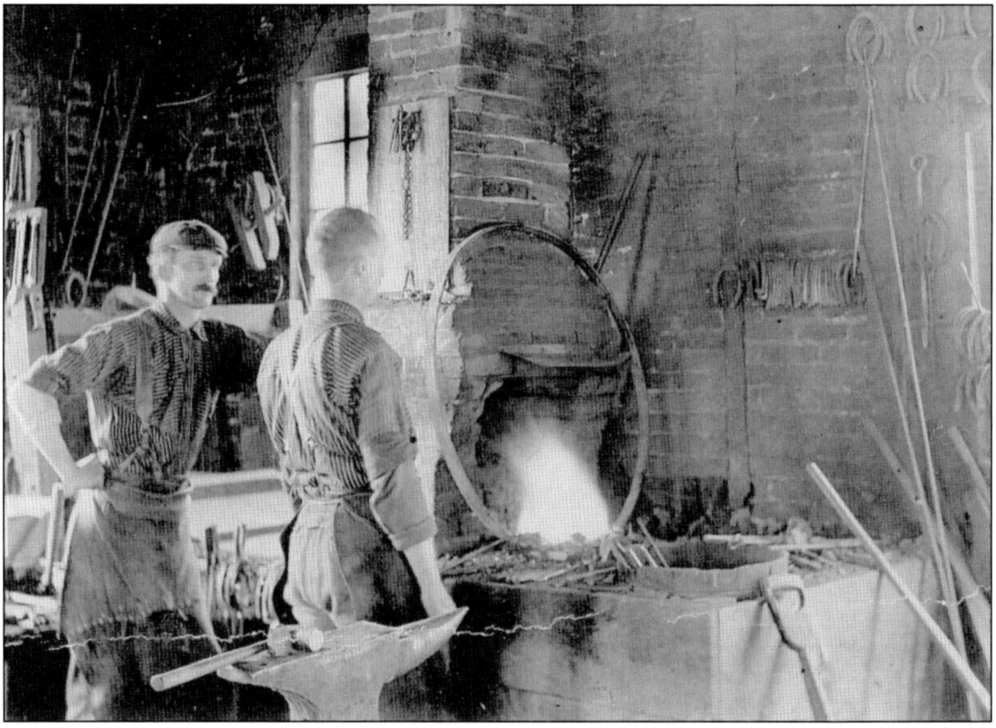

BART WARREN IN BLACKSMITH SHOP. Bart Warren (left) is at his forge around 1901 with another young man inside his blacksmith shop. This location is now the Barber Shop on Route 150, just south of the Four Corners. (JW.)

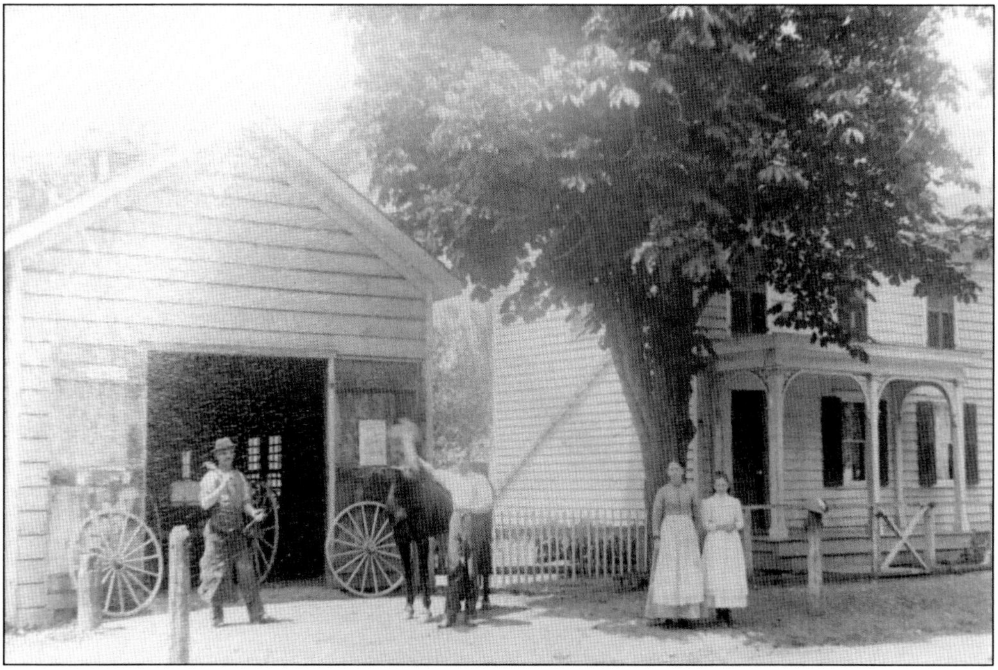

GEORGE EWIG'S BLACKSMITH SHOP. George Ewig ran his blacksmith shop from the late 1800s to the early 1900s. The Ewig property was next to the West Sand Lake Methodist Church, now the Bible Baptist Church on Route 150. (CV.)

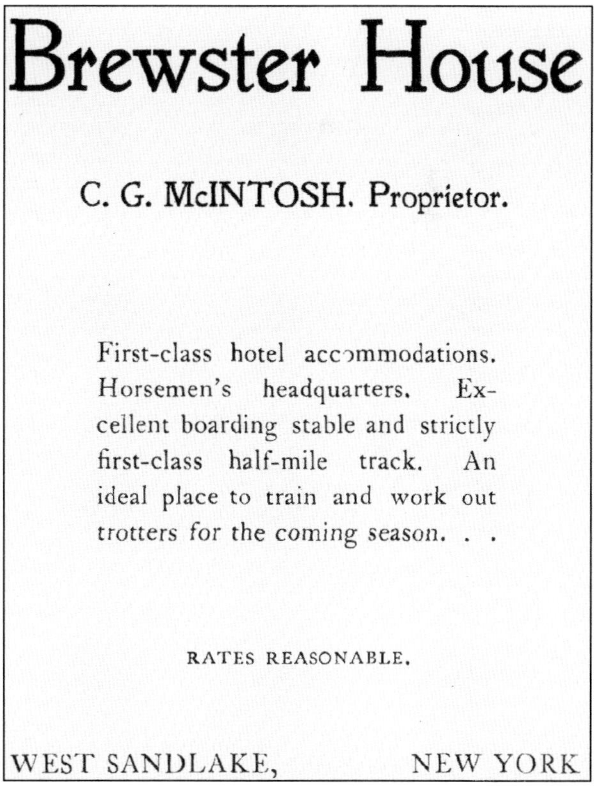

BREWSTER HOUSE ADVERTISEMENT. In the brochure for the 1904 Rensselaer County Agricultural and Horticultural Society Fair, the Brewster House publicizes outstanding accommodations for persons and horses. (SLHSC.)

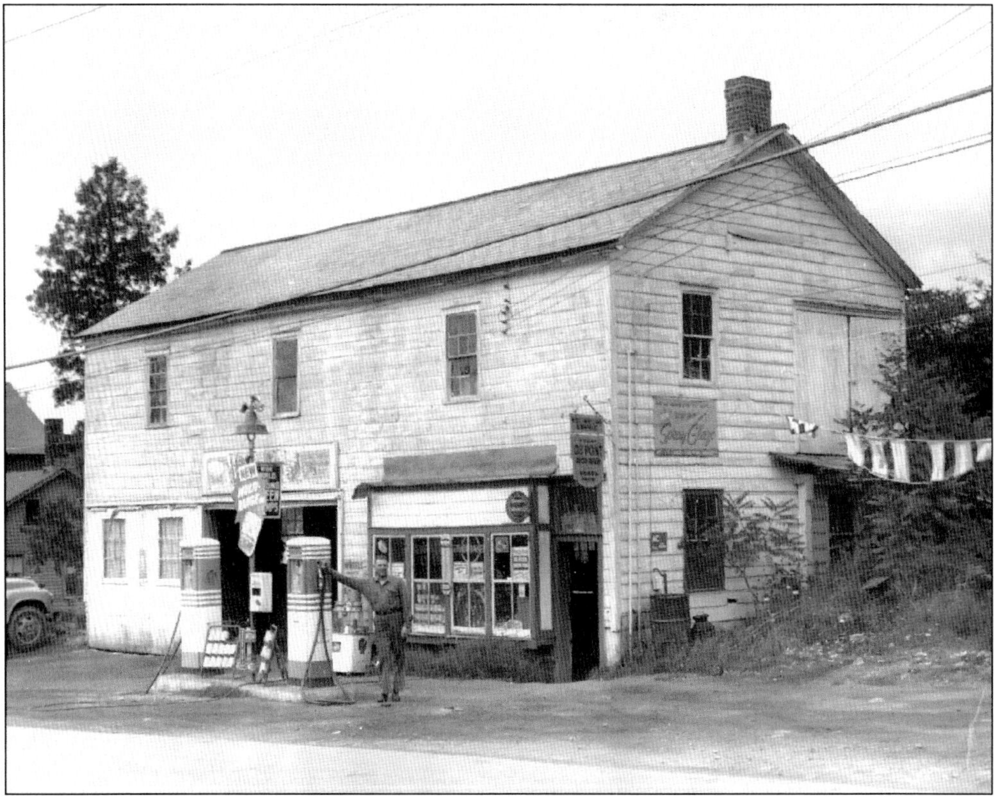

HAROLD FOSTER'S FIRST GARAGE. Harold Foster had his first garage at this location, which is now an apartment house at the corner of Brookview Court (the first left turn traveling east, past the 43 Mall) and Route 43. (JB.)

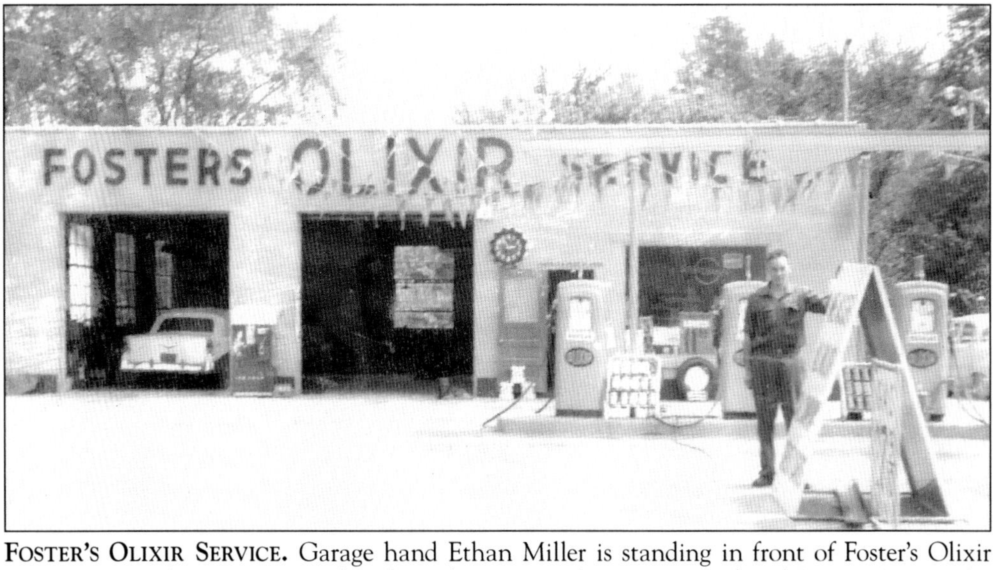

FOSTER'S OLIXIR SERVICE. Garage hand Ethan Miller is standing in front of Foster's Olixir service station (see pages 89 and 125), at the corner of Springer Road and Route 43, now the Sand Lake Ambulance garage. (JB.)

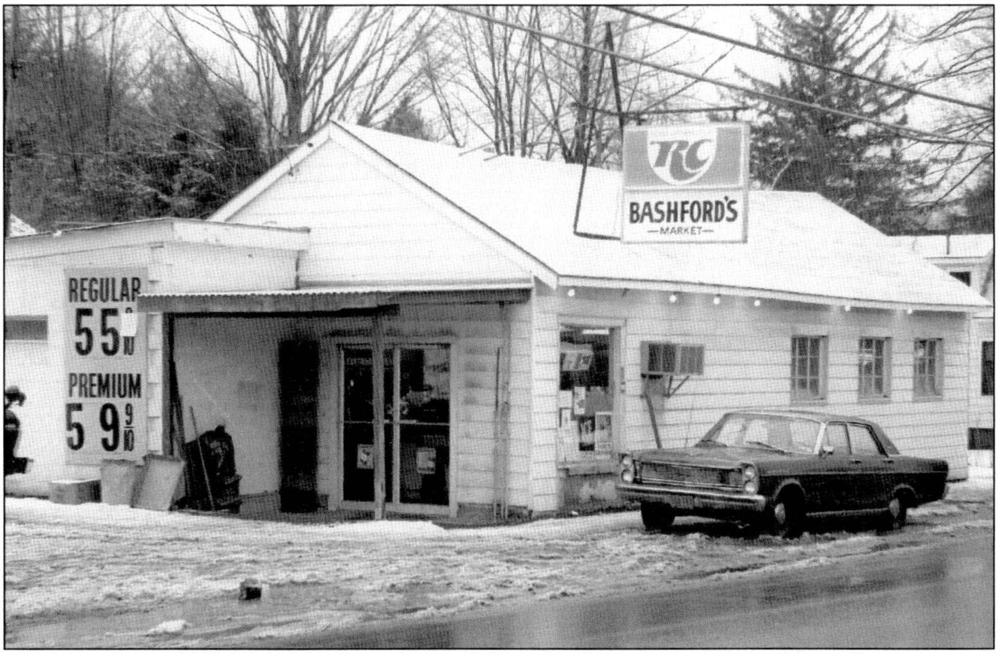

BASHFORD'S MARKET, 1975. Bashford's Market would be today's convenience store and gas station. Notice the price of gas in the "good old days." It is now an apartment house and is located across from Stewart's Shop on Route 43. (CV.)

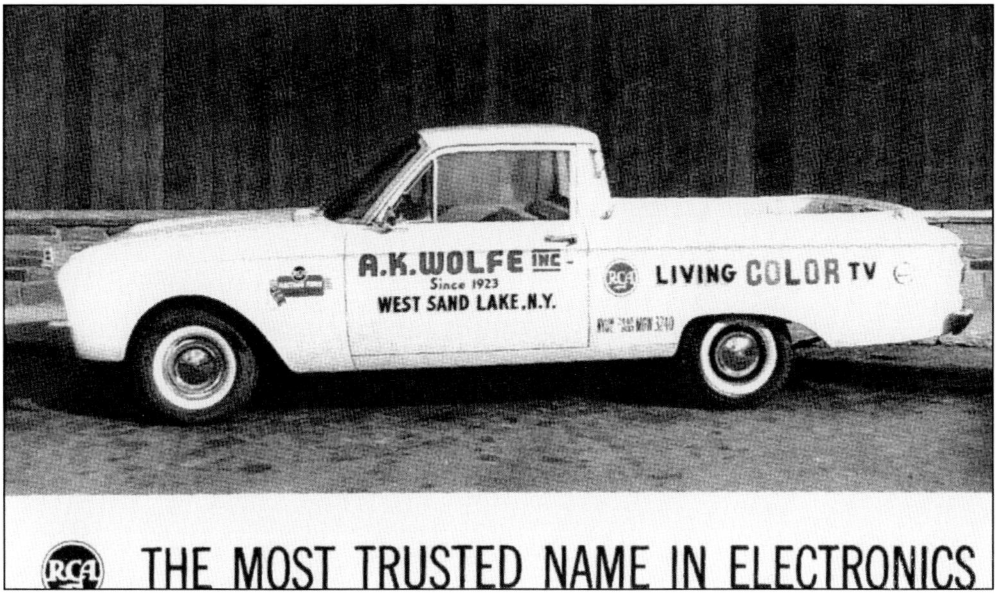

A. K. WOLFE ADVERTISEMENT. This 1960 Ford Falcon Ranchero pickup truck gave salient information on A. K. Wolfe's wares as it was driven around town, as well as being featured on this postcard advertisement. (JC.)

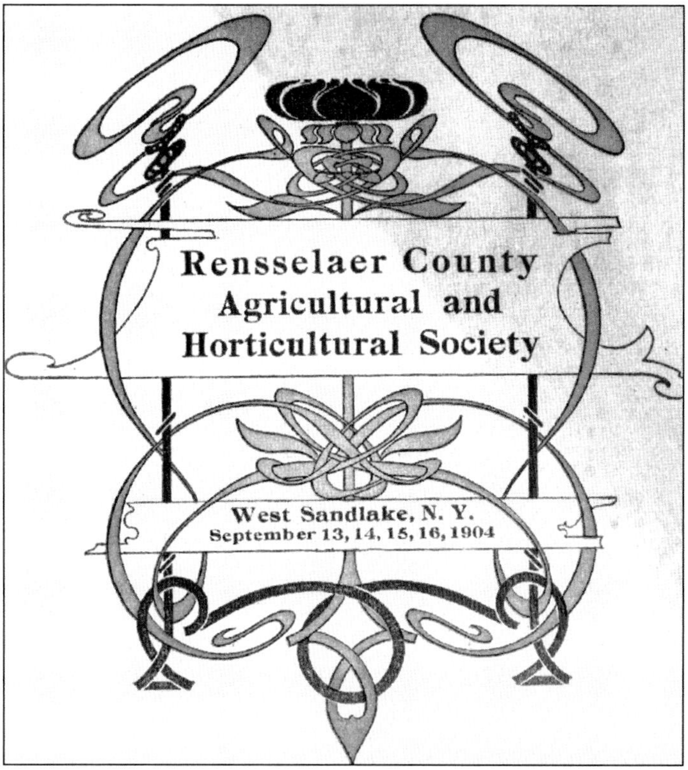

RENSSELAER COUNTY AGRICULTURAL AND HORTICULTURAL SOCIETY FAIR. This is the cover of the brochure for the Rensselaer County Agricultural and Horticultural Society Fair, held at the fairgrounds in West Sand Lake September 13–16, 1904. Several town merchants advertised in the brochure. (SLHSC.)

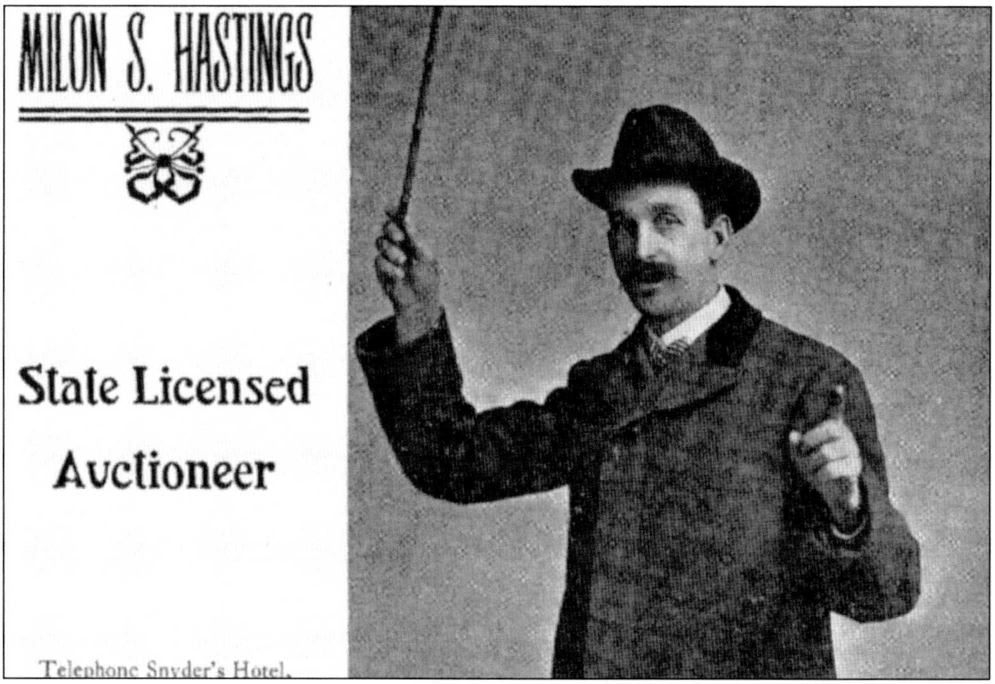

MILON HASTINGS. Advertisement space was purchased in the brochure for the 1904 Rensselaer County Agricultural and Horticultural Society Fair. Milon (also spelled Milan) Hastings was the father of Clifford C. Hastings, who brought electricity to West Sand Lake. (SLHSC.)

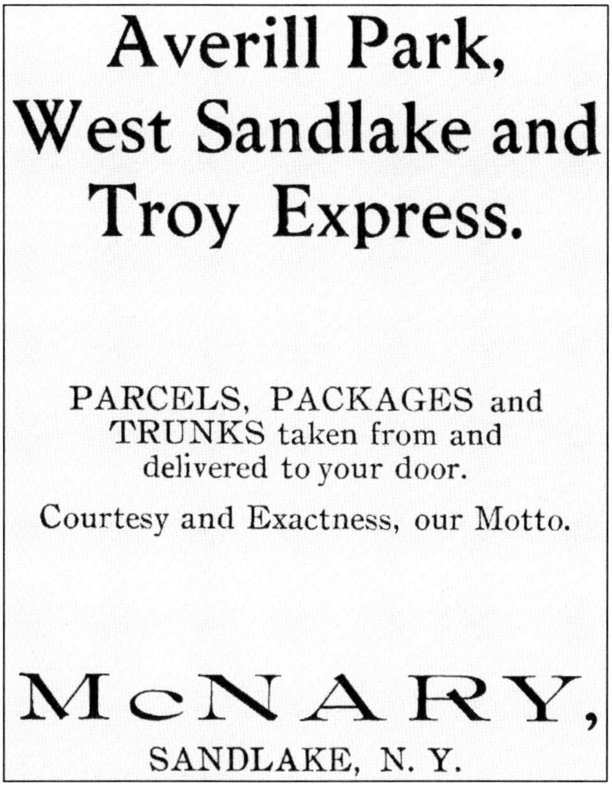

AVERILL PARK, WEST SANDLAKE AND TROY EXPRESS. Advertisement space was purchased in the brochure for the 1904 Rensselaer County Agricultural and Horticultural Society Fair. Samuel McNary later became a partner in the KLWM Bus Company (see *Sand Lake*, page 61). (SLHSC.)

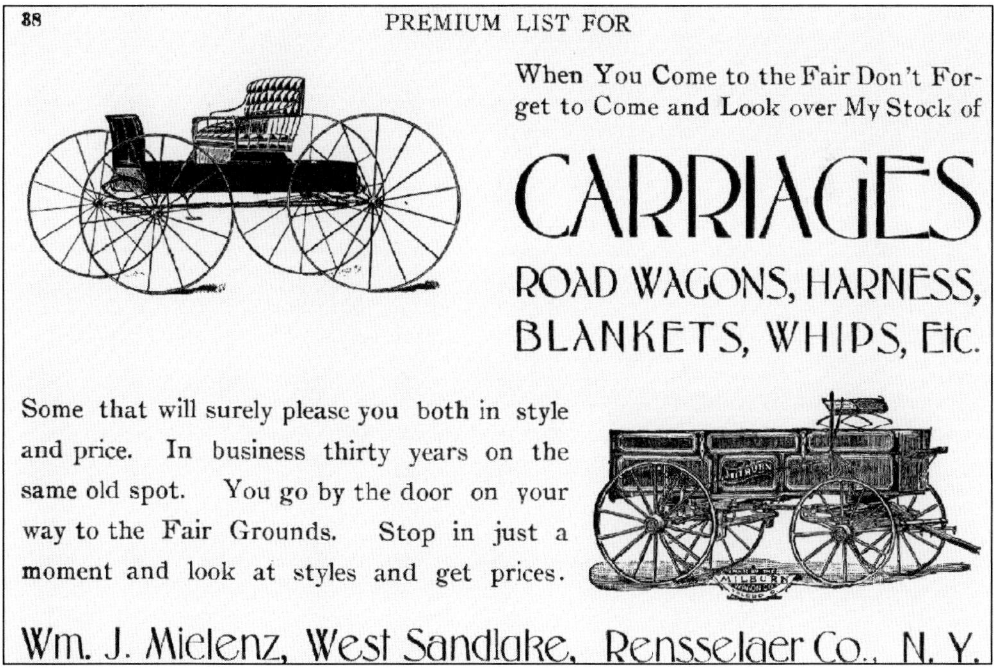

WILLIAM J. MIELENZ. William J. Mielenz advertised his carriages in the brochure for the 1904 Rensselaer County Agricultural and Horticultural Society Fair (see *Sand Lake*, page 26). (SLHSC.)

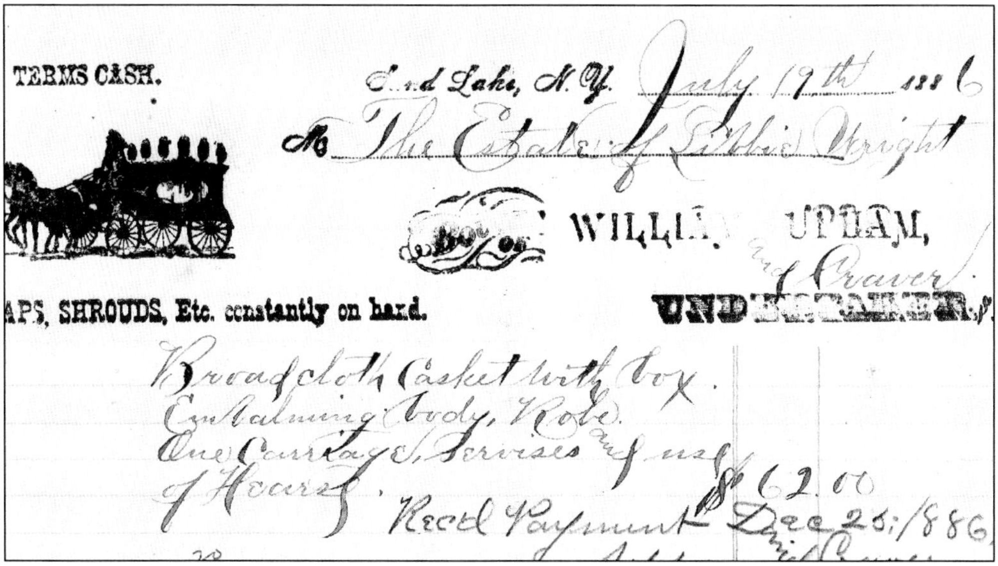

TERMS CASH.

Sand Lake, N.Y. July 19th 1886

M The Estate of Libbie Wright

WILLI... UPHAM, and Craver

UND...

...APS, SHROUDS, Etc. constantly on hand.

Broadcloth Casket with box.
Embalming body, Robe
One Carriage, Services of use of Hearse $62.00
Recd Payment Dec 25/1886

Upham and Craver Funeral Receipt. From this letterhead, Clarence Craver joined William Upham, and the Craver name was written on the receipt. (aG.)

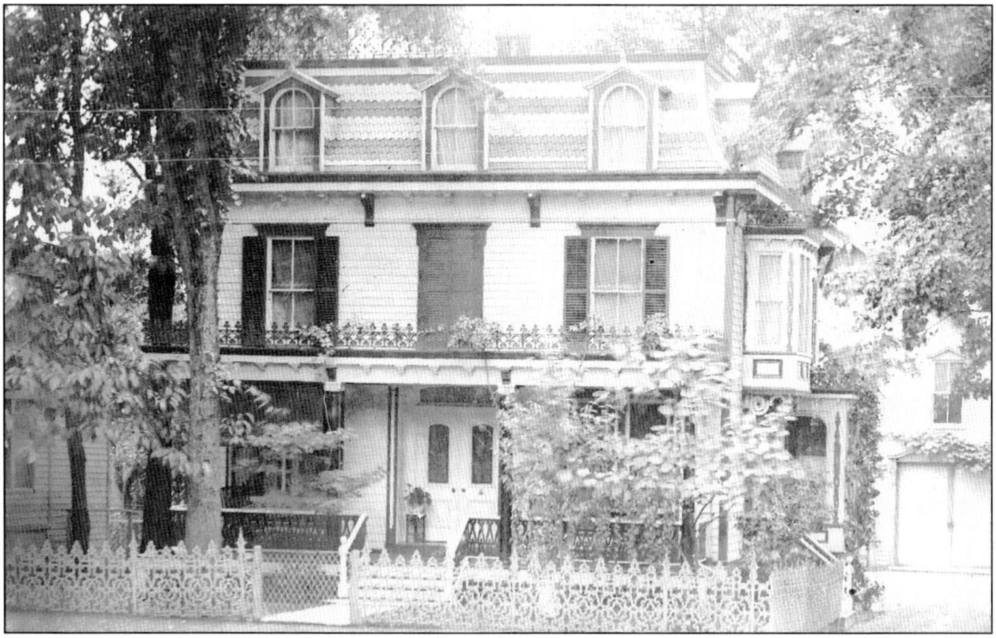

Upham and Craver Undertakers. Going east on Routes 43 and 66, the house next to Jill's Hidden Garden in the hamlet of Sand Lake was the location of Upham and Craver Undertakers. (AT.)

COTTON CHAIRS. Here are two chairs made by James C. Cotton in the 1800s. Restoration of the house where Cotton made his chairs (see *Sand Lake*, page 81) is a project of Girl Scout Troop 181. (SLHSC.)

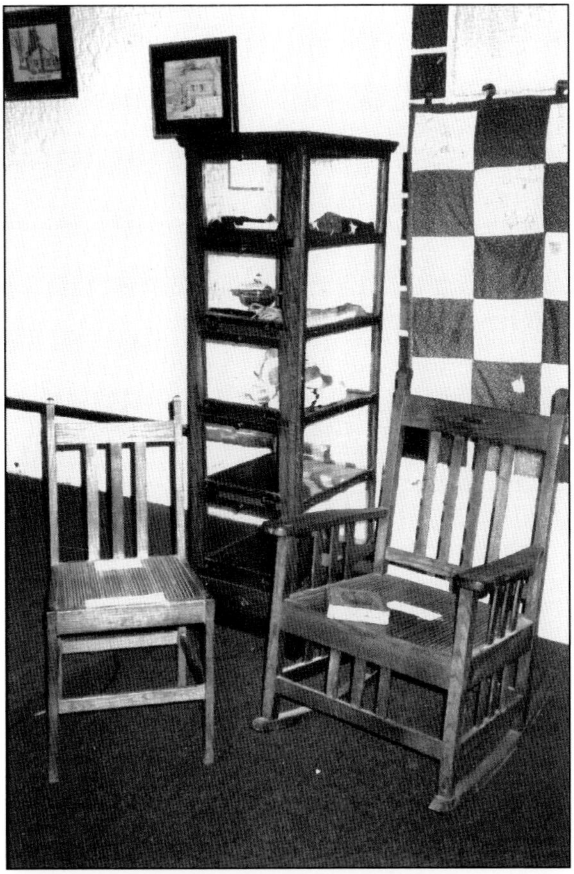

RENSSELAER COUNTY MUTUAL FIRE INSURANCE CO.

DEAR MADAM : SECRETARY'S OFFICE, SAND LAKE, N. Y., AUG. 16, 1909.

The directors having approved of the claims of F. Durr, $454.08; Thomas Galvin, $20; C. Randall, $15; Wm. Moody, $40; A. A. & E. S. Bunce, $27.65; H. Miller, $25; D. Hoffman, $10; H. Holcomb, $2.50; Wm. I. Miller, $25; C. Hoffman, $150; B. Smith, $150; D. R. Burdick, $20; Heirs of S. A. Ferguson, $5; D. Covey, $2; C. Holser, $125; W. Stewart, $10; M. Tremont, $900; A. S. & J. E. Reichard, $1925; Mrs. J. E. Reichard, $2; F. J. Hardick, $250; C A. Smith, $200; M. J. Tucker, $700; Wm. L. Green, $450; M. Therien, $5; C. D. Hall, $8; Geo Teal, $438.40; Geo. Z. Lafleur, $146.07; T. Galvin, $5; Wm. Hunt, $8; Geo. Gile, $400; Wm. E. Phillips, $799.34; F. Hogie, $18.06; J. Whitley, $6.46; A. O. Bink, $20; P. Prediger, $5; T. H. Bendon, $100; W. & L. A. Germond, $25; C. Conant, $2; F. Amidon, $3; Wm. Meilenz, $10; J. McCarty, $26.60; A. Armsby, $75; T. H. Bendon, $350; W. D. Larkin, $25; W. O. Ives, $2; W. H. Atwater, $50; A. Love, $23; M. F. Horton, $50; Wm. E. Link, $30; Bunce Bros., $1150; Mrs. M. F. Chamberlain, $2505; Mrs. A. W. Fish, $271.75; J. Strump, $2; H. Brown, $4.20; P. Donnelly, $470; N. Herrington, $25; J. Schaus, $3; H. Van Allen, $800; W. L. Snyder, $5; J. Launt, $15; W. L. Gibbs, $5; E. Brust, $734.65; V. Stritsman, $10; A. E. Horton, $400; M. A. Bennett, $2000; E. A. Spicer, $598.50; F. Sibley, $17.50; R. Gibson, $120; therefore on July 23rd, 1909, they declared an assessment of 24 cts. on each $100, for each rate.

Your assessment is $. 3.69, which you are required to pay to the Treasurer within thirty days from date of this notice. Make all checks payable to A M. Peck, Treas.

Respectfully yours,

A. M. PECK, Secretary.

Rec'd Payment A. M. Peck. Treas.

Treasurer will be at Grafton, Sept. 6th; at Petersburg, Sept. 7th; at BERLIN HOUSE, Sept. 8th; at VANDERBILT HOUSE, Sept. 9th; at SNYDER HOUSE, Sept. 13th; at WAGAR HOUSE, Sept. 14th, 1909

Members can pay MITCHEL LINK, East Greenbush; WARREN CROPSEY, Speigletown; H. B. CARR, Pittstown; S. J. LENNON, Nassau; JOHN HERRICK, at Schodack Landing; MCCHESNEY & RIFENBURG, at Cropseyville; H. DAWSON, So. Schodack; M. MELIUS, E. Nassau and DEAVITT & HOLCOMB, 130 Congress St., Troy, N. Y

RENSSELAER COUNTY MUTUAL FIRE INSURANCE COMPANY INSURANCE CARD. A 1909 postcard reported all the approved insurance claims for the year and the resulting assessment of $3.69. It was addressed to Melissa E. Gardner of Averill Park. (TSLC.)

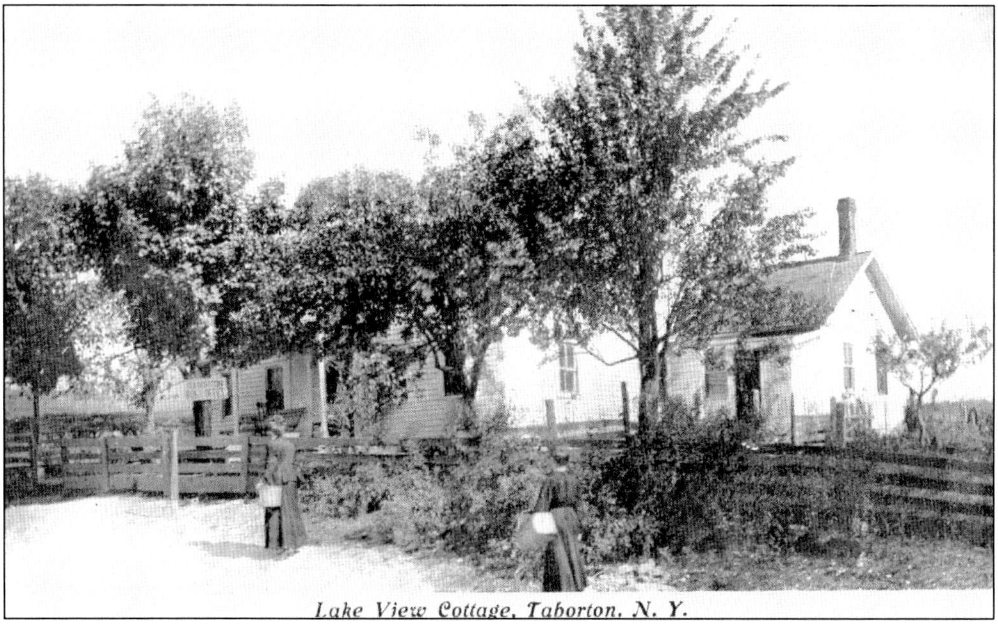

TABORTON POST OFFICE. This cottage on County Route 42 in Taborton has the post office sign in front. Conrad, Gertrude, and Minnie Malkmes (see *Sand Lake*, page 107) served as postmasters. The post office was in service from 1892 to 1942. It was also a convenience store for the people on Taborton Mountain. (A&WM.)

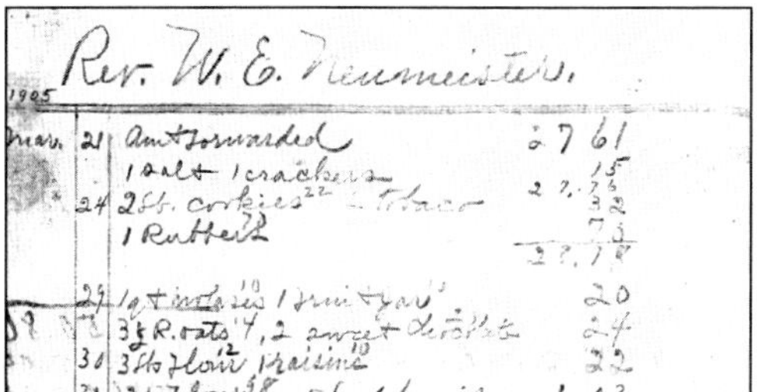
Rev. W. E. Neumeister.

CASHBOOK ENTRY. In the cashbook of Conrad, who ran a store as well as the Taborton Post Office, is a record of Rev. W. E. Neumeister's purchases. Note the price of items in 1905. (BVB.)

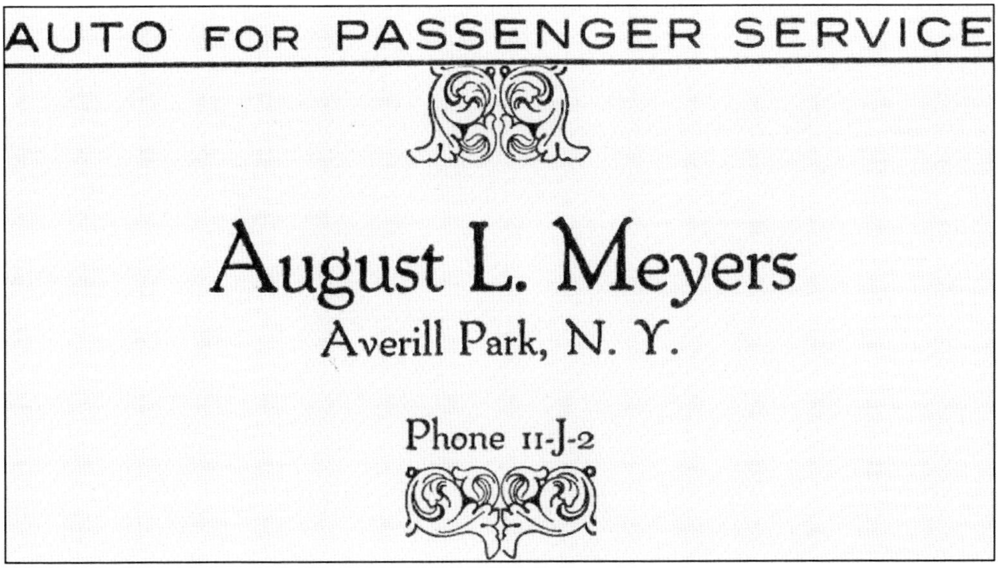

AUTOMOBILE PASSENGER SERVICE. Taborton had a local passenger service with August Meyers as the chauffeur around 1922. (BB.)

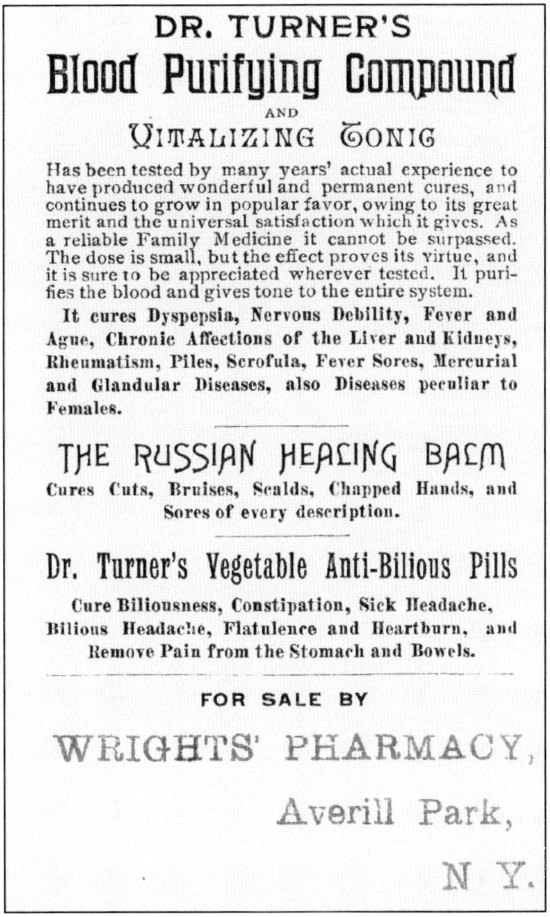

DR. TURNER'S BLOOD PURIFYING COMPOUND. Wrights' Pharmacy in Averill Park is one place to purchase Dr. Turner's Blood Purifying Compound, an advertised "cure all." (A&WM.)

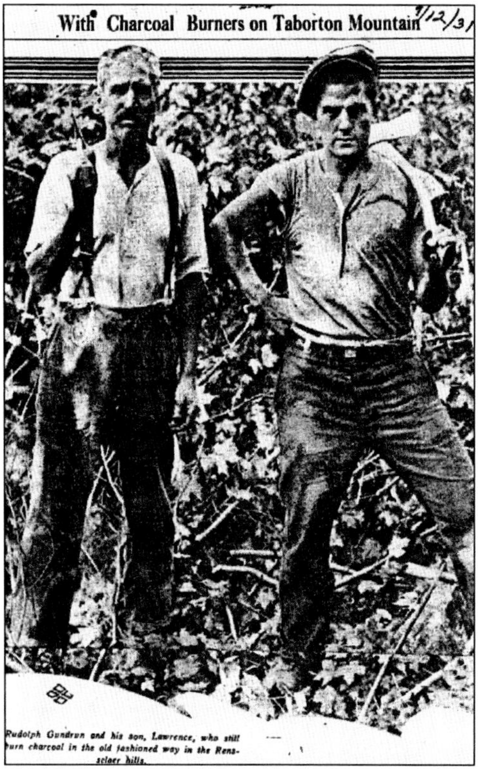

CHARCOAL BURNERS. Charcoal burning was a major industry on Taborton Mountain in East Sand Lake (see *Sand Lake*, page 102). Shown are Rudolph (Rudy) Gundrum and his son Lawrence, two of many charcoal burners in 1931. Others included Frank Vines, August (Gus) Meyers, Joseph Timber, George Dobert, and Nicholas Teal. (TSLC, *Knickerbocker Press* photograph.)

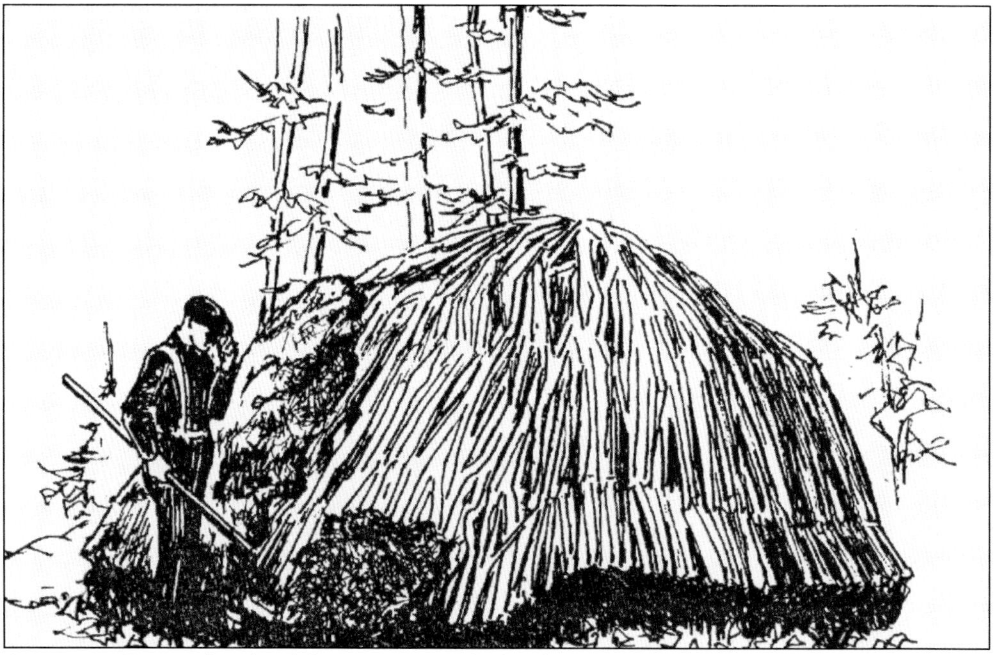

CHARCOAL PIT. In this sketch by Patricia Brock, the charcoal burner known as a collier is covering the pit with earth and sod. This is the last step before the pit is lit and an around-the-clock vigil is kept for a constant, sure burn of the approximately 20 cords of wood stacked in precise order. (SLHSC.)

CHARCOAL BAG OF A. L. MEYERS. August Meyers had his charcoal packaged in quarter-bushel bags. Charcoal was a popular fuel of restaurants and factories in Albany and Troy. (BB.)

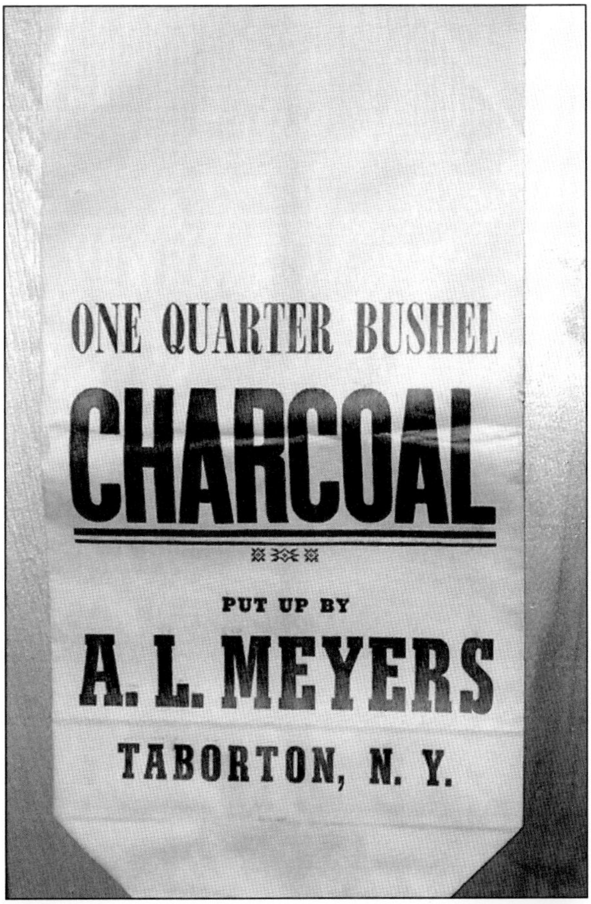

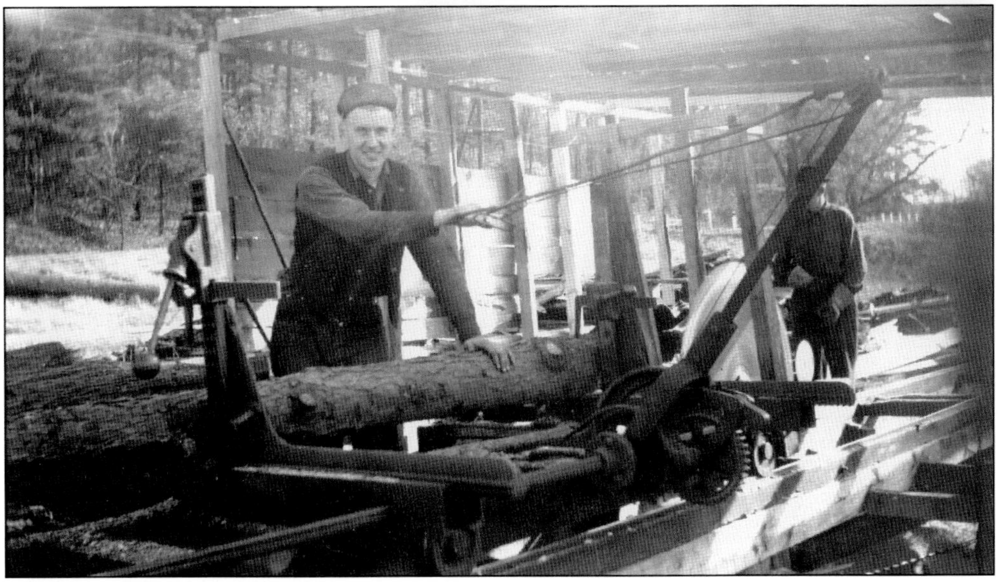

SAWMILL. Howard (left) and Edward Lerch are working at their sawmill. Route 150 can be seen in the background. (BLT.)

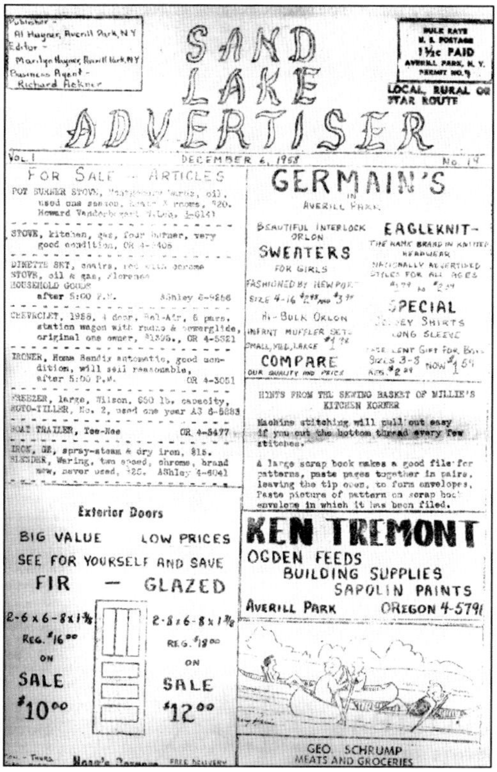

Publisher – Al Hayner, Averill Park, N.Y.
Editor – Marilyn Hayner, Averill Park, N.Y.
Business Agent – Richard Ackner

SAND LAKE ADVERTISER

BULK RATE U. S. POSTAGE 1½c PAID AVERILL PARK, N. Y. PERMIT NO. 9
LOCAL, RURAL OR STAR ROUTE

Vol. I — DECEMBER 6, 1958 — No. 14

FOR SALE – ARTICLES

POT BURNER STOVE, oil, used one season, rooms, $20. Howard Vanderbogart

STOVE, kitchen, gas, four burner, very good condition, OR 4-5405

DINETTE SET, chairs, STOVE, oil & gas, Florence HOUSEHOLD GOODS after 5:00 P.M. AShley 8-9266

CHEVROLET, 1955, 4 door, Bel-Air, 6 pass. station wagon with radio & powerglide, original one owner, $1395., OR 4-5521

IRONER, Home Bendix automatic, good condition, will sell reasonable, after 5:00 P.M. OR 4-3051

FREEZER, large, Wilson, 650 lb. capacity, ROTO-TILLER, No. 2, used one year AS 8-8883

BOAT TRAILER, Tee-Nee OR 4-5477

IRON, GE, spray-steam & dry iron, $15. BLENDER, Waring, two speed, chrome, brand new, never used, $25. AShley 4-6041

GERMAIN'S IN AVERILL PARK

BEAUTIFUL INTERLOCK ORLON SWEATERS FOR GIRLS FASHIONED BY NEWPORT SIZE 4-16

HI-BULK ORLON INFANT MUFFLER SETS SMALL, MED., LARGE

COMPARE OUR QUALITY AND PRICE

EAGLEKNIT – THE HAWK BRAND IN KNITTED HEADWEAR NATIONALLY ADVERTISED STYLES FOR ALL AGES

SPECIAL JERSEY SHIRTS LONG SLEEVE EXCELLENT GIFT FOR BOYS SIZES 3-8

HINTS FROM THE SEWING BASKET OF MILLIE'S KITCHEN KORNER

Machine stitching will pull out easy if you cut the bottom thread every few stitches.

A large scrap book makes a good file for patterns, paste pages together in pairs, leaving the tip open, to form envelopes. Paste picture of pattern on scrap book envelope in which it has been filed.

Exterior Doors
BIG VALUE LOW PRICES
SEE FOR YOURSELF AND SAVE
FIR — GLAZED
ON SALE ON SALE

KEN TREMONT
OGDEN FEEDS
BUILDING SUPPLIES
SAPOLIN PAINTS
AVERILL PARK OREGON 4-5791

GEO. SCHRUMP MEATS AND GROCERIES

SAND LAKE *ADVERTISER*. Marilyn and Al Hayner started the *Sand Lake Advertiser* in 1958 from their kitchen table. Advertisements were hand-drawn or typed and printed by mimeograph. It became the *Advertiser* in the late 1960s, when neighboring communities asked to advertise and have their events published in this weekly newspaper. It has always been mailed free to area residents. Alyson Hayner Regan began as associate editor 30 years ago and became managing editor and editor in chief in 1986. Al (her father) continued as consultant. (SLHSC.)

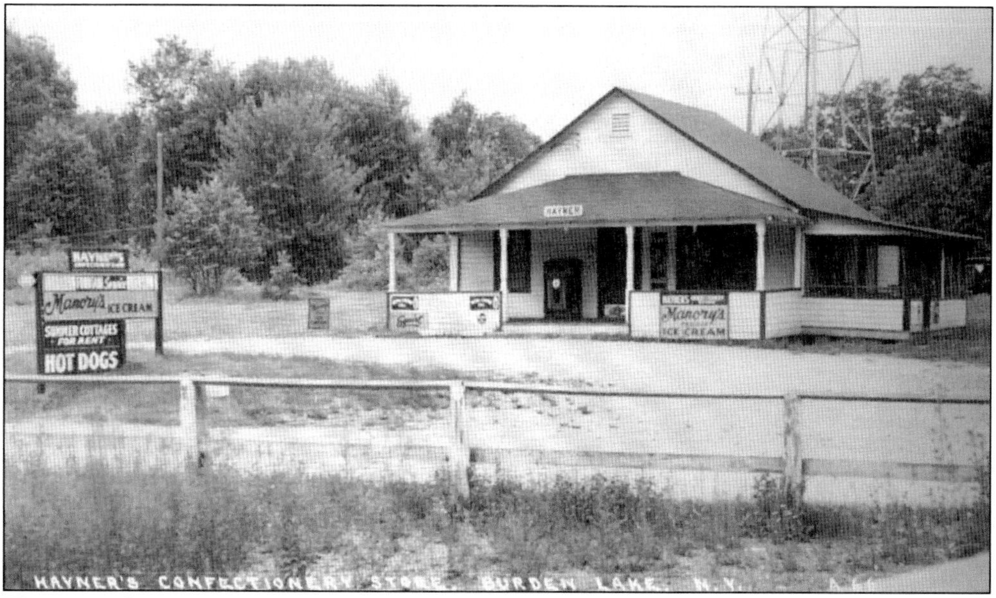

HAYNER'S CONFECTIONERY STORE. Al began Hayner's Confectionery Store in 1942 when he was 15 years old. Manory's Ice Cream gave him the first ice-cream order on consignment. A big drawing card was the jukebox on the porch for dancing. Hot dogs, fountain service, and groceries were also available. Advertising leaflets were dropped over the area from an airplane piloted by Al. When 100 leaflets were gathered, they could be turned in for a free ice-cream cone. (TSLC.)

Three

RECREATION

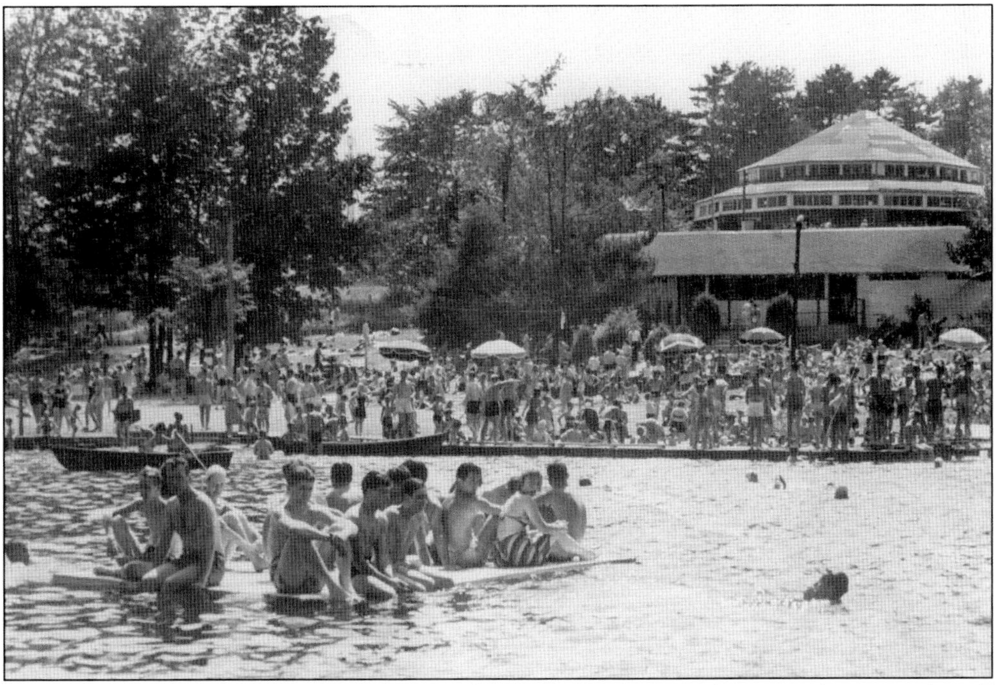

CRYSTAL LAKE BEACH AND CAROUSEL. There was quite a population explosion at Averill Park during the summer months. This day, Crystal Lake Beach was living up to its nickname of "Upstate Coney Island." For some it was a one-day excursion, a round-trip trolley ride, or, at a later date, a United Traction Company bus ride to and from Albia on the outskirts of Troy. Many others would stay at the hotels in the area for extended vacations. Fishing, hunting, hiking, boating, and camping were available at the seven lakes within the town and could be interspersed with more visits to the carousel and other rides (see *Sand Lake*, pages 58 and 59). (CV.)

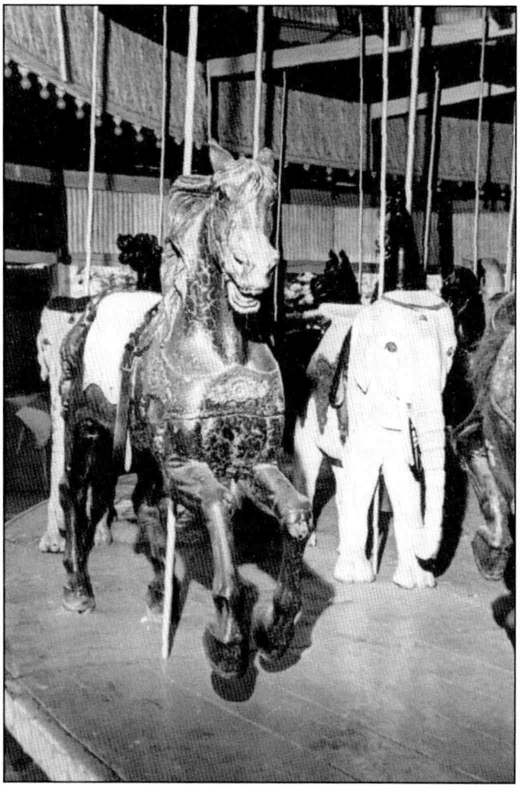

Carousel Horse and Elephant. The horse ride had a feature the elephant ride did not have. The horse had a real horsehair tail. If patrons rode often enough, they might display their expertise by stepping on the stirrup and swinging a leg over the horse's back. (CV.)

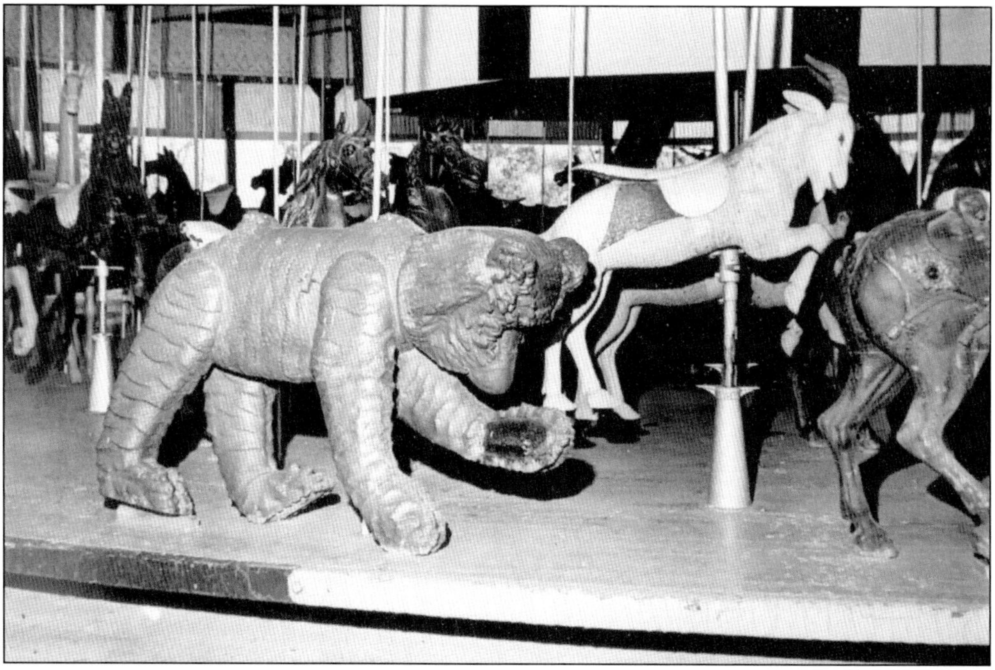

Carousel Bear and Goat. Other choices for rides were the bear or goat. All the animals were hand-carved. The carousel was sold in 1947 and subsequently dismantled. One of the bears made its way to a museum. (CV.)

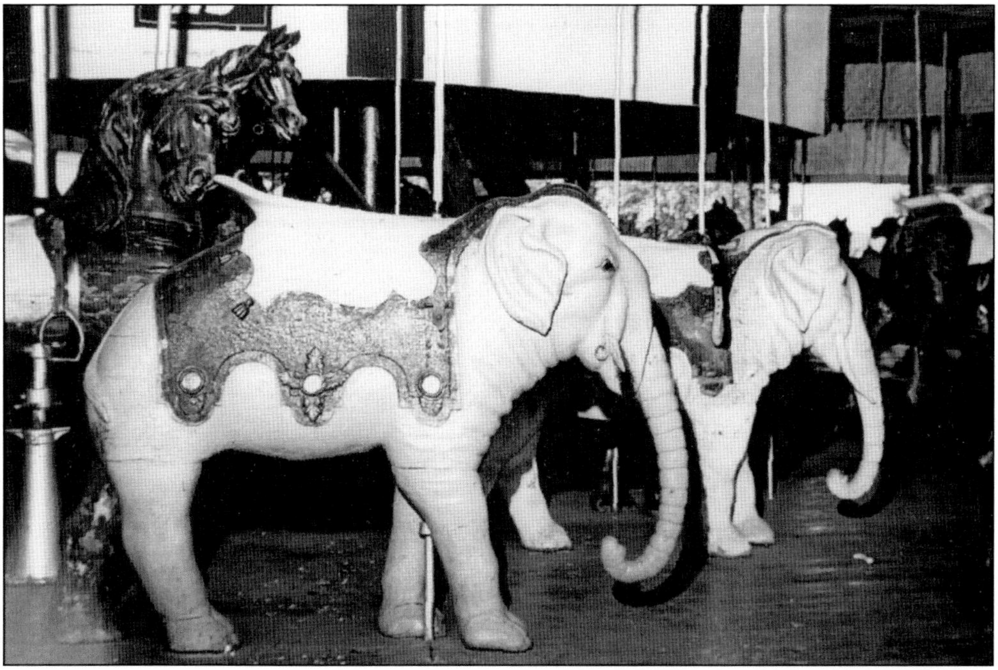

Carousel Elephants. The elephants had to have a seat extension on their backs so the rider could stay upright and not slide off. (CV.)

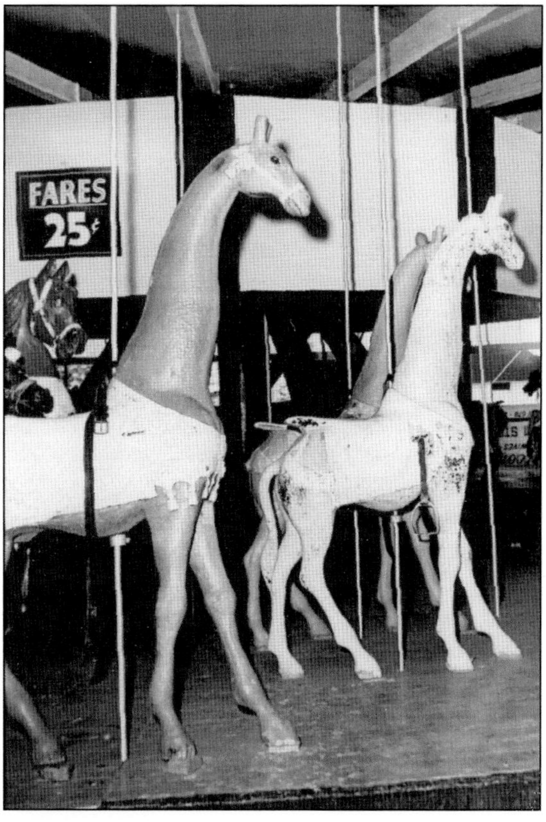

Carousel Giraffes. These giraffe rides appear to be walkers. Other rides like the horses were called jumpers and went up and down. Individuals especially wanted to ride on the outside to try for a brass ring, which brought the reward of a free ride. (CV.)

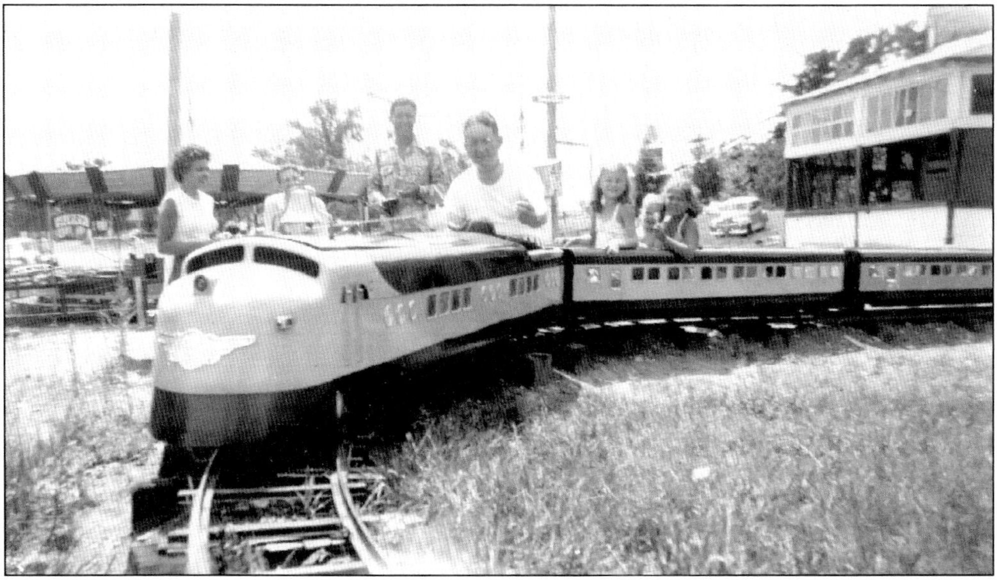

MINIATURE TRAIN RIDE. Armand St. Germain was often a helper to Bernard Mantha, owner of the Crystal Lake Beach. Here he is the driver for the miniature train ride. The carousel is also close by for the passengers' next ride. (MSt.G.)

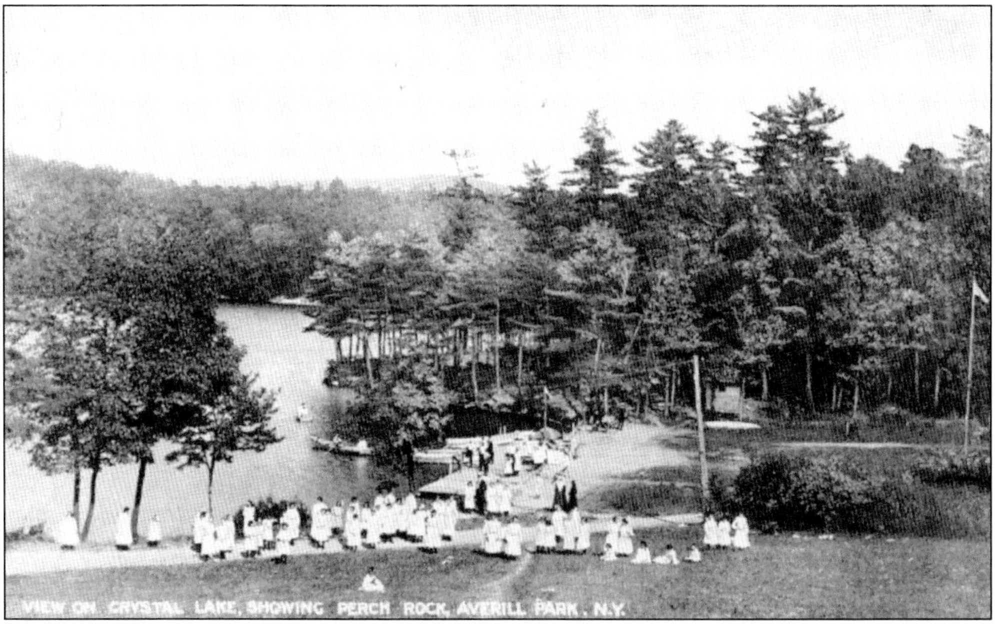

CRYSTAL LAKE BEACH AND PERCH ROCK. The open space on the far shore was known as Perch Rock. It was a popular swimming and fishing spot for local residents. It would seem that the long white dresses and black stockings and shoes are a uniform for the girls enjoying their day at the beach. (AT.)

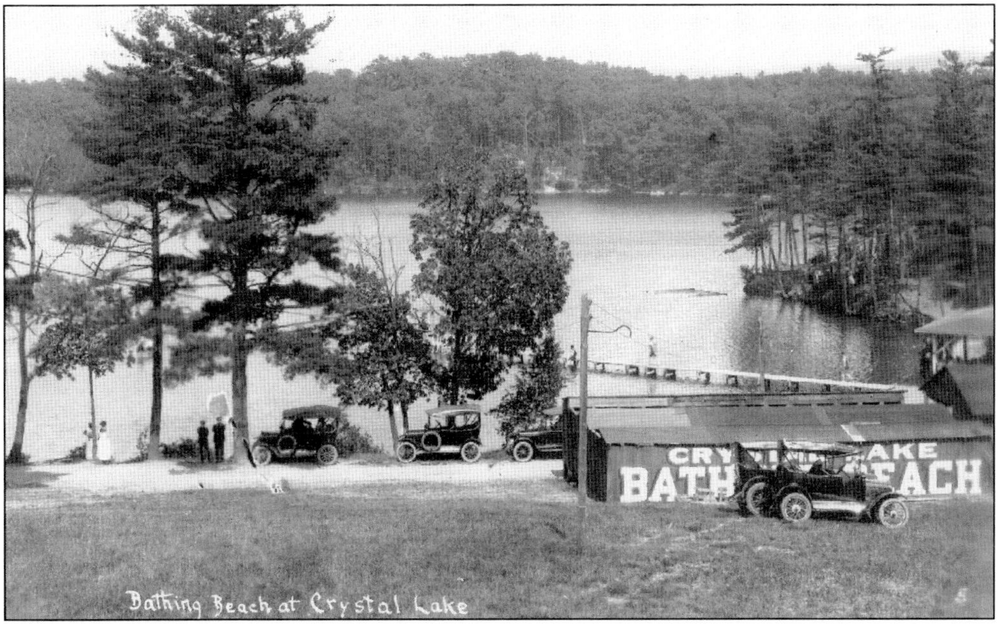

CRYSTAL LAKE BEACH. With private cars becoming more popular, the need for taxis to the trolley station would be decreasing. (LH.)

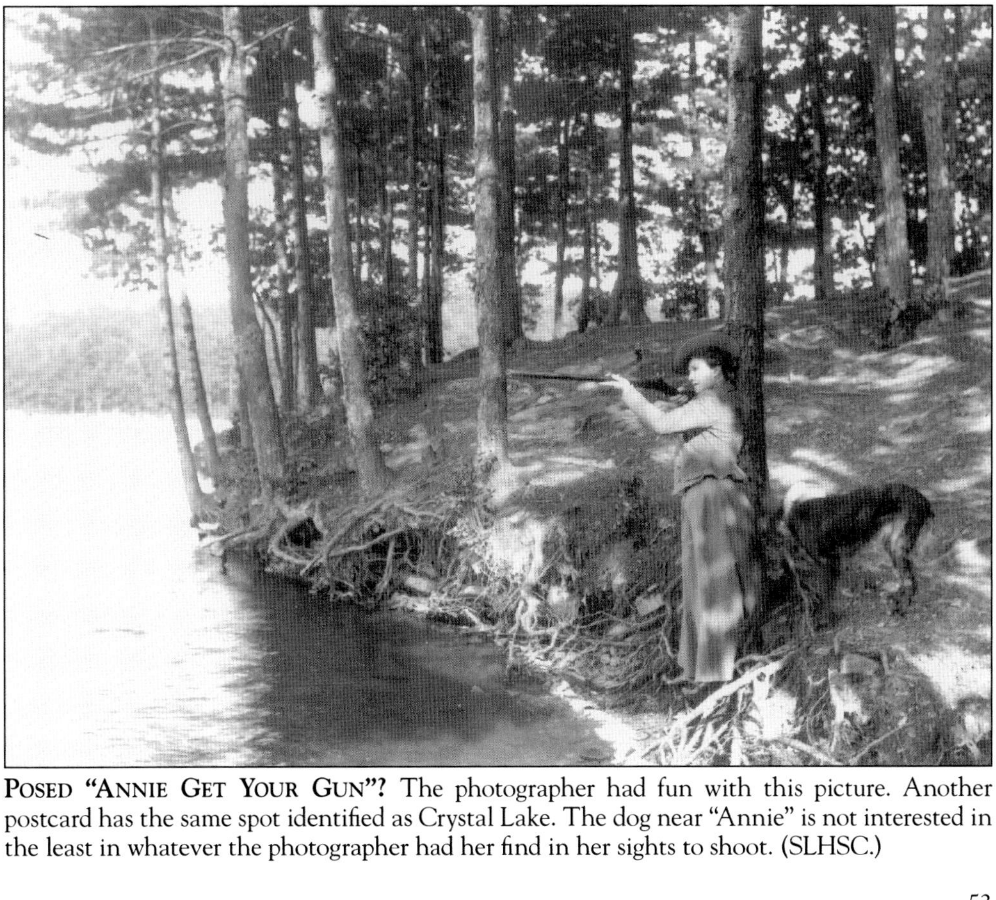

POSED "ANNIE GET YOUR GUN"? The photographer had fun with this picture. Another postcard has the same spot identified as Crystal Lake. The dog near "Annie" is not interested in the least in whatever the photographer had her find in her sights to shoot. (SLHSC.)

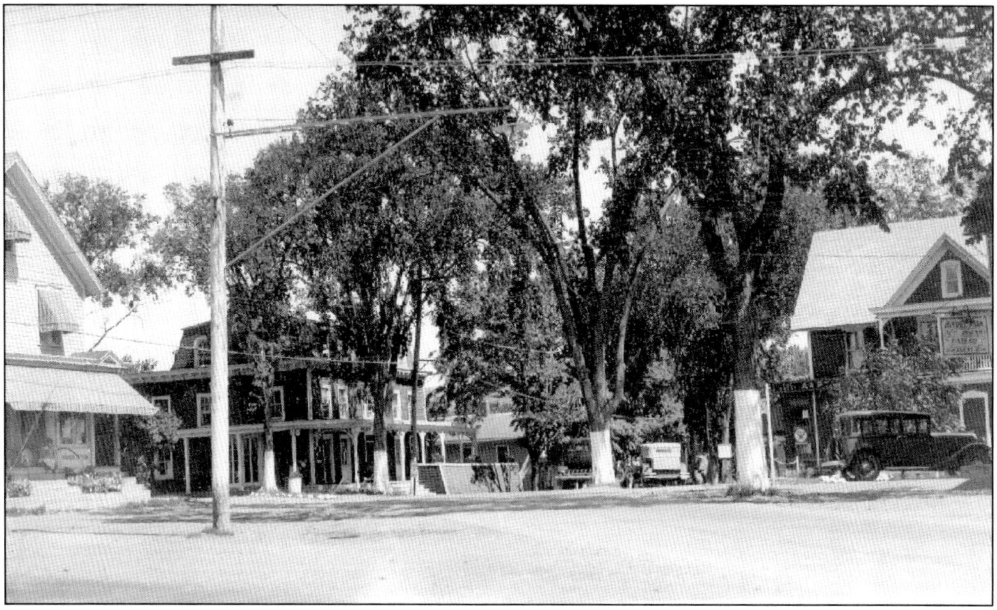

MAIN STREET AVERILL PARK. In the center of Averill Park hamlet are, from left to right, Stout's Hardware Store, Lake View Hotel, and, across the street, the A&P. Stout's Hardware is now Legenbauer Gas and Oil Company. (MSt.G.)

¶ Open the Year 'Round : Rates Two Dollars per Day : Special Rates by the Week to Summer Boarders. ¶ Crystal Lake 100 feet from Hotel : Good Boating and Fishing Covered Dancing Pavilion on Lake Shore : Picnic Grove, Boat Livery, Tennis Court : 1000 feet above Sea Level.

Lake View Hotel

B. F. CUSACK, PROPRIETOR

AVERILL PARK, RENSSELAER COUNTY, NEW YORK

¶ Three hundred feet from Electric Railroad : Long Distance Telephone. ¶ Large Hall in Hotel : Annex for Entertainments : Trolley Parties.

B. F. CUSACK'S LAKE VIEW HOTEL ADVERTISEMENT. This advertisement gives all the amenities of the Lake View Hotel when B. F. Cusack was proprietor. (AT.)

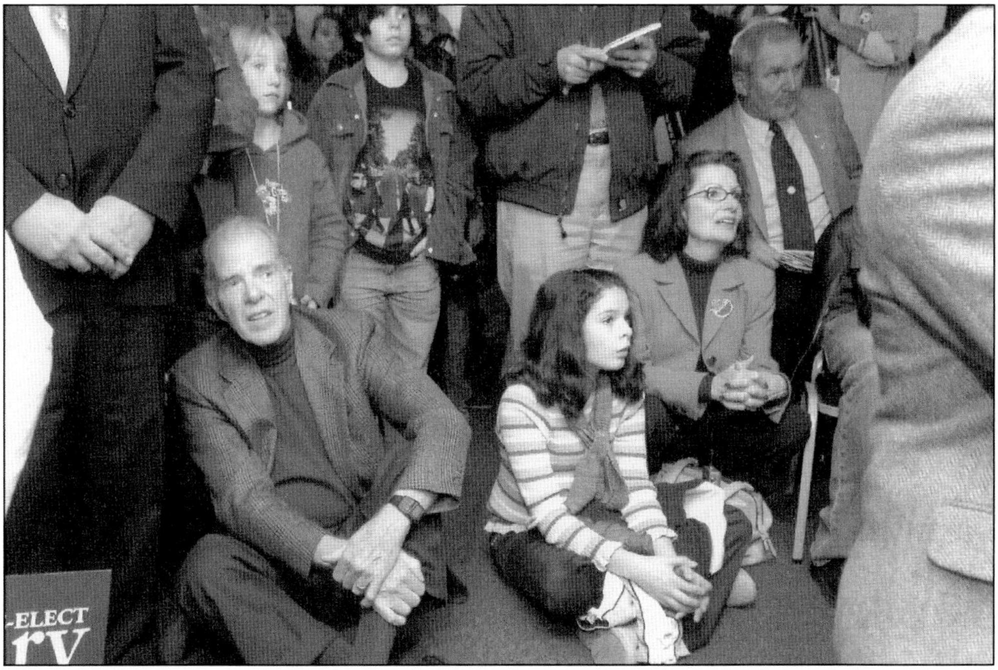

WILLIAM KENNEDY AT LAKEVIEW ON CRYSTAL LAKE. The Lakeview on Crystal Lake Restaurant was chosen by the Democrats in October 2006 for an election rally with Sen. Hillary Rodham Clinton as a big drawing card. With standing room only, Sand Lake resident and Pulitzer Prize–winner William Kennedy found a seat on the floor to listen. (BW, Tom Killips photograph for the *Record*.)

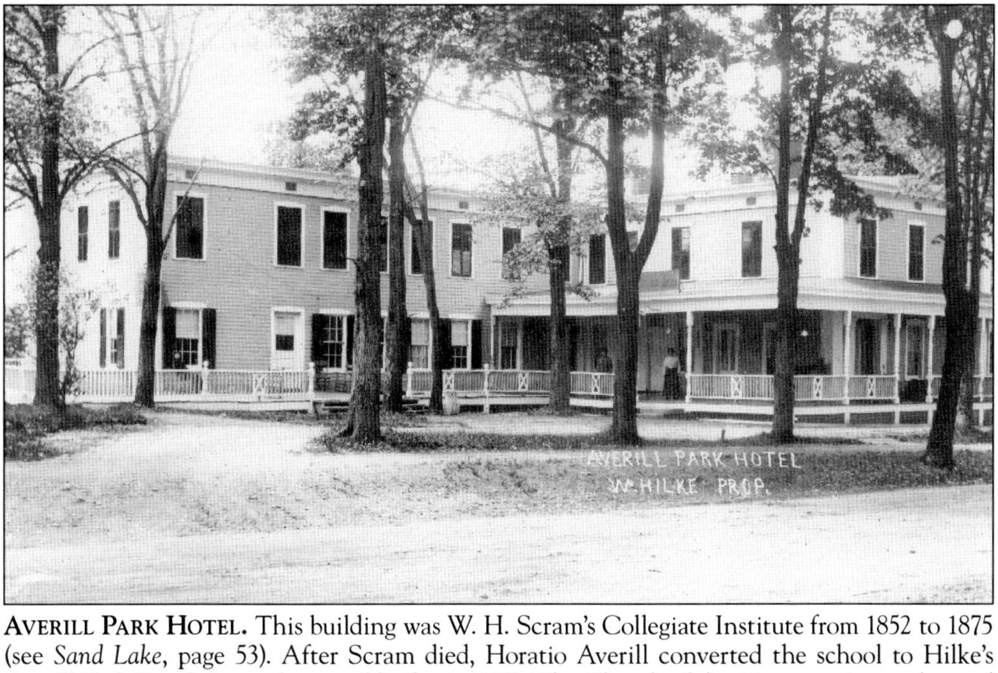

AVERILL PARK HOTEL. This building was W. H. Scram's Collegiate Institute from 1852 to 1875 (see *Sand Lake*, page 53). After Scram died, Horatio Averill converted the school to Hilke's Averill Park Hotel. It was destroyed by fire in 1921. The Church of the Covenant is now located on this site. (AT.)

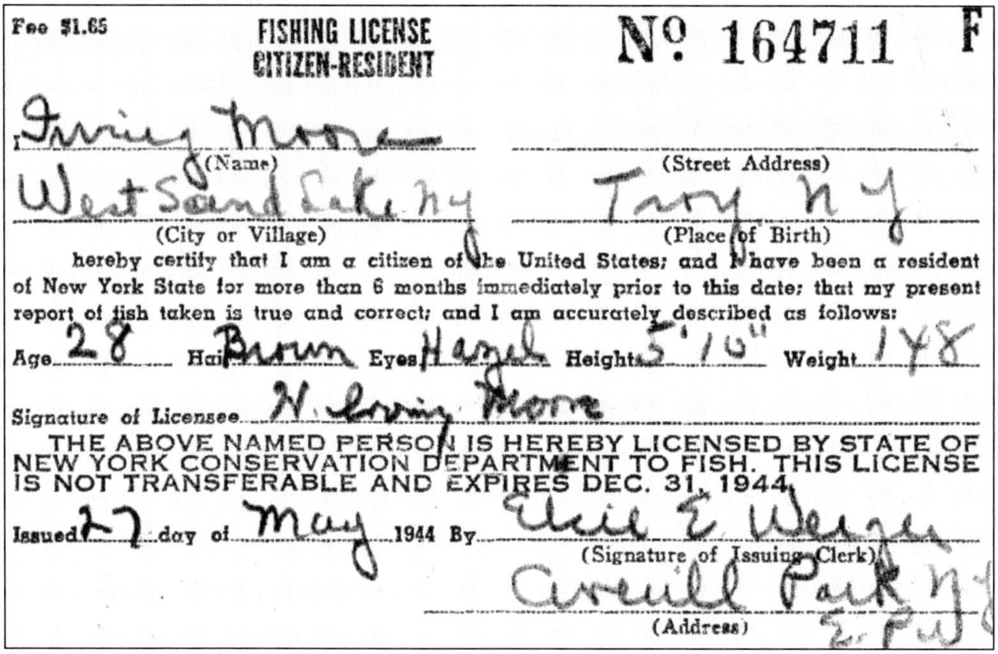

Fee $1.65 FISHING LICENSE CITIZEN-RESIDENT Nº 164711 F

Irving Moore (Name) (Street Address)

West Sand Lake NY (City or Village) Troy N Y (Place of Birth)

hereby certify that I am a citizen of the United States; and have been a resident of New York State for more than 6 months immediately prior to this date; that my present report of fish taken is true and correct; and I am accurately described as follows:

Age 28 Hair Brown Eyes Hazel Height 5'10" Weight 148

Signature of Licensee H. Irving Moore

THE ABOVE NAMED PERSON IS HEREBY LICENSED BY STATE OF NEW YORK CONSERVATION DEPARTMENT TO FISH. THIS LICENSE IS NOT TRANSFERABLE AND EXPIRES DEC. 31, 1944.

Issued 27 day of May 1944 By Elsie E Werger (Signature of Issuing Clerk)

Averill Park N Y (Address)

FISHING LICENSE. In 1944, Robert Moore's father, H. Irving Moore, paid $1.65 for his fishing license. (RIM.)

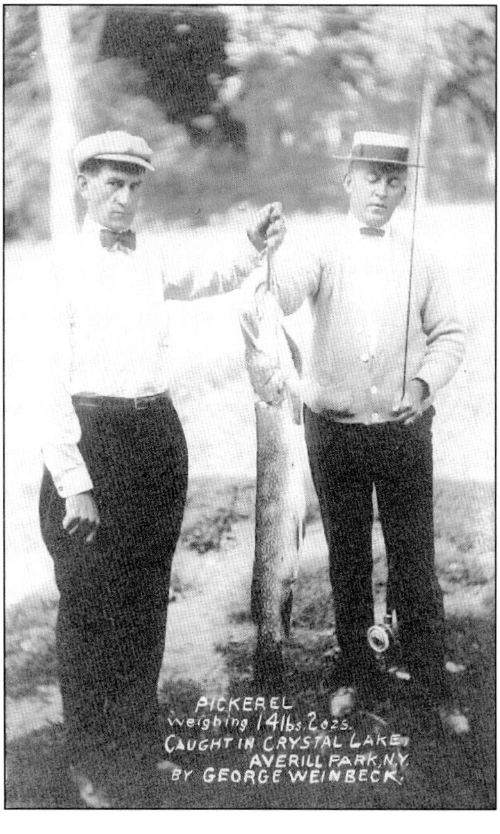

GEORGE WEINBECK WITH HIS 14-POUND PICKEREL. George Weinbeck lived in a boardinghouse located near the old firehouse on Route 43. It was run by Anna Werger for persons who worked in Faith Mills. Weinbeck proudly displays the 14-pound, 2-ounce pickerel he caught in Crystal Lake. Having a postcard of such a fine catch would certainly be good advertisement for other fishermen. (AT.)

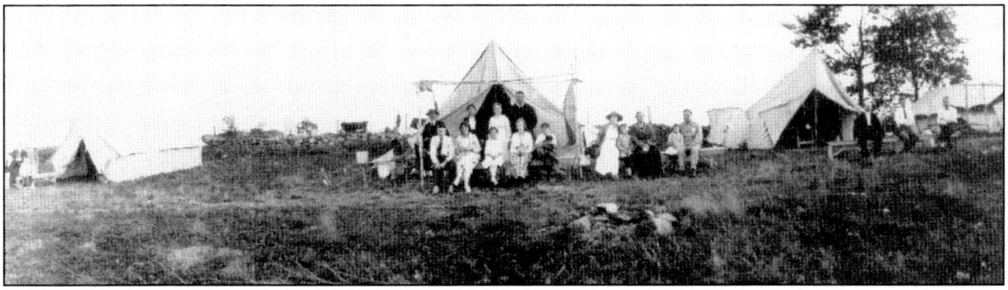

METHODIST FARM. Camping at the Methodist Farm on Crooked Lake was very rustic between 1915 and 1920. (SLHSC.)

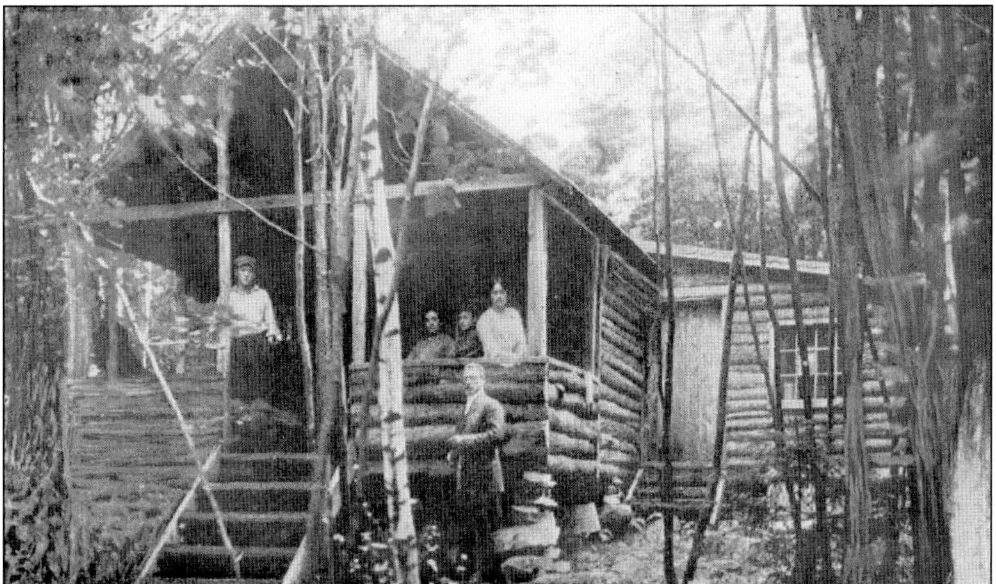

CAMP FUHRMANN ON BIG BOWMAN POND. Camp Fuhrmann was built in 1908 on the east shore of Big Bowman Pond. Since his childhood, Edward Fuhrmann had attended Sunday school and services during the summer at the "Taborton Church." After becoming an Evangelical and Reformed clergyman, Reverend Fuhrmann substituted for Rev. Oscar Egli. After Egli's death, Fuhrmann became the pastor of Zion's Evangelical and Reformed Church of Taborton. (LH.)

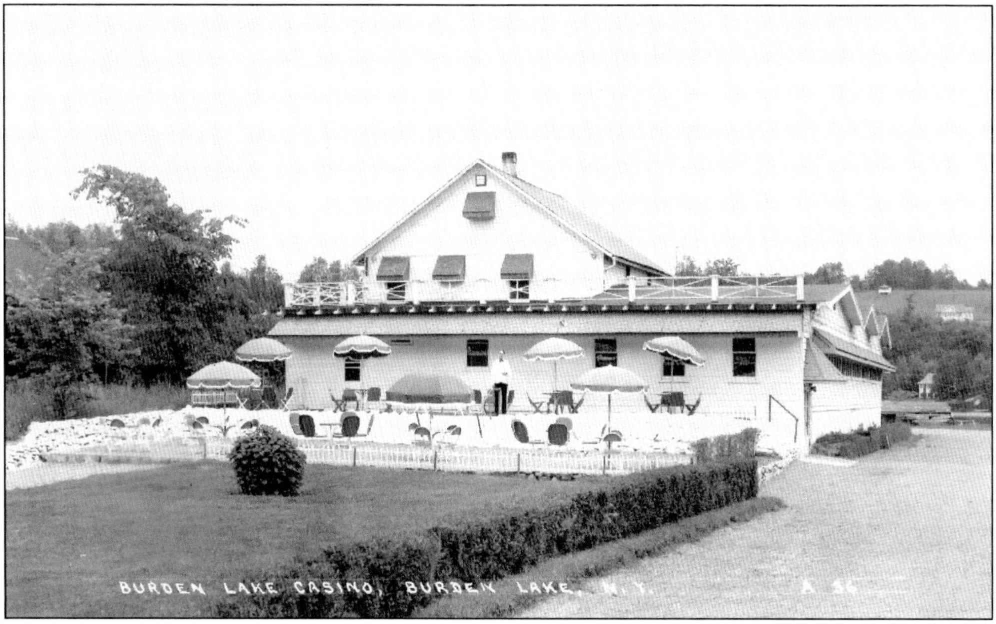

BURDEN LAKE CASINO. Begun first as Fisherman's Rest, this site later became the Burden Lake Hotel and Burden Lake Casino. It was located on the second lake on Burden Lake Road. (JC.)

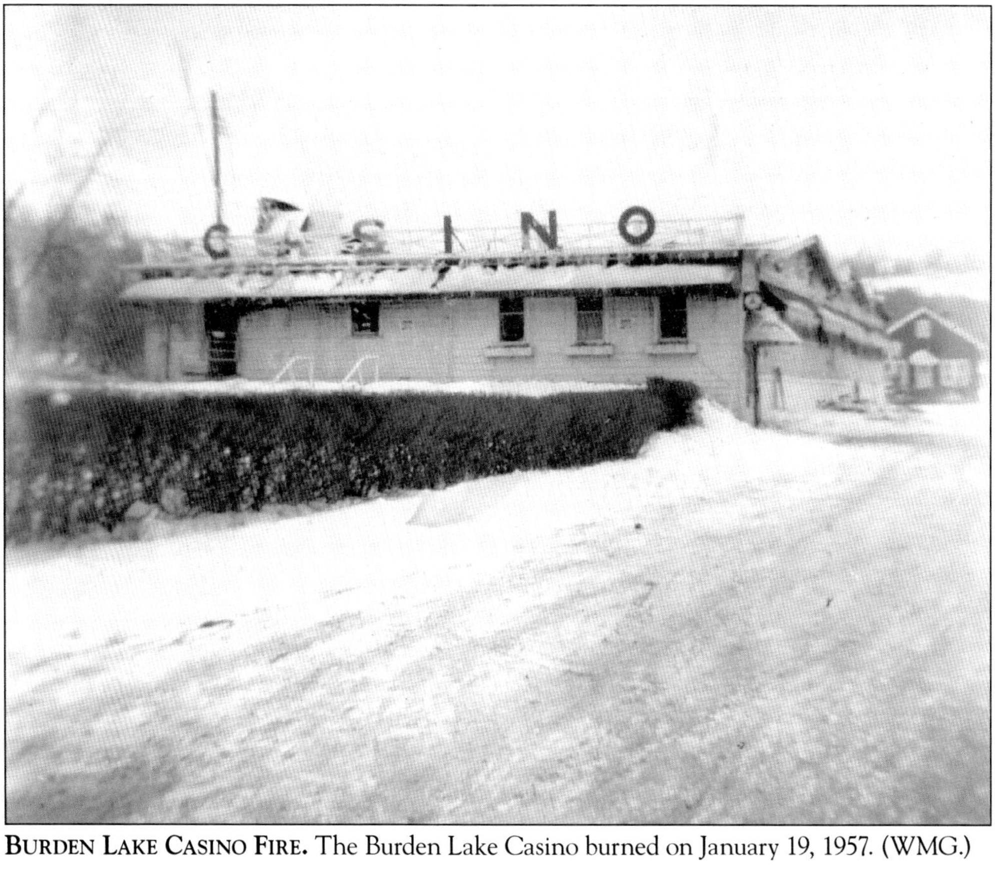

BURDEN LAKE CASINO FIRE. The Burden Lake Casino burned on January 19, 1957. (WMG.)

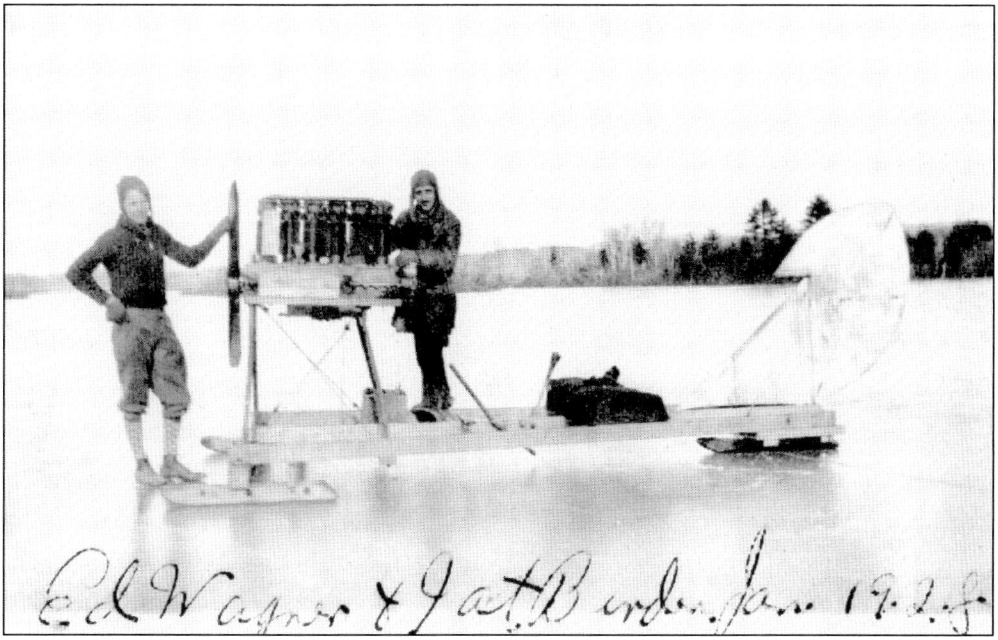

ICEBOAT. John Arekian Sr. (right) gives Edward Wagner a ride on Burden Lake in the iceboat built by Arekian and Ralph Sleicher. The boat, driven by a Franklin air-cooled motor with an airplane propeller attached, could reach 80 miles per hour. It was picked up for speeding when it went that fast on the Hudson River. (JA.)

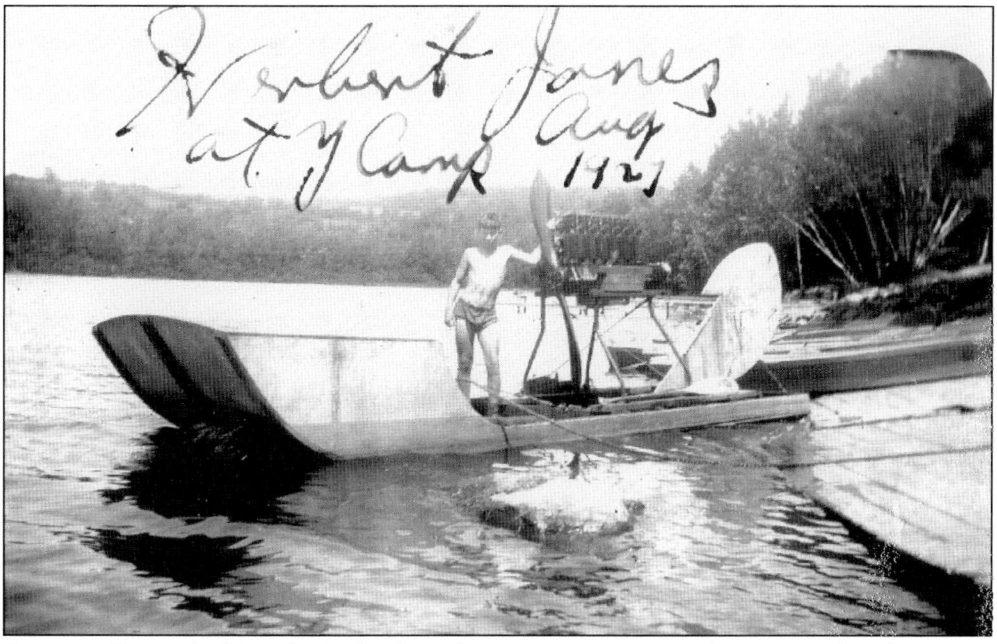

AREKIAN BOAT. Arekian also built a boat for summertime use on the water and paid a visit to the YMCA Camp Van Schoonhoven. Herbert Jones poses for this picture. (JA.)

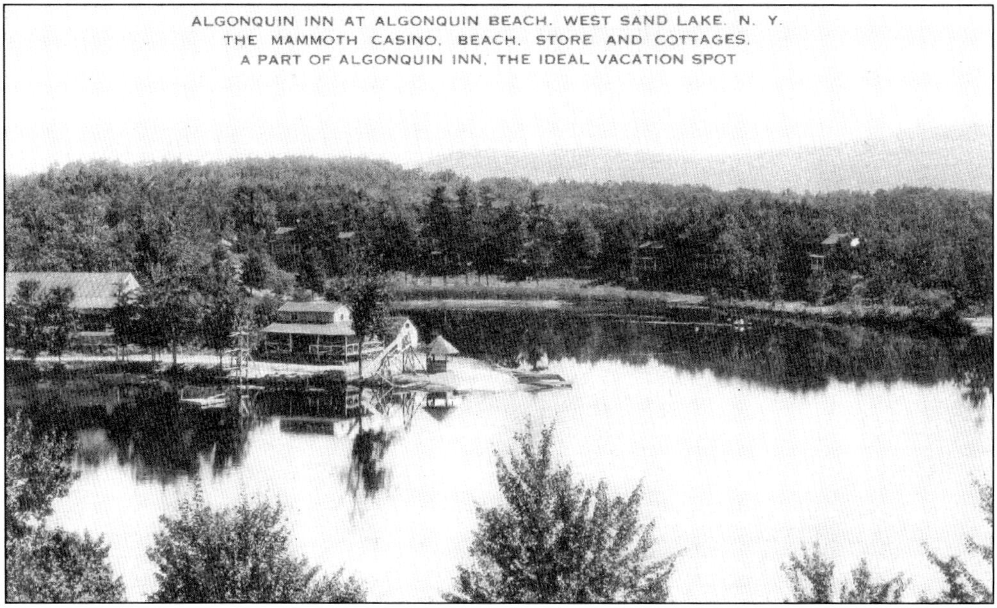

ALGONQUIN INN. Advertised on the front of this postcard is the variety of facilities available at Algonquin Inn. (RS.)

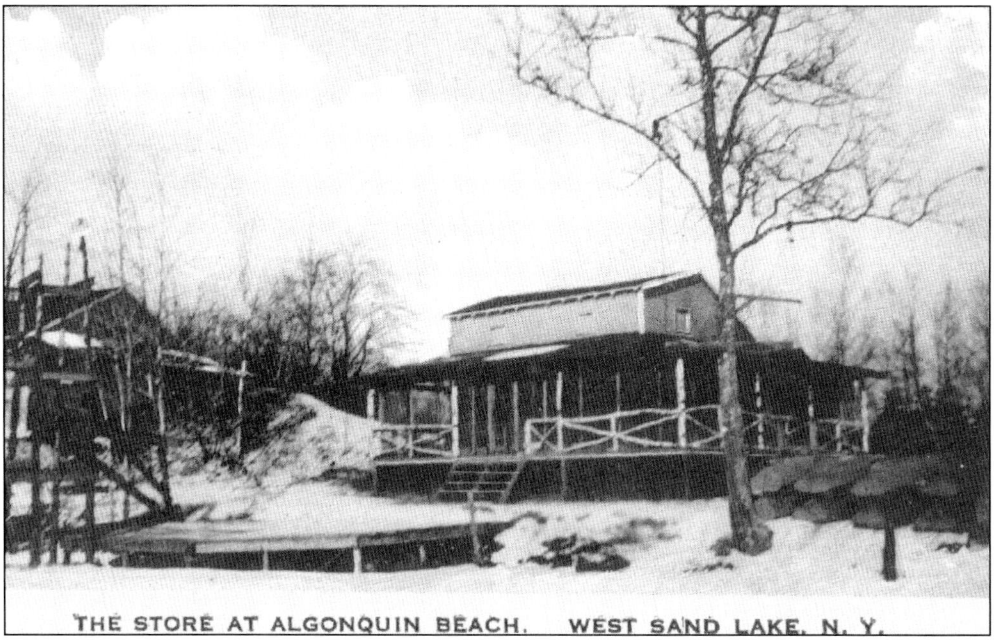

ALGONQUIN STORE AT ALGONQUIN INN. This postcard advertised, "We have Canoes, Boats, Diving Towers, Spring Boards, Bath Houses, Suits For Rent, Fishing Tackle, Store Dance Hall, Free." (LH.)

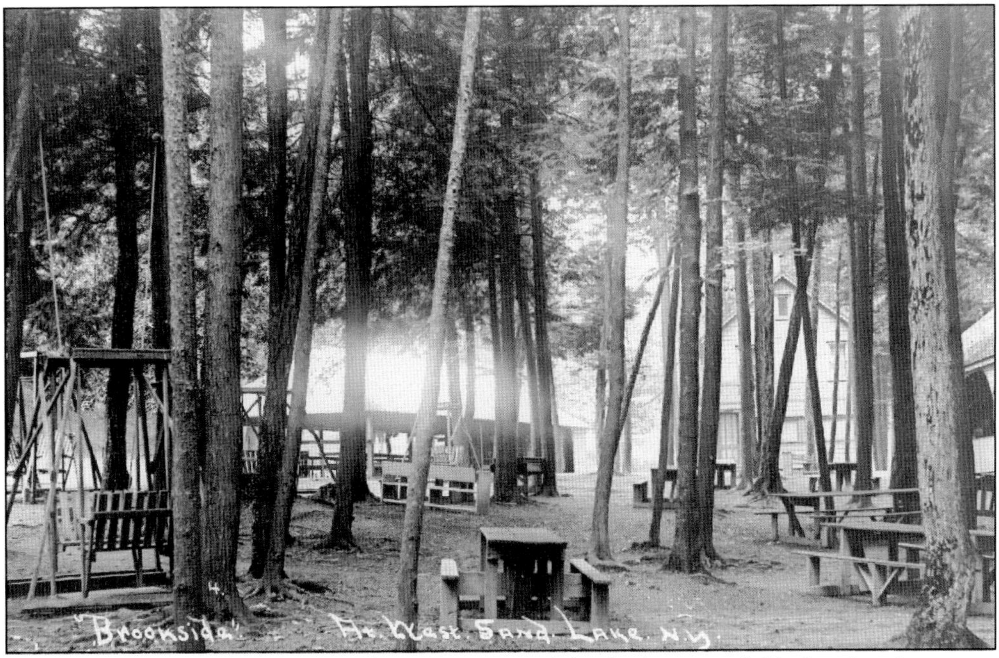

BROOKSIDE PARK. This photograph gives a view of the facilities available for church picnics, family picnics, and other organizational outings at Brookside Park in West Sand Lake. (JC.)

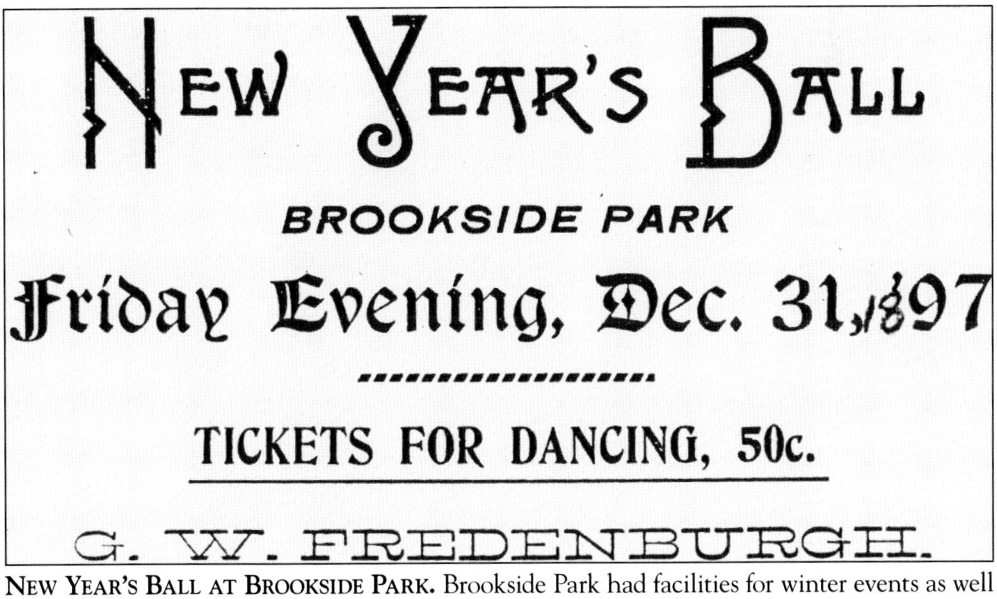
NEW YEAR'S BALL

BROOKSIDE PARK

Friday Evening, Dec. 31, 1897

TICKETS FOR DANCING, 50c.

G. W. FREDENBURGH.

NEW YEAR'S BALL AT BROOKSIDE PARK. Brookside Park had facilities for winter events as well as being available all summer. (CV.)

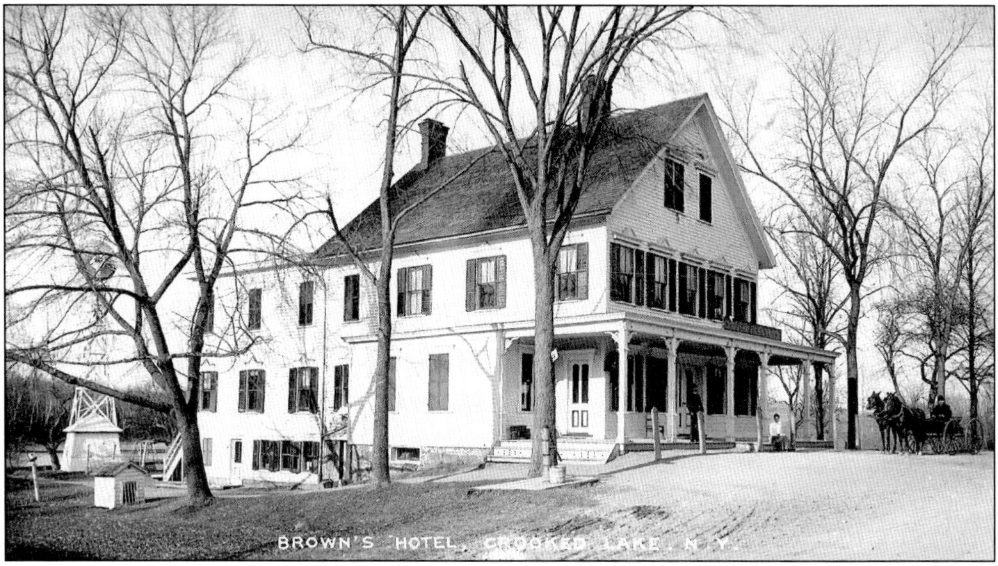

BROWN'S CROOKED LAKE HOUSE. Most generally, the hotel Willet Brown purchased in 1860, after it had been rebuilt by James M. Mosher, has been called Brown's Crooked Lake House. Its claim to fame was that Gov. Theodore Roosevelt was a frequent guest (see *Sand Lake*, page 94). (AT.)

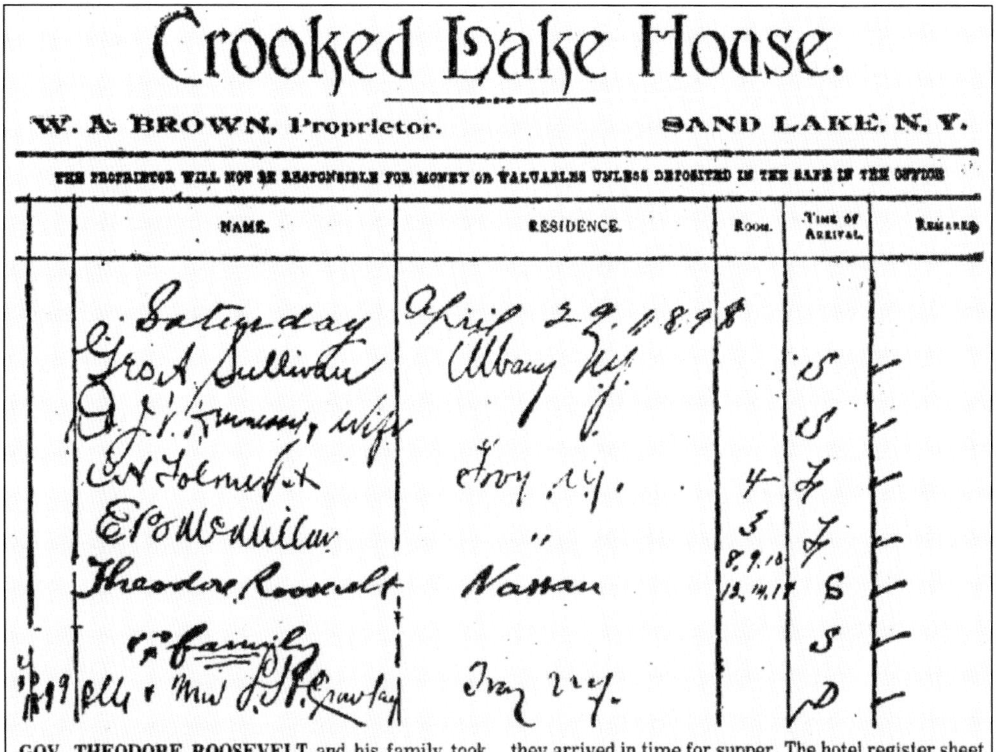

Crooked Lake House.

W. A. BROWN, Proprietor. SAND LAKE, N. Y.

THE PROPRIETOR WILL NOT BE RESPONSIBLE FOR MONEY OR VALUABLES UNLESS DEPOSITED IN THE SAFE IN THE OFFICE

NAME	RESIDENCE	ROOM	TIME OF ARRIVAL	REMARKS
Saturday	April 29. 1898			
Geo. A. Sullivan	Albany N.Y.		S	
[illegible] & Wife	"		S	
C. H. Tolme [illegible]	Troy N.Y.	4	T	
E. P. McMillan	"	3	T	
Theodore Roosevelt	Nassau	8, 9, 10, 12, 14, 17	S	
& family			S	
Mr & Mrs [illegible] Crowley	Troy N.Y.		D	

GOV. THEODORE ROOSEVELT and his family took they arrived in time for supper. The hotel register sheet

GOV. THEODORE ROOSEVELT'S SIGNATURE. An article in the *Troy Record* publicized the Crooked Lake House register sheet with Gov. Theodore Roosevelt's signature, with the six rooms the family would occupy, and that they arrived for supper. (TSLC.)

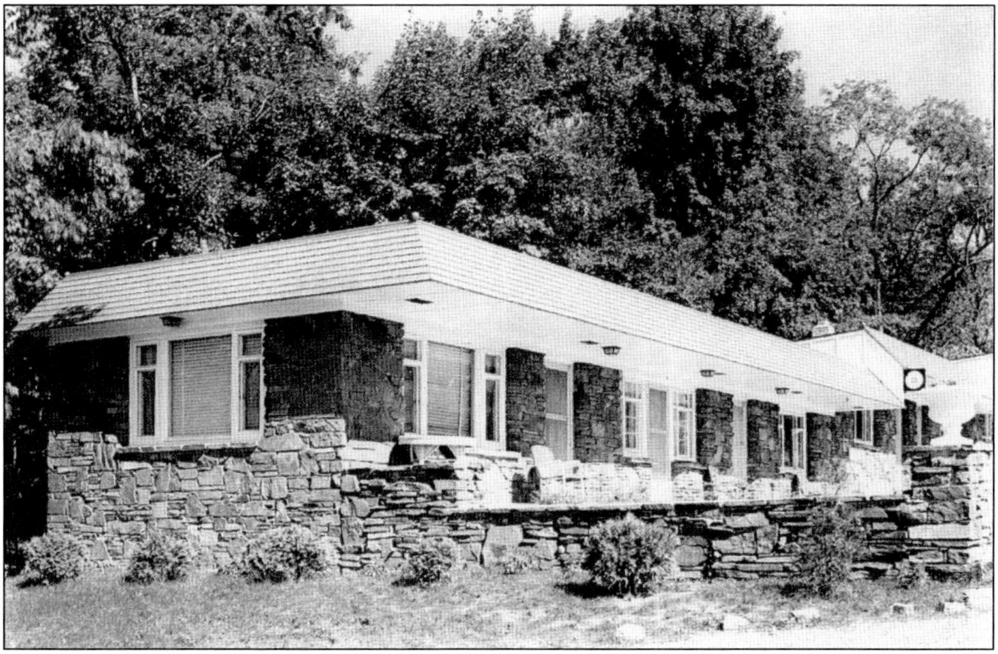

CROOKED LAKE MOTEL. The Crooked Lake Motel was built in 1957 on the hill opposite the hotel and had 35 units and a commanding view of the lake. (AT.)

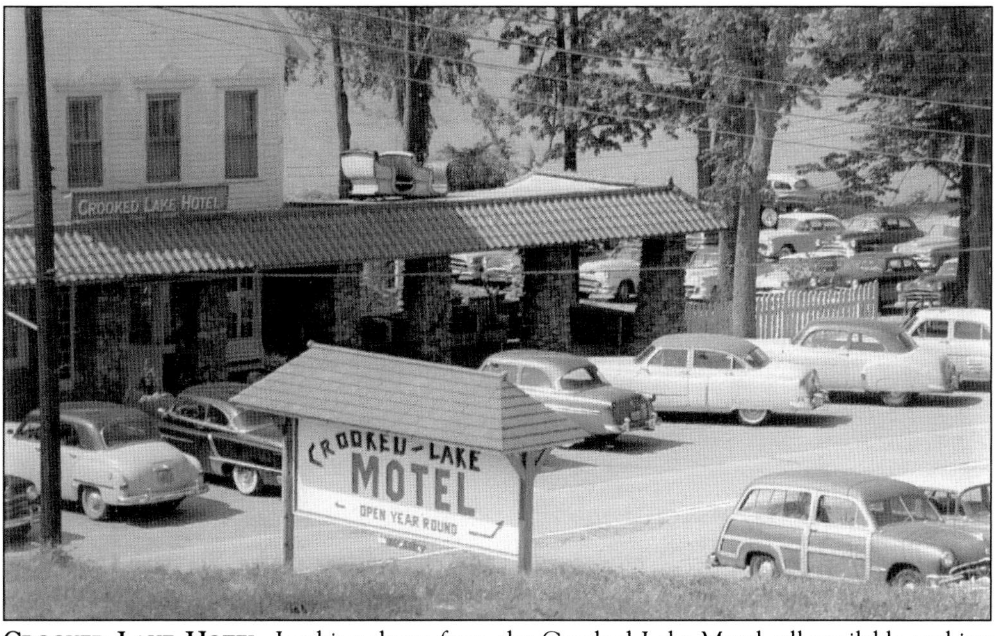

CROOKED LAKE HOTEL. Looking down from the Crooked Lake Motel, all available parking space is being used for the occasion being hosted at the hotel. (JC.)

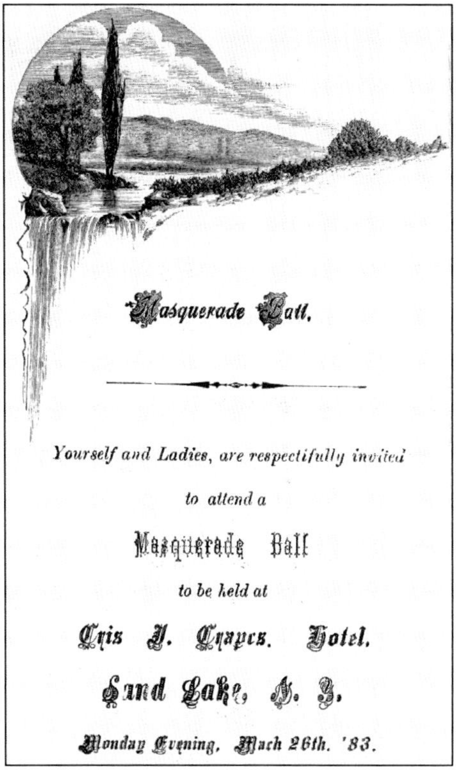

Masquerade Ball.

Yourself and Ladies, are respectifully invited

to attend a

Masquerade Ball

to be held at

Cris Y. Crapes. Hotel,

Sand Lake, N. Y.

Monday Evening, Mach 26th. '83.

MASQUERADE BALL. On "Mach" 26, 1883, "Yourself and Ladies" were "respectifully" invited to the masquerade ball at "Cris Y. Crapes Hotel." One wonders whether Crist Crape paid full price for the spelling errors in this otherwise attractive program. (TSLC.)

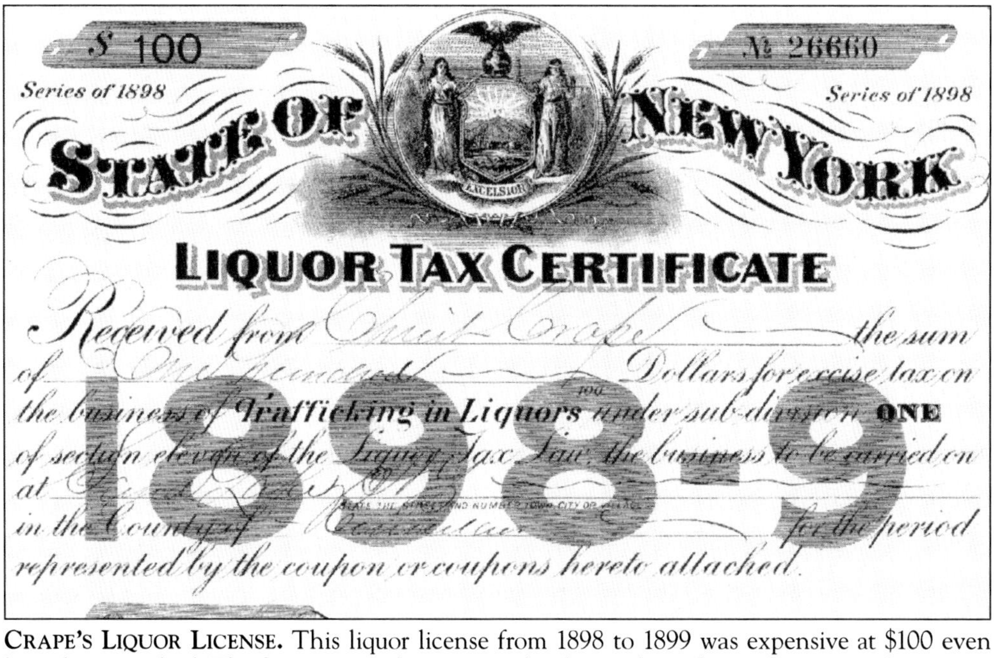

$ 100 — № 26660

Series of 1898 — Series of 1898

STATE OF NEW YORK

LIQUOR TAX CERTIFICATE

1898-9

Received from Crist Crape the sum of One Hundred Dollars for excise tax on the business of Trafficking in Liquors under sub-division ONE of section eleven of the Liquor Tax Law, the business to be carried on at Sand Lake, N.Y. in the County of Rensselaer for the period represented by the coupon or coupons hereto attached.

CRAPE'S LIQUOR LICENSE. This liquor license from 1898 to 1899 was expensive at $100 even by today's standard. The fine print at the top stated, "If a window adjoins the principal entrance to your place, post this certificate therein so that it may be readily seen from the street." At the bottom it read, "Severe penalties are imposed for neglect or refusal to place and keep this certificate conspicuously in your place of business." (TSLC.)

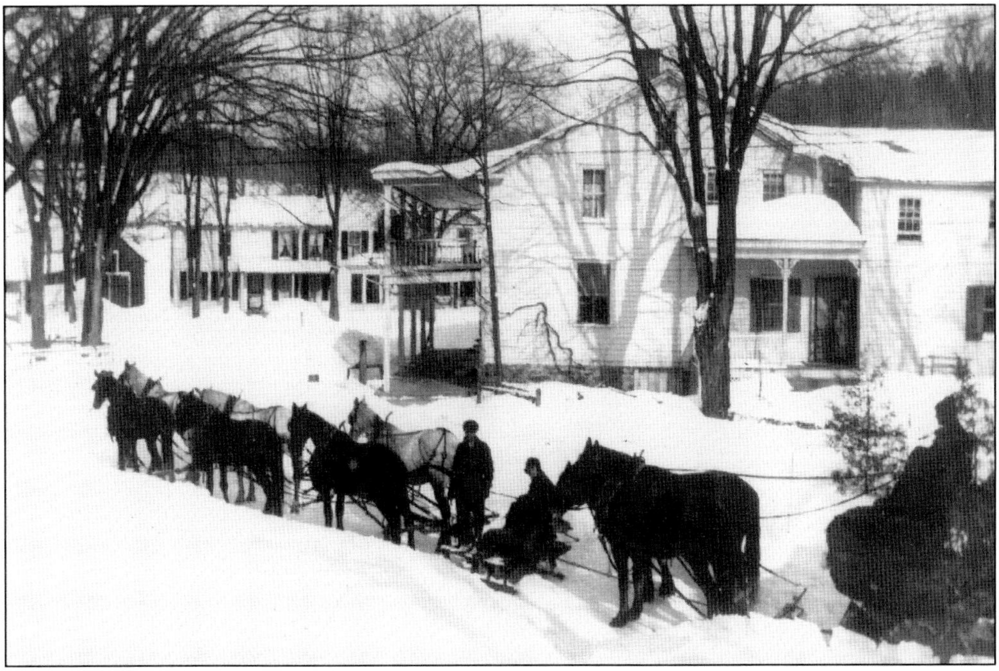

CRAPE'S HOTEL IN WINTER. The depth of this scene shows some of the hotel's 22 rooms. Oswald Biittig Jr. owned the hotel building as his home from around 1945 to 1955. His daughter Gladys Corbeil verified a rectangular metal bar extended from floor to ceiling in her bedroom. According to oral history, during a hotel stopover with prisoners, they would be handcuffed to that metal bar. A soprano soloist, Corbeil also attested to the excellent acoustics of the ballroom. (TSLC.)

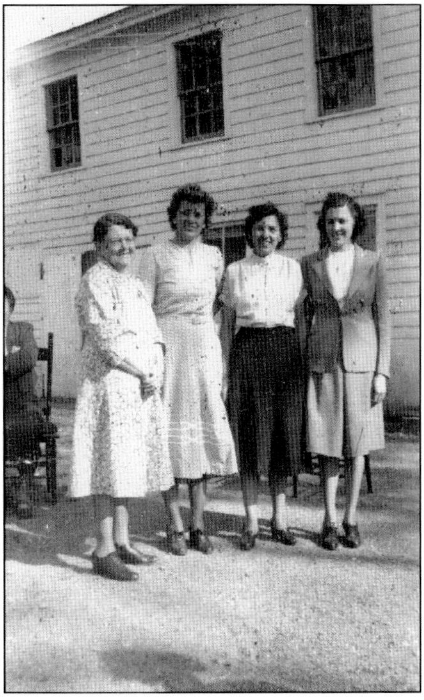

CARRIE GUNDRUM AND DAUGHTERS. Seen here are, from left to right, Carrie Gundrum (see page 46) and daughters Mildred Smyth, Luella Shoemaker, and Iona Mosher. Seated on the left is her son John's wife, Rachel Gundrum. Carrie rented one of the 22 rooms in Crape's Hotel building from Oswald Biittig Jr. Families of her three daughters and eight sons would get together on Mother's Day and her birthday, November 11. (DG.)

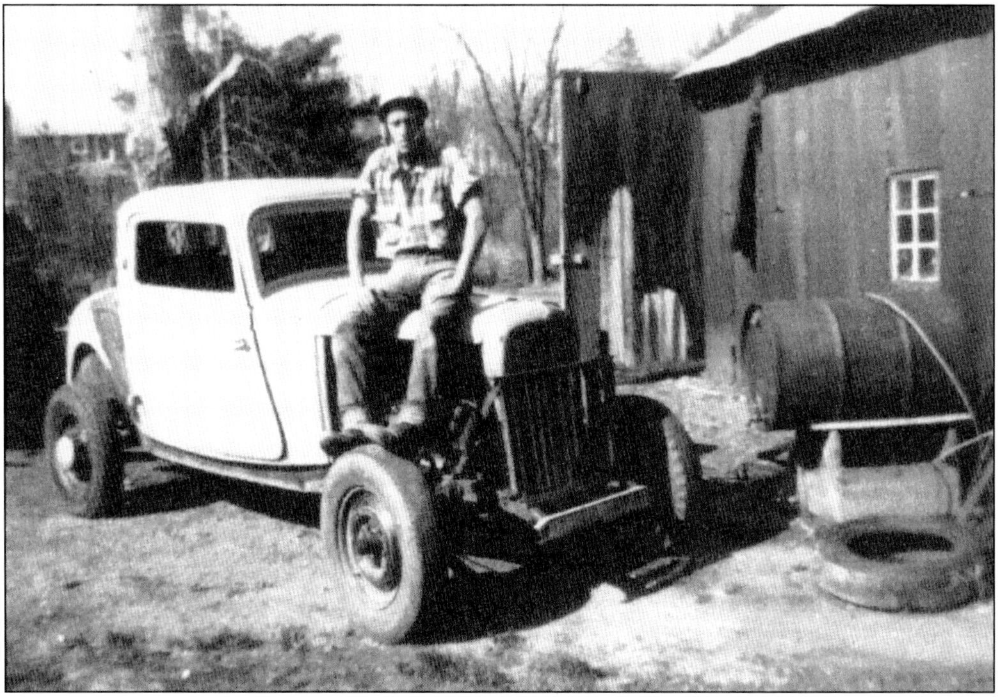

John Leavenworth's Stock Car. The hood of John Leavenworth's stock car makes a good seat for him in this picture. He ran in races at Pine Bowl and Burden Lake Speedways. (SLHSC.)

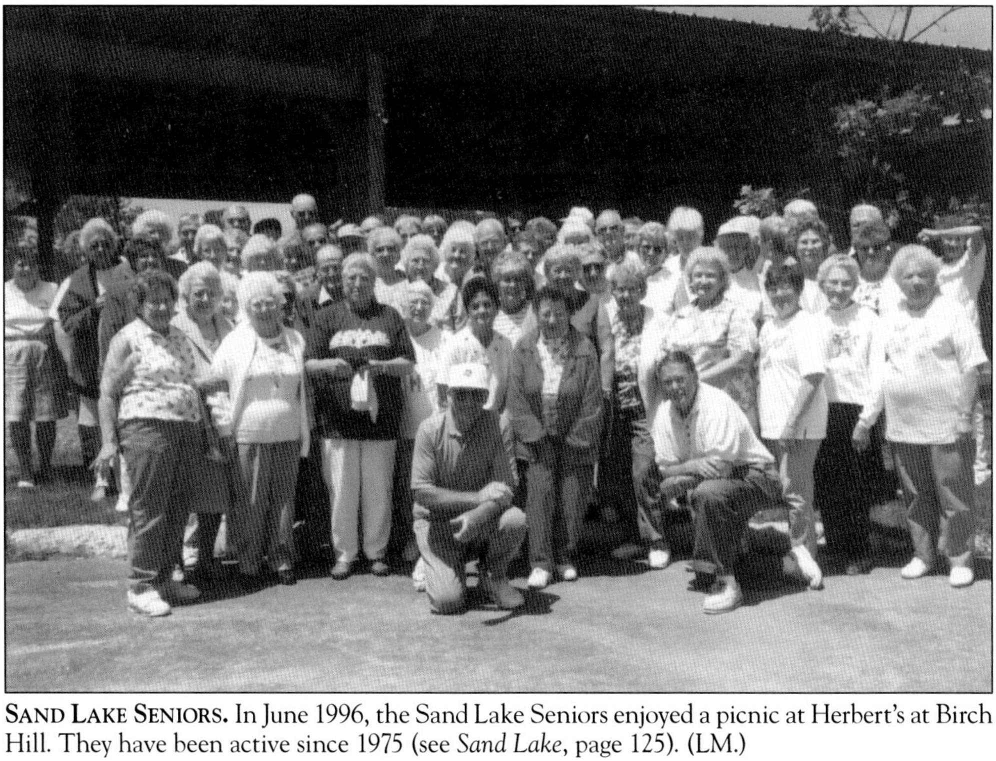

Sand Lake Seniors. In June 1996, the Sand Lake Seniors enjoyed a picnic at Herbert's at Birch Hill. They have been active since 1975 (see *Sand Lake*, page 125). (LM.)

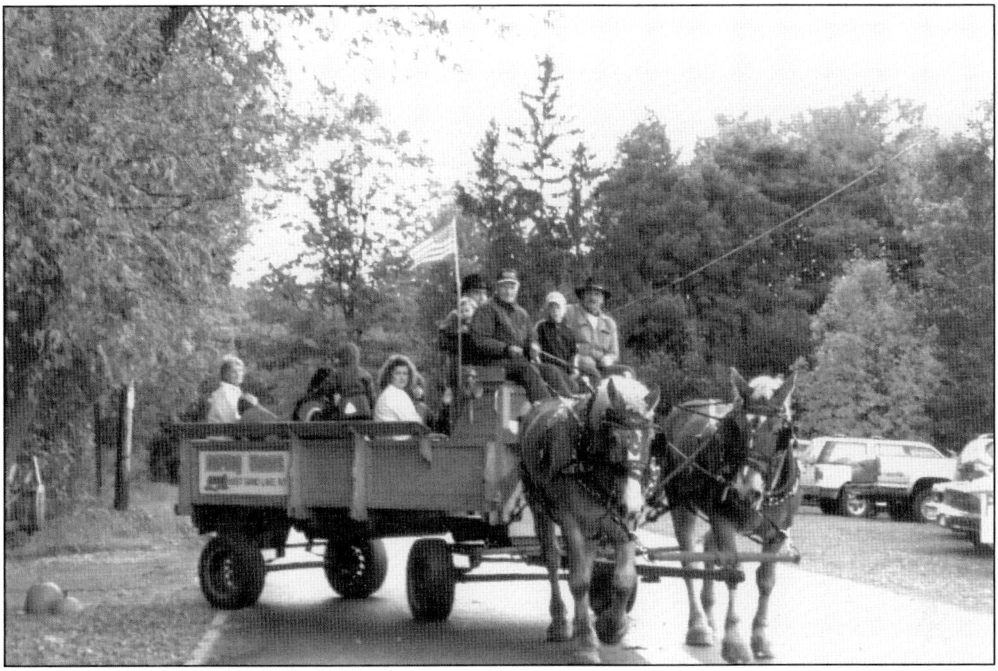

RIDE AT HOFFAY'S FARM. William Hoffay welcomed people to his farm with horse-drawn rides through the meadows around 1998–2005. On the driver's seat are, from left to right, William Green Jr., his great-grandson Nicholas Concra, and William Hoffay. Seated directly behind the driver's seat is William Green's daughter Sharon Green. The reins must have felt familiar to William Green, who used horses in his ice-harvesting business. (WMG.)

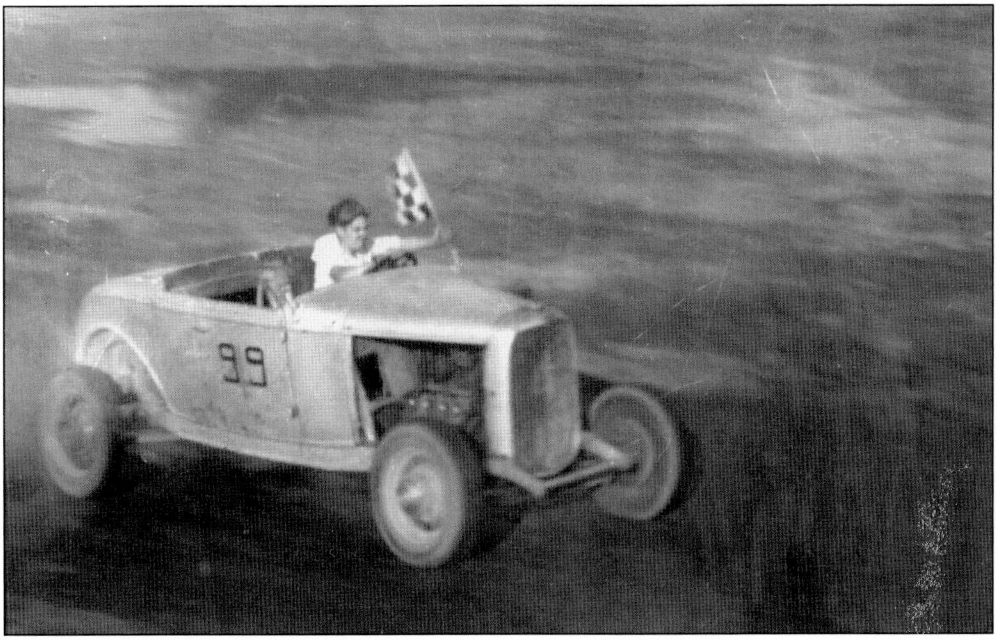

IRVING SEWELL, STOCK CAR WINNER, C. 1949. Irving Sewell holds the winner's flag proudly at Burden Lake Speedway on Garner Road. During World War II, there were no stock car races because of the gas shortage. (IS.)

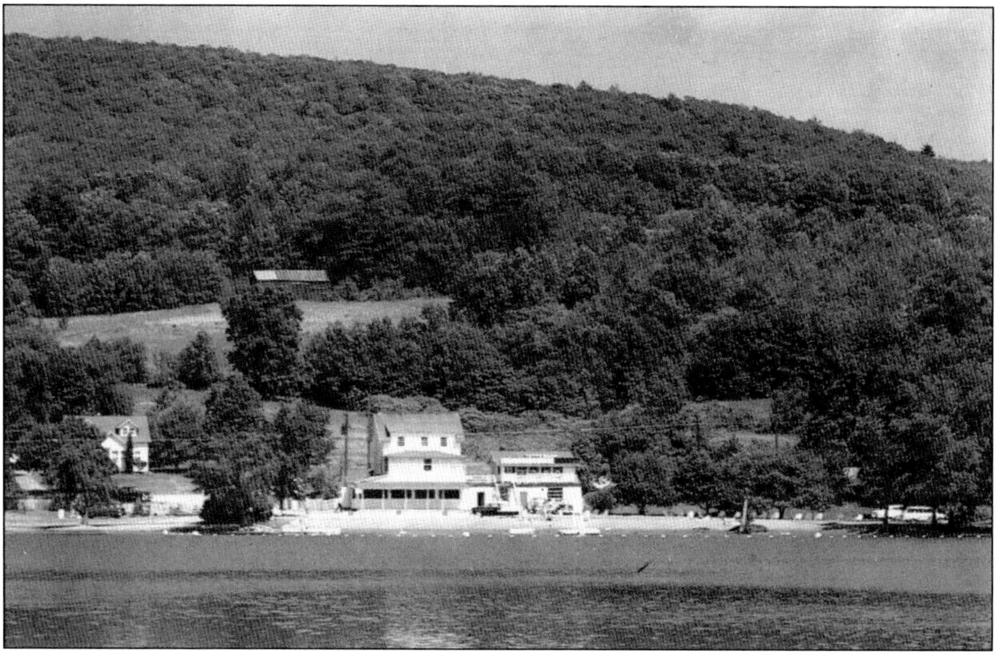

Tifft's Beach. A panoramic view of Tifft's Beach and the hills on the other side of Routes 43 and 66 can be seen from the opposite side of Glass Lake. (AT.)

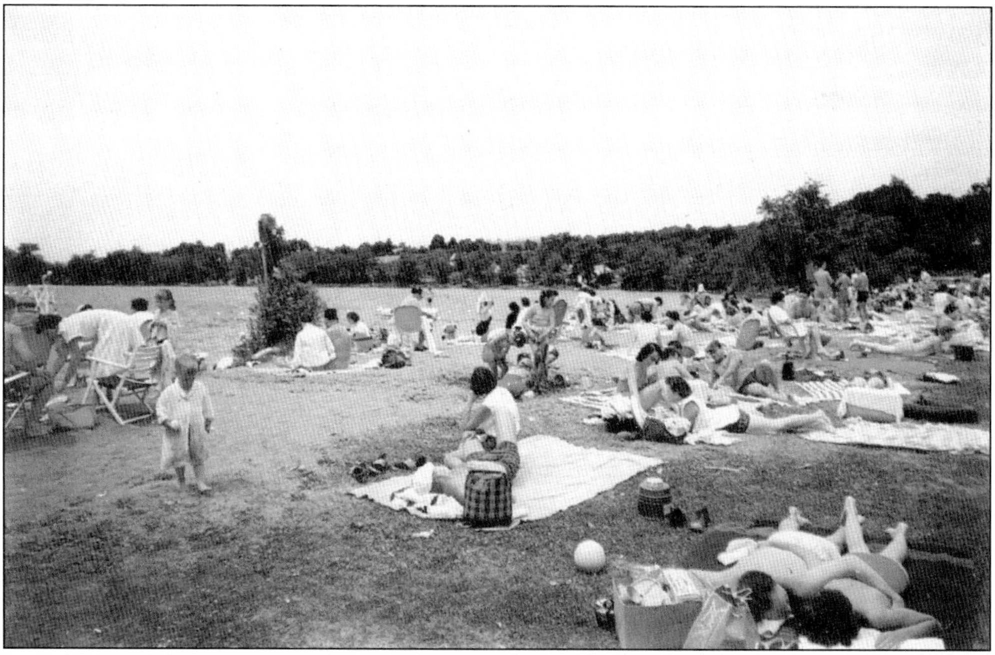

Tifft's Beach Sunbathers. From 1945 to 1992, Harold and Alice Tifft operated Tifft's Beach, a very popular spot for picnics and water activities on the shore of Glass Lake. This unique area provided an outstanding wide-angle view of Glass Lake. (AT.)

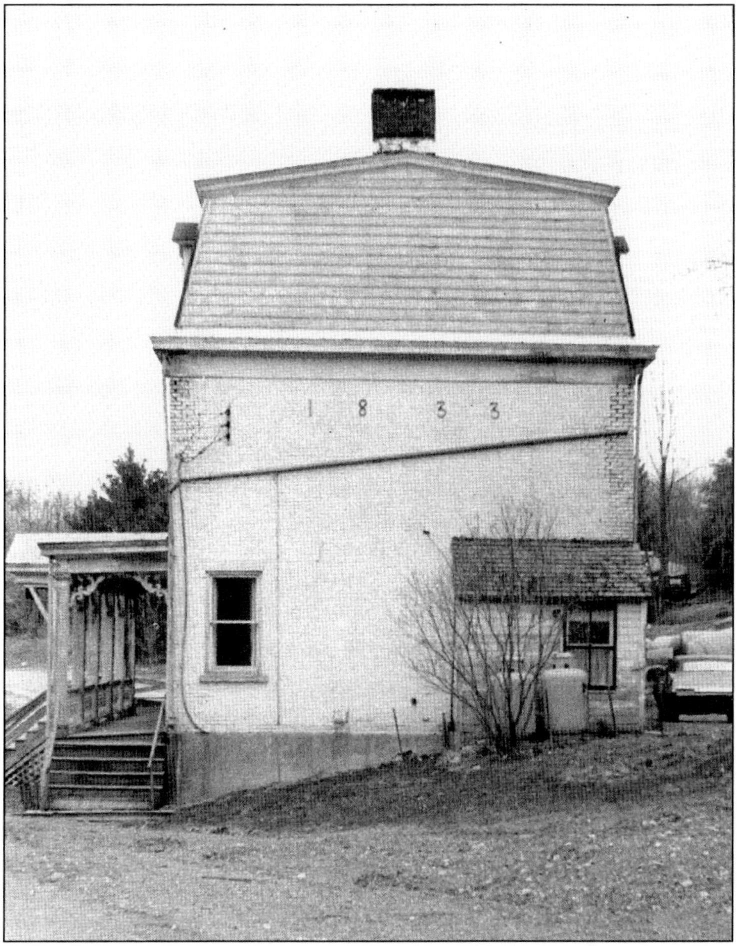

BRICK END OF CEDARHURST. The iron numbers 1833 on the east end of Cedarhurst denote the year in which J. Westfall and Son built the brick portion of Cedarhurst. The numbers have been painted over but can still be seen up close. The Westfalls also built five brick houses of Georgian design in Sand Lake (see *Sand Lake*, page 74.) (CV.)

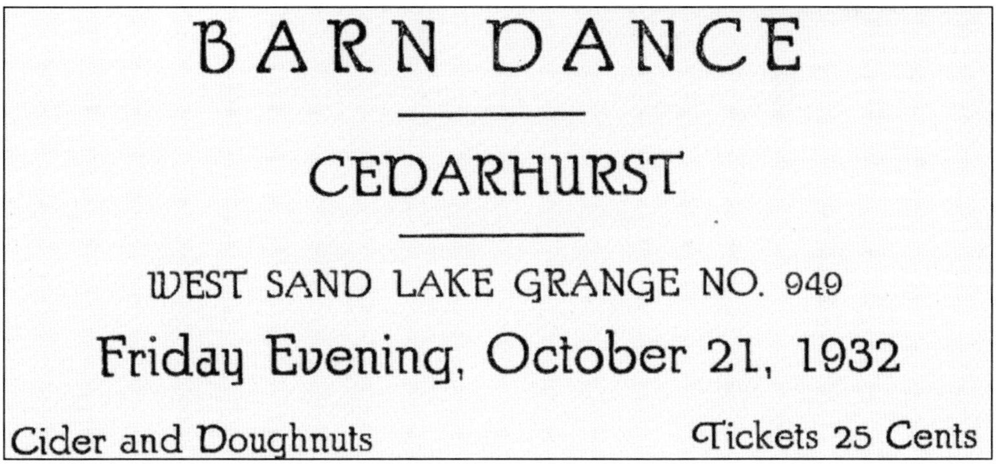

BARN DANCE

CEDARHURST

WEST SAND LAKE GRANGE NO. 949

Friday Evening, October 21, 1932

Cider and Doughnuts — Tickets 25 Cents

CEDARHURST TICKET. With this ticket, entrance was gained to the barn dance sponsored by West Sand Lake Grange No. 949 at Cedarhurst. The West Sand Lake Grange owned Cedarhurst from 1932 to 1968. It was usually called Grange hall but would often be referred to as Cedarhurst, which it was from 1833 to 1895. (aG.)

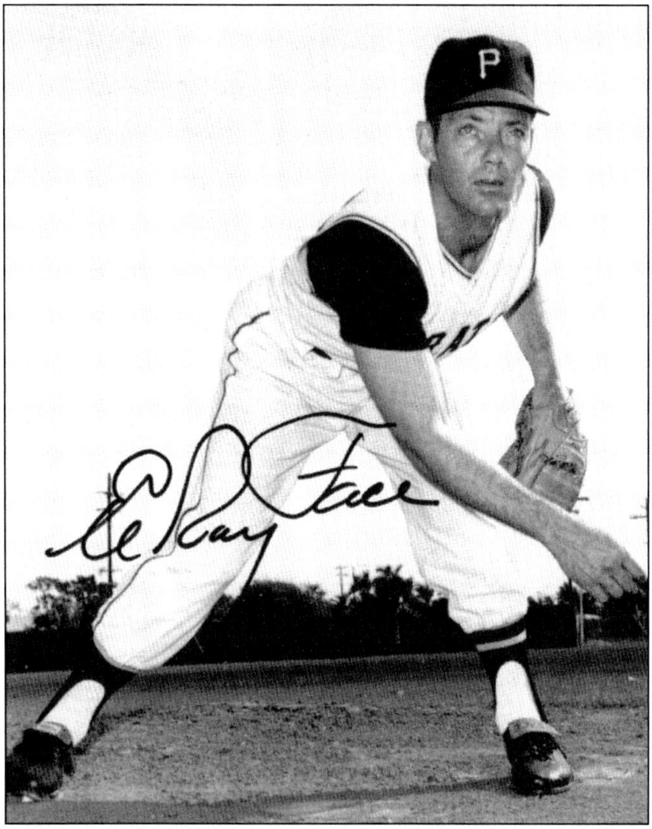

ELROY FACE. ElRoy Face lived across from the Faith Mills. His mother ran a boardinghouse for the mill workers. His record as a major-league relief pitcher is a testimony to the American dream. (JC.)

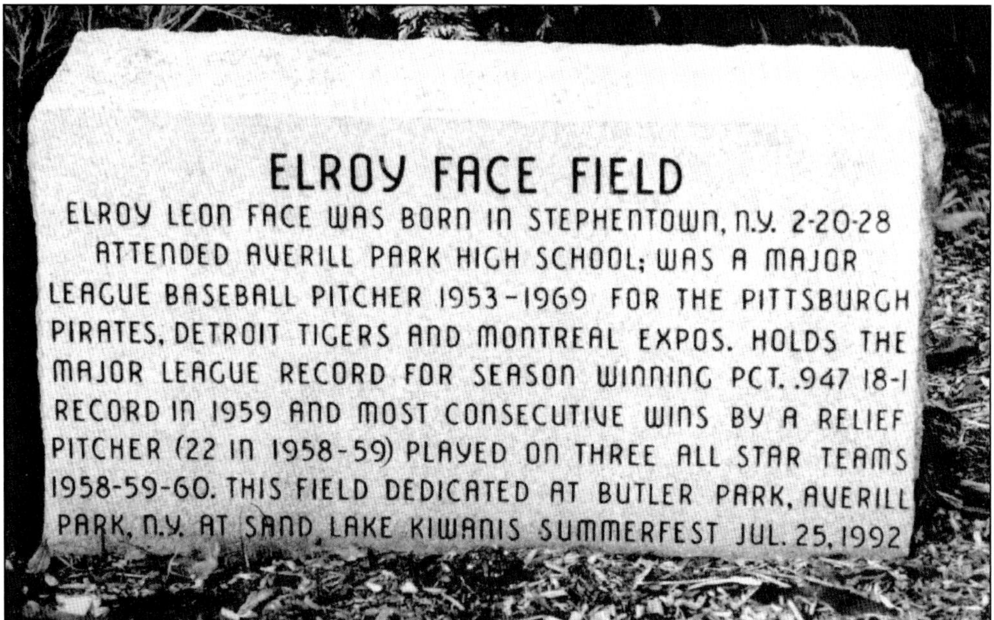

ELROY FACE FIELD. This plaque, denoting the ElRoy Face Field at Butler Park, gives the highlights of Face's baseball career. (SLHSC.)

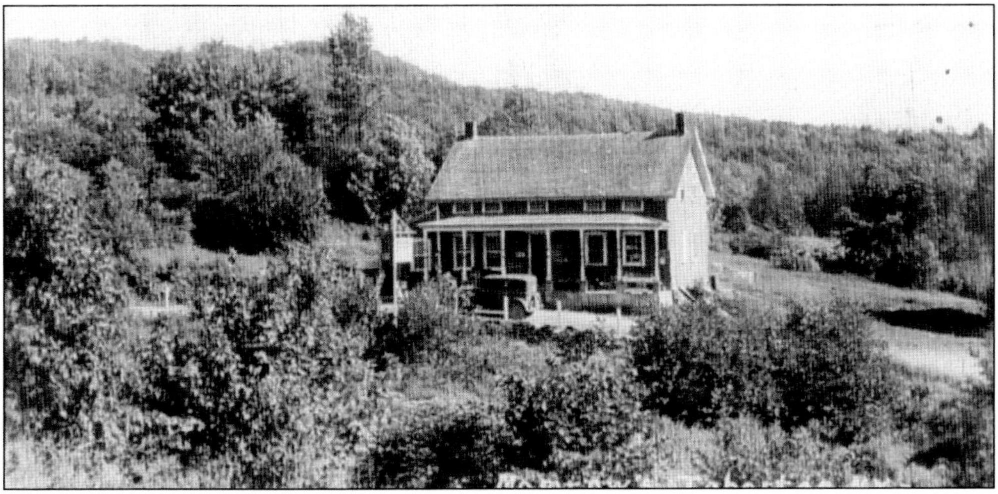

MOMROW'S GRILL, C. 1934. Taborton House, owned by Fred and Mary Leffler Momrow, was known by most regular customers as Mary Momrow's Grill. (VB.)

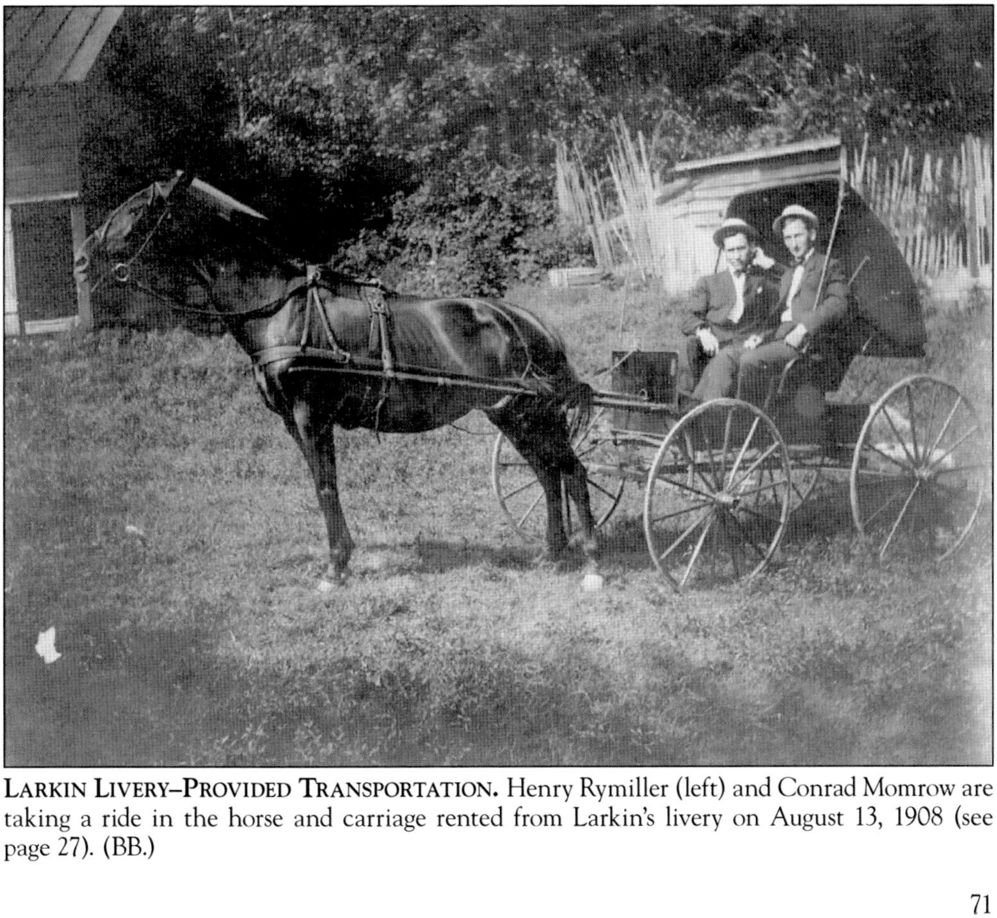

LARKIN LIVERY–PROVIDED TRANSPORTATION. Henry Rymiller (left) and Conrad Momrow are taking a ride in the horse and carriage rented from Larkin's livery on August 13, 1908 (see page 27). (BB.)

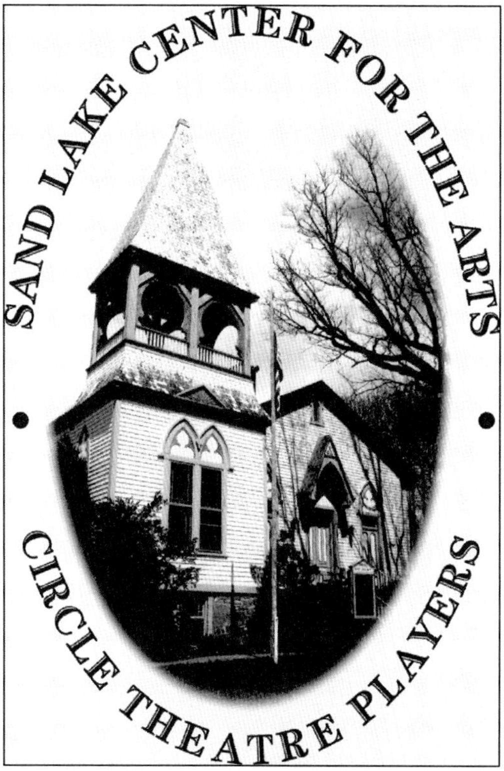

LOGO OF SAND LAKE CENTER FOR THE ARTS-CIRCLE THEATRE PLAYERS. Expanding each year, Squire Jacobs Coffeehouse has provided concerts with nationally and internationally known performers. The Circle Theatre Players' dramatic performances have been consistent award winners. Visual arts are on display from local artists. Theater, music and art workshops, the annual Kids for Kids play performed by middle and senior high school students, and the Fine Arts Fair are among the offerings of this gem within the town. (SLCA/CTP.)

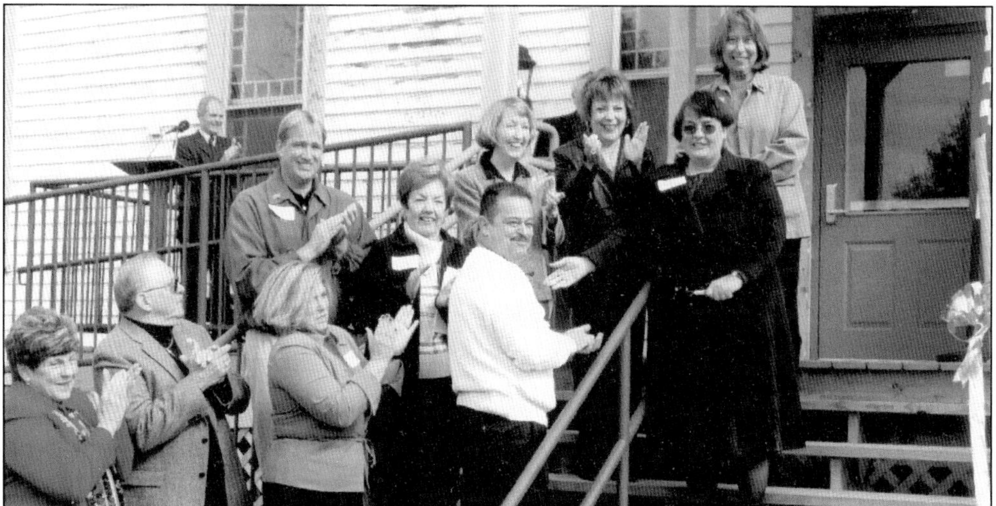

SAND LAKE CENTER FOR THE ARTS DEDICATION. At the dedication ceremony on October 18, 2003, town supervisor Steve Robelotto (foreground left) is handing Center for the Arts president Joan Fuess a 25-year lease from the town to use the former Sand Lake Presbyterian Church and later town hall for Center of the Art's new home. Standing behind are, from left to right, town clerk Christine Kronau, council members Jack Welcome, Flora Fasoldt, John Glasser, and Nancy Dunn, Rensselaer County executive Kathleen Jimino, county legislator Virginia O'Brien, and capital campaign chairman Mary Hall. At the podium is Jack Casey, Rensselaer County Republican chairman. (SLCA/CTP.)

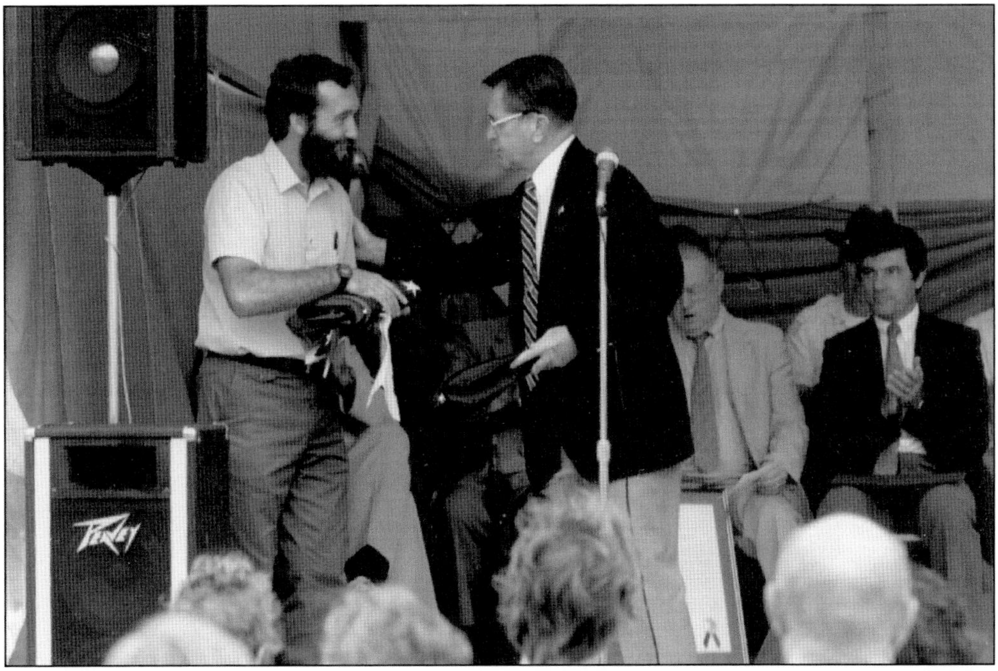

TOWN SUPERVISOR DOUGLAS KELLEY AND CONGRESSMAN GERALD SOLOMON. At the 175th anniversary celebration of the Town of Sand Lake at Butler Park on August 22, 1987, Congressman Gerald Solomon presents town supervisor Douglas Kelley with a flag that flew over the United States Capitol. (TSLC.)

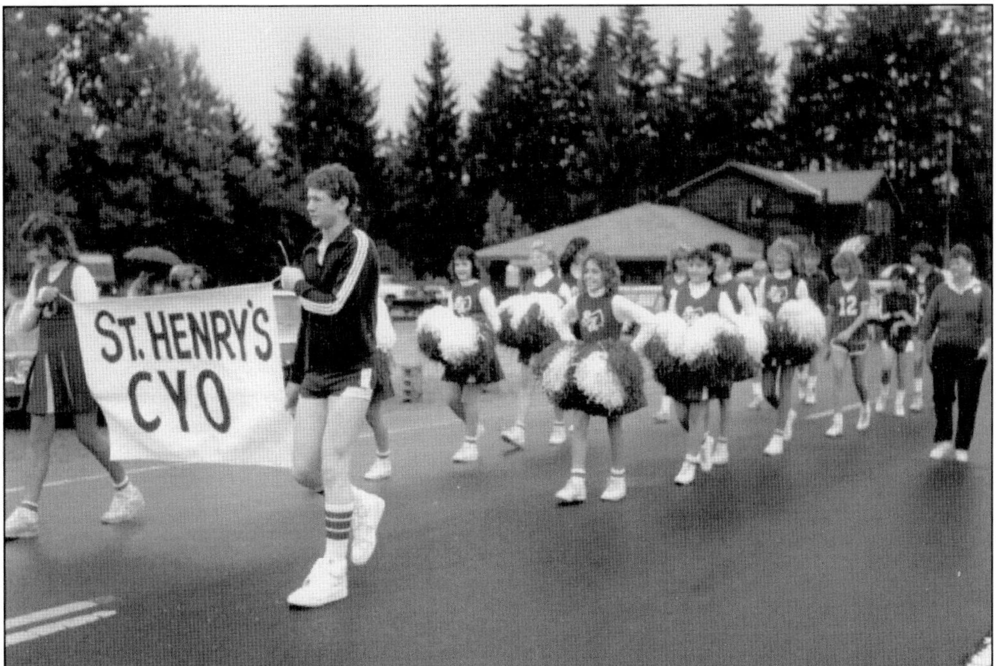

ST. HENRY'S CYO. One of the many organizations marching in the parade for the 175th anniversary of the town was St. Henry's Catholic Youth Organization (CYO). (TSLC.)

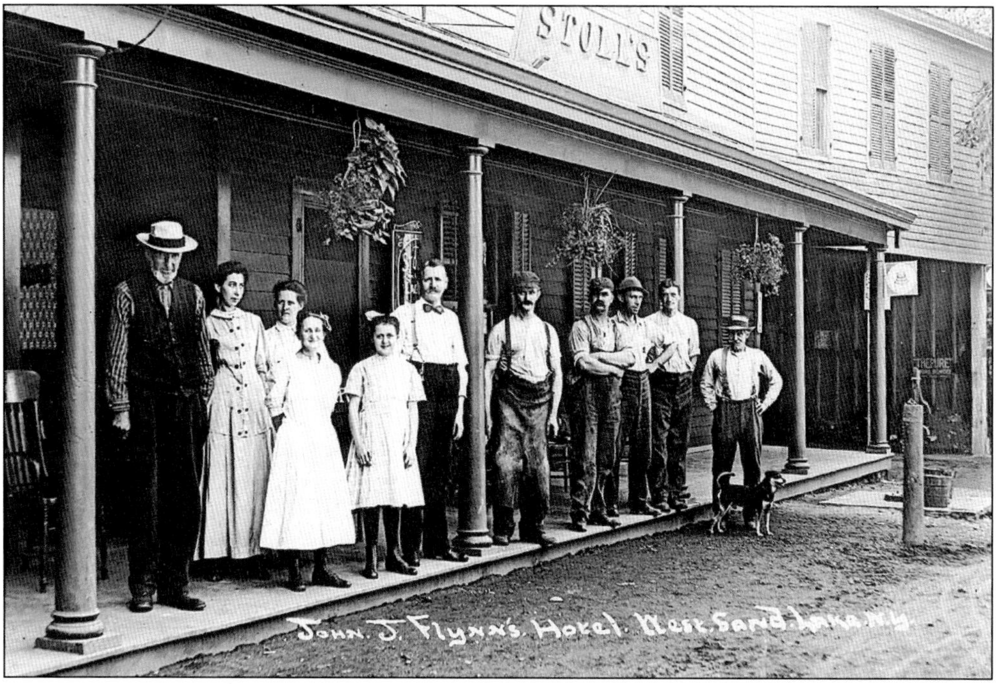

BREWSTER HOUSE. The Brewster House was owned by John J. Flynn around 1901. Seventh from the left is Bart Warren in his blacksmith apron (see page 36) standing beside the Flynn family members. (JW.)

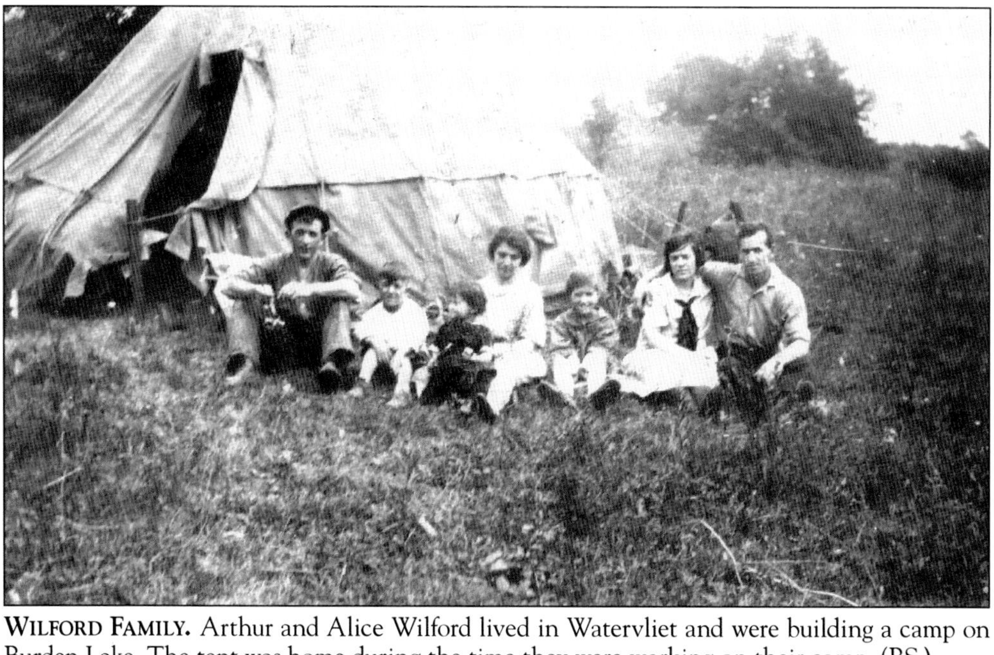

WILFORD FAMILY. Arthur and Alice Wilford lived in Watervliet and were building a camp on Burden Lake. The tent was home during the time they were working on their camp. (BS.)

Four

COMMUNITY SERVICES

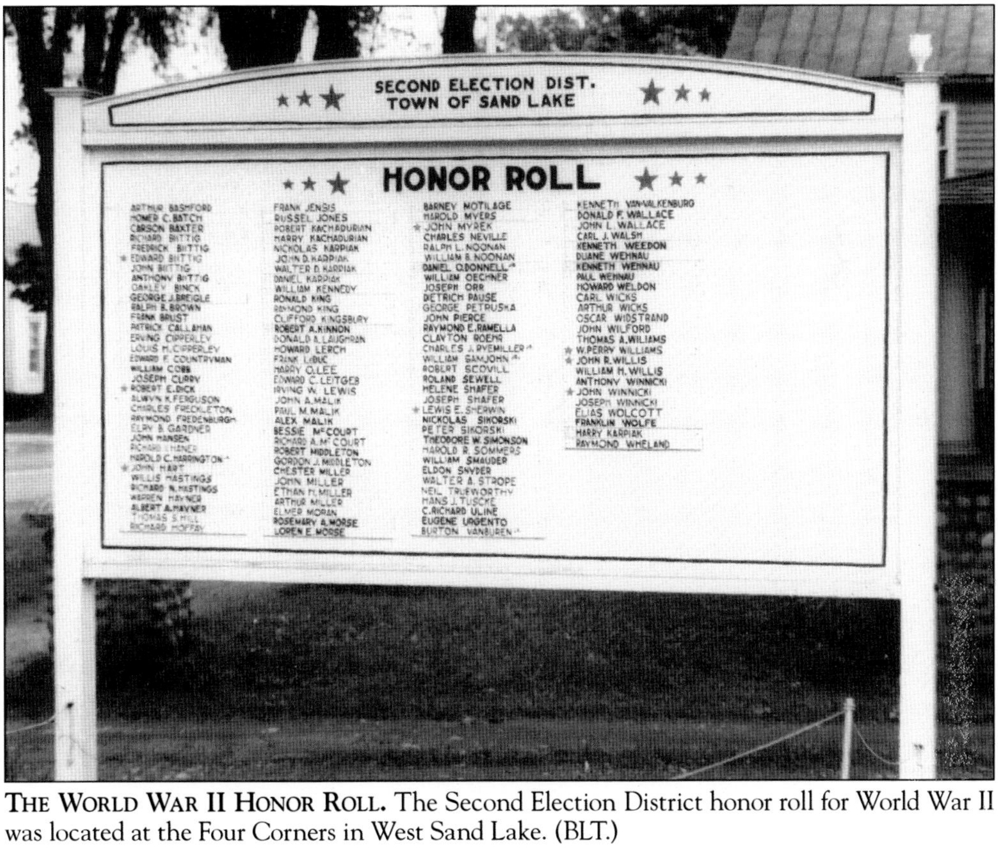

THE WORLD WAR II HONOR ROLL. The Second Election District honor roll for World War II was located at the Four Corners in West Sand Lake. (BLT.)

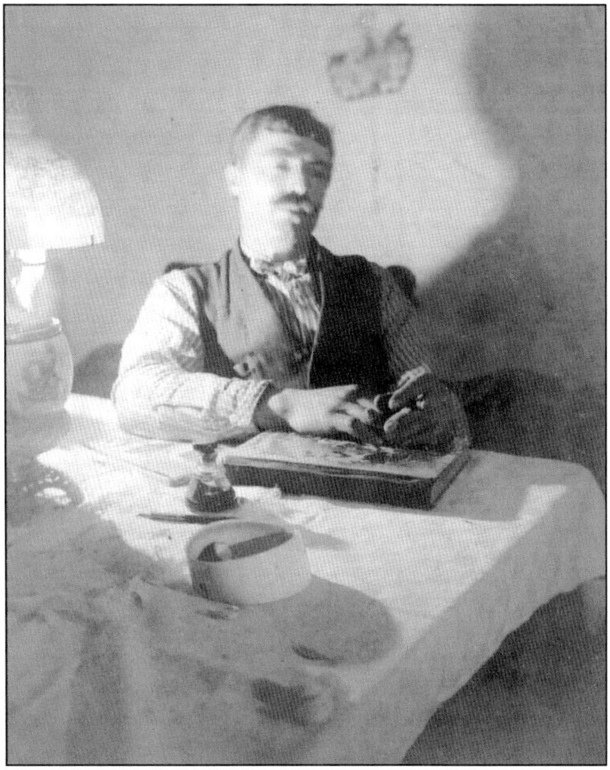

John Henry Meyers. Best known as Henry Meyers, he came to America from Germany. Serving in the Union army earned him his citizenship. Inexpensive land drew him to Taborton. He sent to Germany for his wife-to-be, Mary Elizabeth Sauerbrei. He worked at logging, cutting ice, and blacksmithing. He leased the house and property at the corner of Taborton and Lawson Roads in the 1870s and bought it 1882. They had four children. John Henry died in 1906, leaving Mary to support herself, her children, and the farm. (BB.)

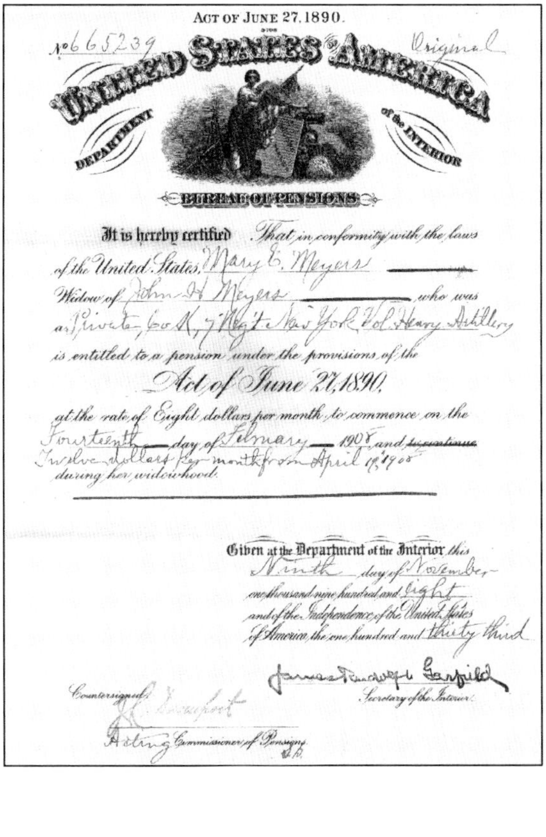

Act of June 27, 1890.

No 665239 Original

United States of America

Department of the Interior

Bureau of Pensions

It is hereby certified That in conformity with the laws of the United States, Mary E. Meyers Widow of John H Meyers who was a Private Co K, 7 Regt New York Vol Heavy Artillery is entitled to a pension under the provisions of the

Act of June 27, 1890,

at the rate of Eight dollars per month to commence on the Fourteenth day of February 1908 and ~~to continue~~ Twelve dollars per month from April 1908 during her widowhood.

Given at the Department of the Interior this Ninth day of November one thousand nine hundred and eight and of the Independence of the United States of America the one hundred and thirty third

James Rudolph Garfield
Secretary of the Interior

Countersigned:
Acting Commissioner of Pensions.

Mary E. Meyers Civil War Pension Papers. Mary, widow of John Henry, received a pension of $8 per month beginning on February 14, 1908, and $12 per month beginning in April 1908. The document dated November 9, 1908, gives a further date of "the Independence of the United States of America the one hundred and thirty third." It was signed by Secretary of the Interior James Rudolph Garfield, son of Pres. James A. Garfield. An unanswered question would be whether the amount of the first check included February to November allotments. (BB.)

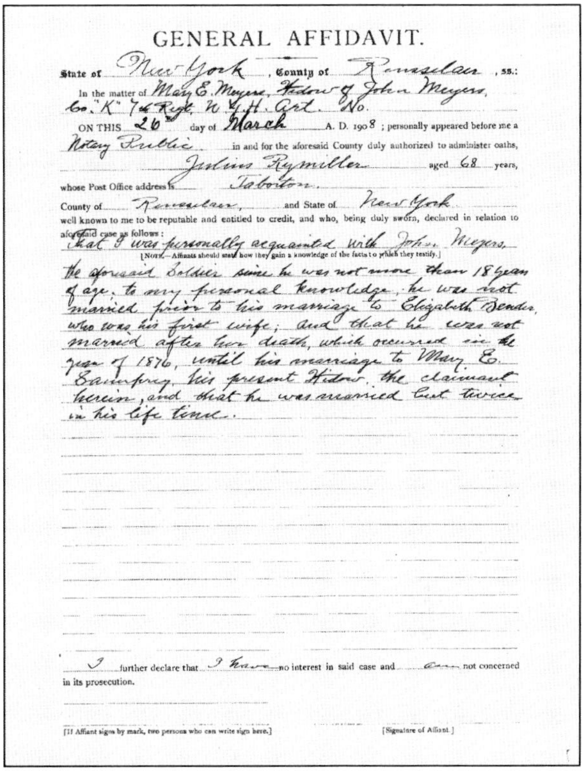

GENERAL AFFIDAVIT.

State of New York, County of Rensselaer, ss.:

In the matter of Mary E. Meyers, Widow of John Meyers, Co. "K" 7th Regt. N.Y.H. Art. No.

ON THIS 26th day of March A. D. 1908; personally appeared before me a Notary Public in and for the aforesaid County duly authorized to administer oaths, Julius Rymiller aged 68 years, whose Post Office address is Taborton, County of Rensselaer, and State of New York, well known to me to be reputable and entitled to credit, and who, being duly sworn, declared in relation to aforesaid case as follows:

[NOTE—Affiants should state how they gain a knowledge of the facts to which they testify.]

That I was personally acquainted with John Meyers, the aforesaid Soldier since he was not more than 18 years of age, to my personal knowledge, he was not married prior to his marriage to Elizabeth Bender, who was his first wife; and that he was not married after her death, which occurred in the year of 1876, until his marriage to Mary E. Sainfrey, his present Widow, the claimant herein, and that he was married but twice in his life time.

I further declare that I have no interest in said case and am not concerned in its prosecution.

[If Affiant signs by mark, two persons who can write sign here.] [Signature of Affiant.]

PENSION AFFIDAVIT. Julius Rymiller gave an affidavit for the marriage status of John Henry Meyers needed for his wife to receive a pension for his Civil War service. He served with Company K, 7th Regiment, New York Volunteer Heavy Artillery. His survival as a prisoner of war was attributed to his being useful as a blacksmith. He was mustered out in Baltimore, was transported to Yorktown, and had to walk home from there. (BB.)

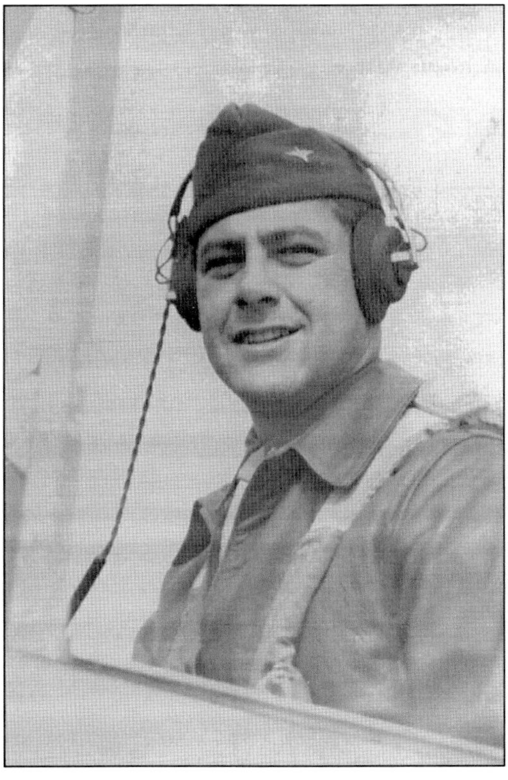

DR. JOHN DUNN. Dr. John Dunn was a decorated officer with the U.S. Air Corps during World War II in Italy, Africa, and Egypt. He opened his dentistry practice in Averill Park at the intersection of Eastern Union Turnpike and Johnnycake Lane (see page 121) in 1949 and practiced there until 1987. (TSLC.)

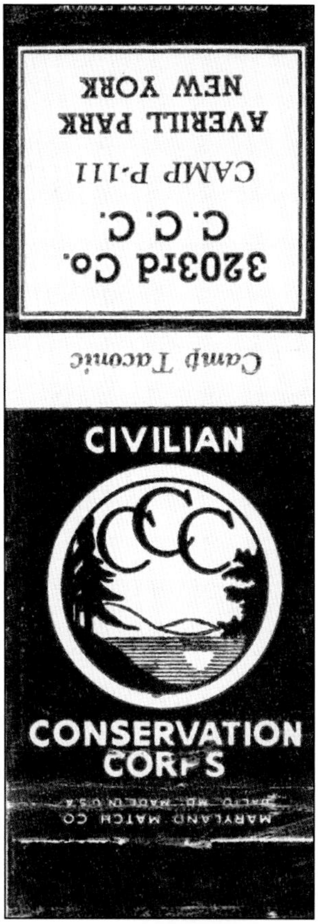

CCC MATCHBOOK. Company 3203 P-111 of the Civilian Conservation Corps (CCC) was based at Camp Taconic in the hamlet of Alps. Sand Lake residents who belonged were Sidney Gallant, John "Tarz" Albanese, and Clifford "Curly" Vigus. The CCC provided work and training for unemployed men during the Great Depression. Family support was aided by part of their pay. Their jobs included reclaiming wastelands, replanting forests, flood control, rescuing lost persons, and developing state and national parks. (JC.)

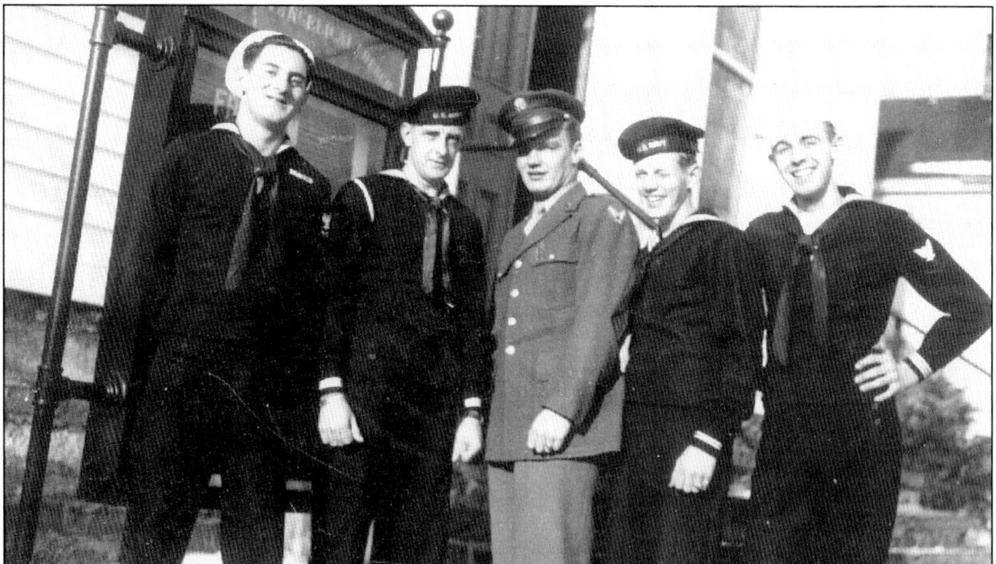

HOME ON LEAVE, DECEMBER 1944. Seen here are, from left to right, Ronald King, William Smauder, Richard Uline, Donald Oliver, and Eldon Snyder, all in uniform and home on leave. In October 2006, this picture was included in an album for Donald Oliver's 80th birthday. (JO.)

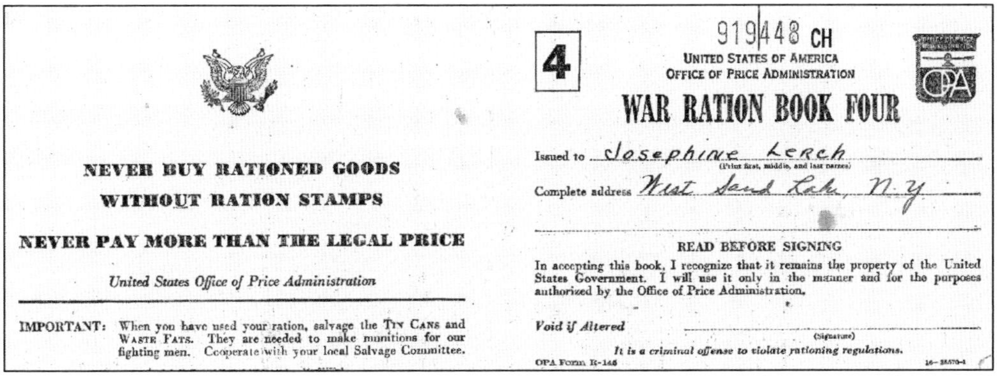

NEVER BUY RATIONED GOODS
WITHOUT RATION STAMPS

NEVER PAY MORE THAN THE LEGAL PRICE

United States Office of Price Administration

IMPORTANT: When you have used your ration, salvage the TIN CANS and WASTE FATS. They are needed to make munitions for our fighting men. Cooperate with your local Salvage Committee.

919448 CH

4

UNITED STATES OF AMERICA
OFFICE OF PRICE ADMINISTRATION

WAR RATION BOOK FOUR

Issued to Josephine Lerch
(Print first, middle, and last names)

Complete address West Sand Lake, N.Y.

READ BEFORE SIGNING

In accepting this book, I recognize that it remains the property of the United States Government. I will use it only in the manner and for the purposes authorized by the Office of Price Administration.

Void if Altered

(Signature)

It is a criminal offense to violate rationing regulations.

OPA Form R-145

WORLD WAR II RATION BOOK. Josephine (Middleton) Lerch was urged to save tin from used cans and waste fat for munitions as part of the war effort in the message on the back of her ration book. (BLT.)

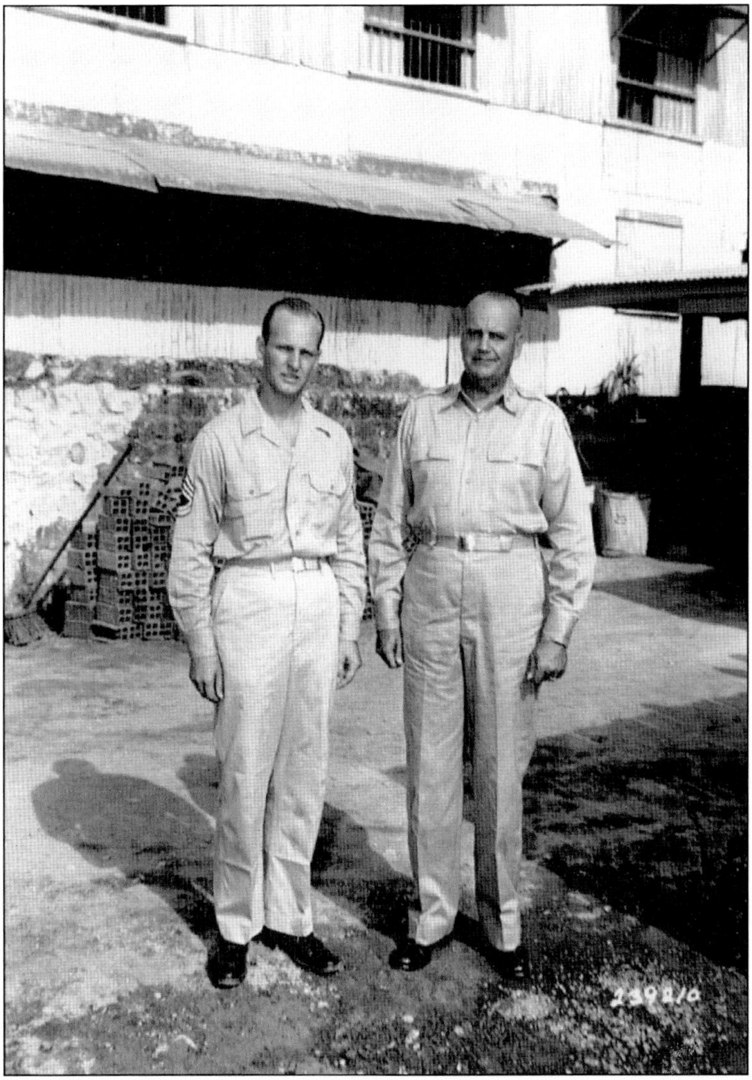

EDWARD T. ZERONDA. In 1945, TSgt. Edward T. Zeronda (left) and Lt. Gen. Wilhelm Styer are at the Enlisted Men's Club in Manila, Philippines, during World War II. Zeronda became owner of Miller's Market in West Sand Lake from May 1952 to January 1981. (KZ.)

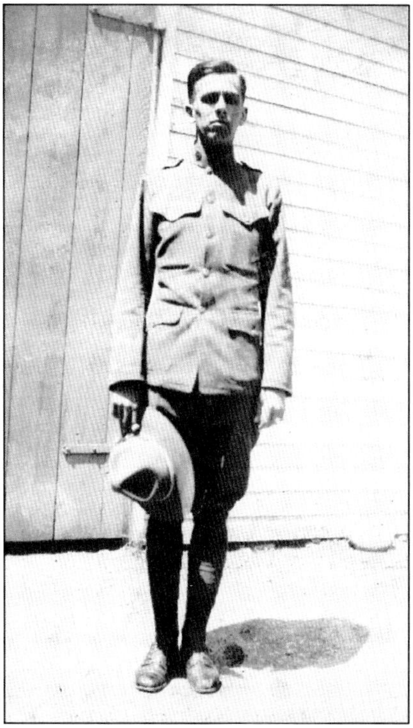

Enoch Lloyd French. The letters that Enoch Lloyd French sent home when he served in World War I were typed by his sister Edith and given to the town historian's office by his son Gordon French. (GF.)

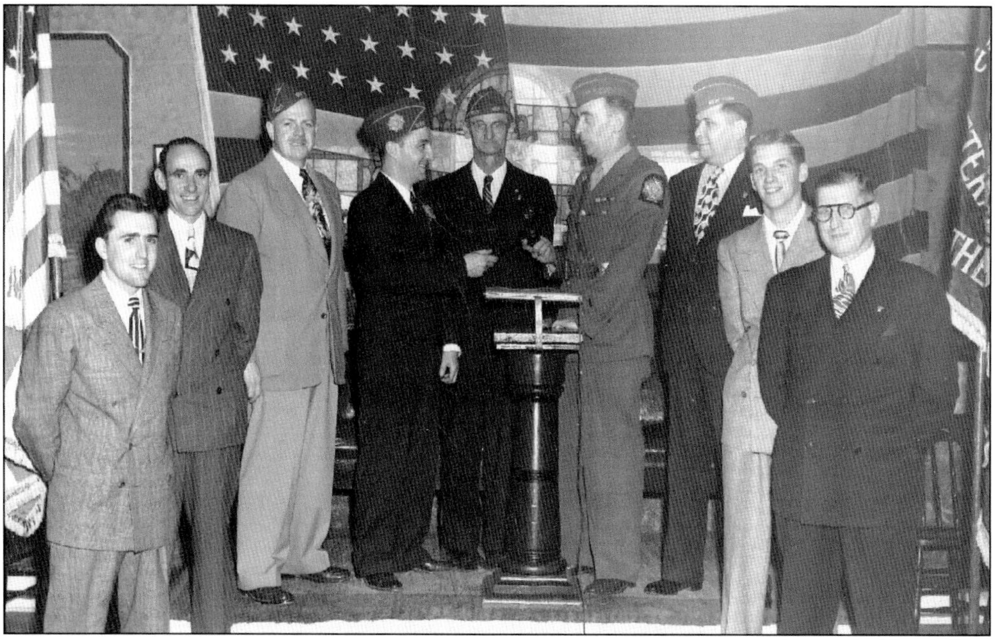

Lt. Perry Williams VFW Post. This Veterans of Foreign Wars (VFW) post began on October 5, 1945, and was named in honor of Lt. Perry Williams, who was killed in action in 1944. The VFW is open to any veteran who has served overseas in war action. Seen here are, from left to right, unidentified, Carson Baxter, William Burlingham, Kenneth Coonradt, Emerson Williams (father of Perry Williams), unidentified installing officer, Kenneth Van Valkenburg, Edward Peters, and Raymond Bedell. Coonradt is being installed as post commander in 1948. (MDW.)

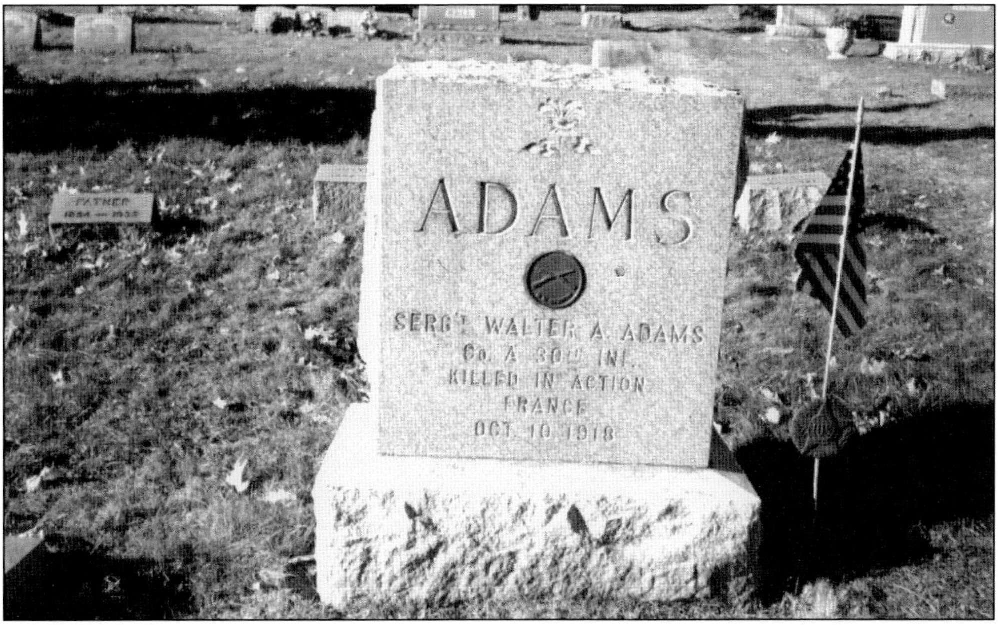

Sgt. Walter A. Adams American Legion Post Unit 1021. This American Legion post formed in October 1931 was named in memory of Sgt. Walter A. Adams, who was killed in action in France on October 10, 1918. Meetings are held in the former District No. 7 School (see *Sand Lake*, page 54). Two of the many tenets in the preamble to the constitution call upon the members to "preserve the memories and incidents of our associates in the Great Wars" and to "safeguard and transmit to posterity the principles of justice, freedom and democracy." (SWAAALPU.)

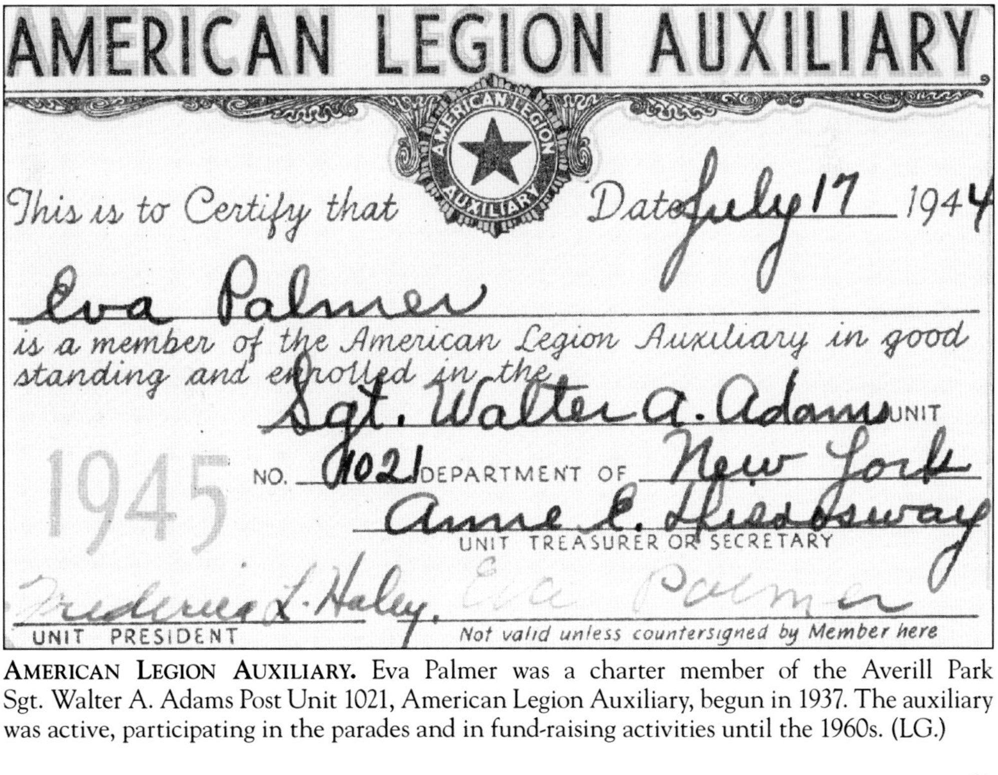

American Legion Auxiliary. Eva Palmer was a charter member of the Averill Park Sgt. Walter A. Adams Post Unit 1021, American Legion Auxiliary, begun in 1937. The auxiliary was active, participating in the parades and in fund-raising activities until the 1960s. (LG.)

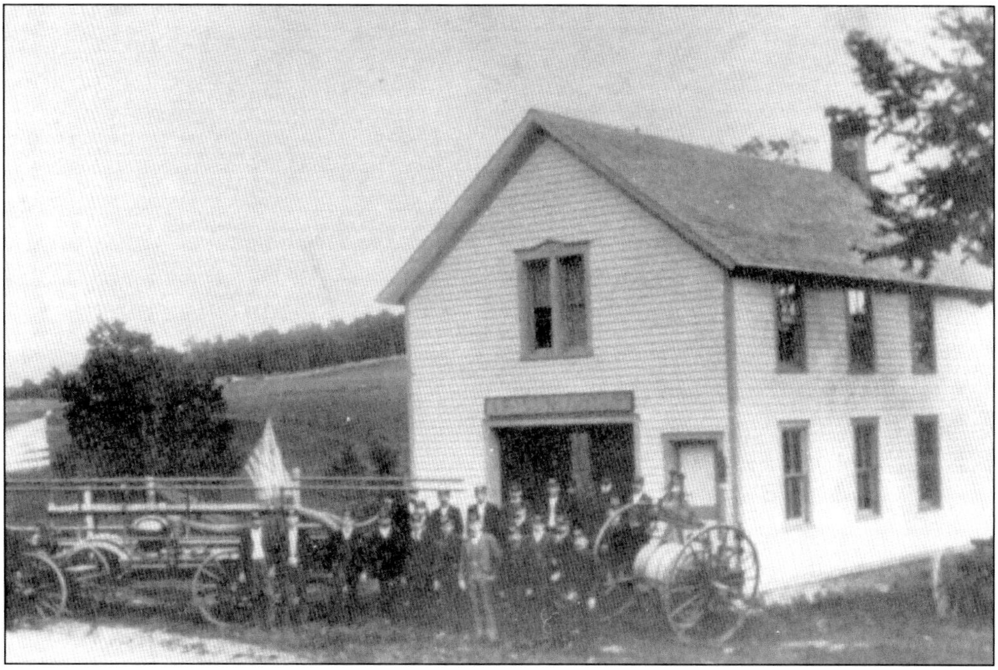

OLD FIREHOUSE, c. 1904. Members of the Averill Park and Sand Lake Volunteer Fire Company No. 1 are in front of the old engine house on Route 43 when there was no house next to it. The hand-pumped fire engine known as "Nickwackett" (meaning river horse) and the two-wheeled, hand-drawn hose cart are the equipment available. (EP.)

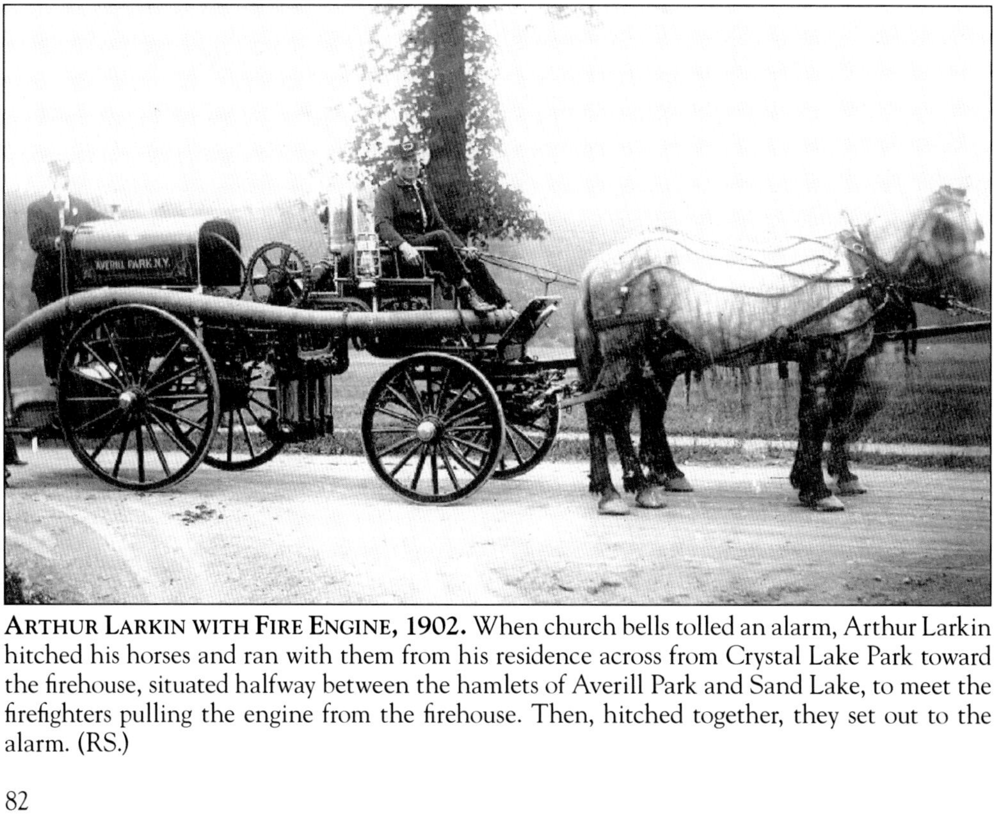

ARTHUR LARKIN WITH FIRE ENGINE, 1902. When church bells tolled an alarm, Arthur Larkin hitched his horses and ran with them from his residence across from Crystal Lake Park toward the firehouse, situated halfway between the hamlets of Averill Park and Sand Lake, to meet the firefighters pulling the engine from the firehouse. Then, hitched together, they set out to the alarm. (RS.)

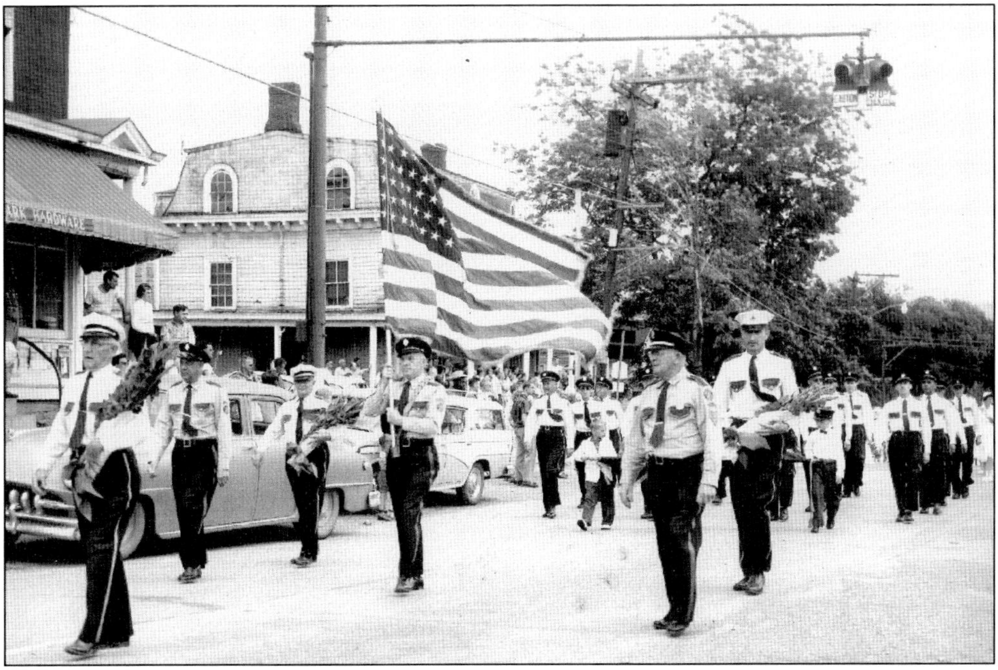

FIREMEN'S FIELD DAY, AUGUST 1958. Seen here are, from left to right, volunteer firemen Frank Hack, Lloyd French, Edward Guy, Harry Barnum (holding the flag), Chauncey Bradway, and Ernest Hoffman in the Averill Park and Sand Lake Fire Company field day parade. (MSt.G, Morris Gerber photograph.)

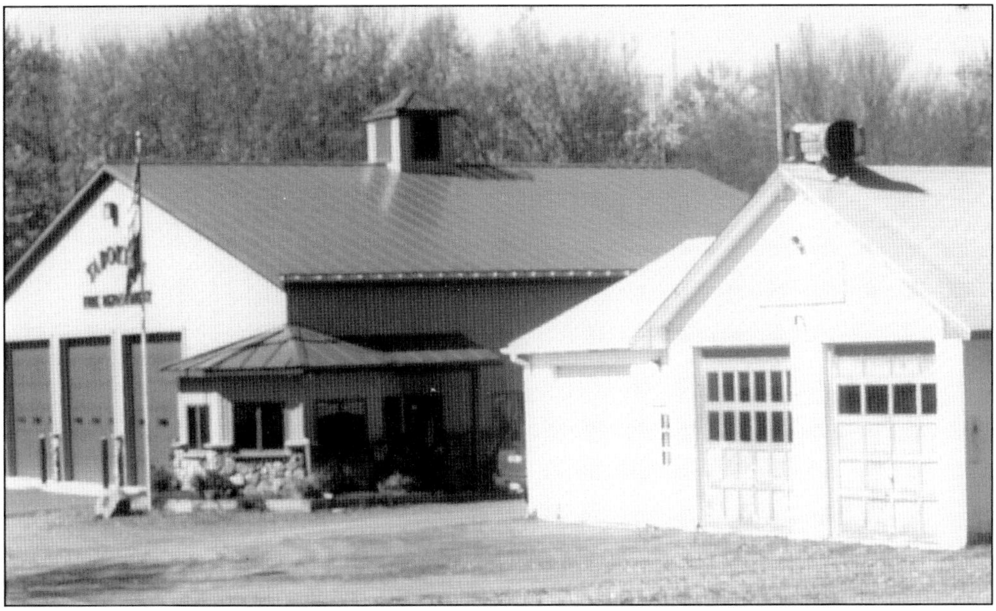

TABORTON FIREHOUSE. The Taborton Volunteer Fire Company received its incorporation papers on May 31, 1958. It has grown from August (Gus) Meyers allowing the fire truck to be stored in one of his buildings to the company dedicating its new four-bay station on September 28, 2002. The company operates three pieces of apparatus for Sand Lake Fire District No. 3, two for fire and an ambulance used as a light rescue/first response emergency medical service vehicle. (SLHSC.)

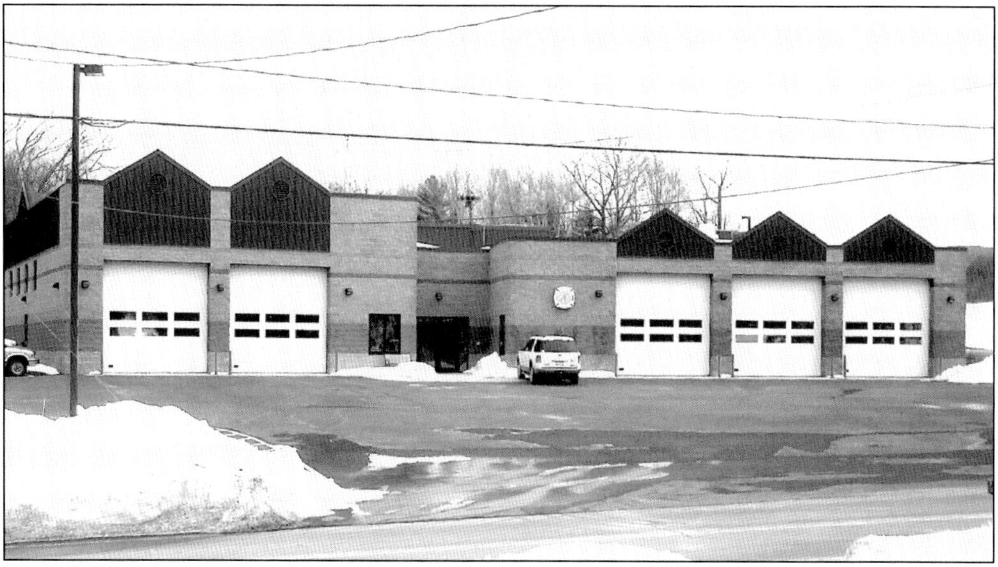

AVERILL PARK AND SAND LAKE FIREHOUSE EXPANDED. The current firehouse, built in 1968 (see *Sand Lake*, page 63), was greatly expanded in 2006. Now it will accommodate any newer, larger fire apparatus to meet the needs of the fire district in this century and beyond. (SLHSC.)

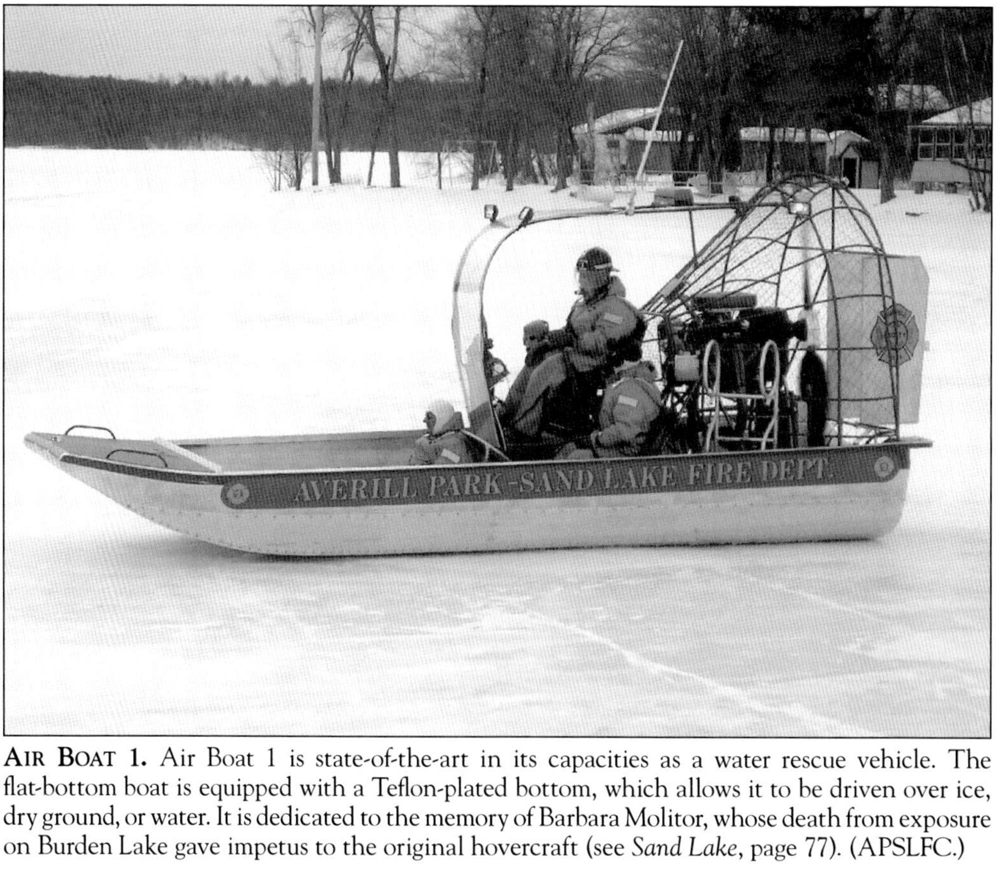

AIR BOAT 1. Air Boat 1 is state-of-the-art in its capacities as a water rescue vehicle. The flat-bottom boat is equipped with a Teflon-plated bottom, which allows it to be driven over ice, dry ground, or water. It is dedicated to the memory of Barbara Molitor, whose death from exposure on Burden Lake gave impetus to the original hovercraft (see *Sand Lake*, page 77). (APSLFC.)

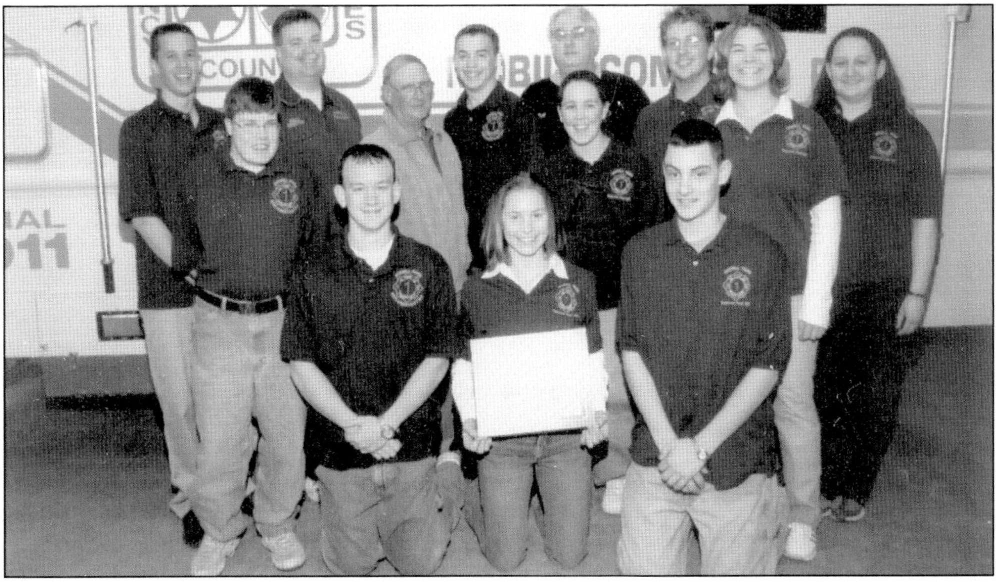

Explorer Post 911. In April 2002, Explorer Post 911 received a certificate of accommodation from the Rensselaer County Bureau of Emergency Service for cleaning and painting the county's fire communications vehicle. Seen here are, from left to right, (first row) John Colin, Robert Blaauw, Danielle Barbour, and Bradley Engwer; (second row) Christopher Cowan, Kelly Paslow, director of the Rensselaer County Bureau of Emergency Services Ivan Wager, Rensselaer County fire coordinator Robert Barbour, Explorer Post 911 advisor Robert Shuey, Drew Smead, Norman Warner III, Teresa Barbour, and Casey Caldwell. (APSLFC.)

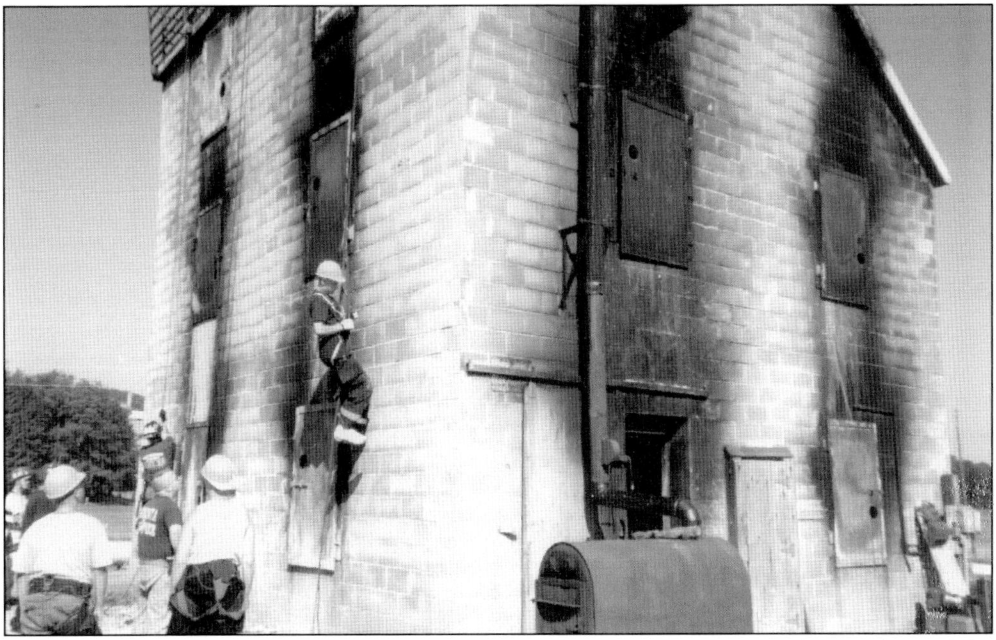

Explorer Post 911 Training. Open to young adults from ages 14 to 20, the members of the Explorers Post 911 receive the same training as career firefighters. From this experience, many have become members of the volunteer fire departments in the communities where they live. Some have made firefighting a career. (APSLFC.)

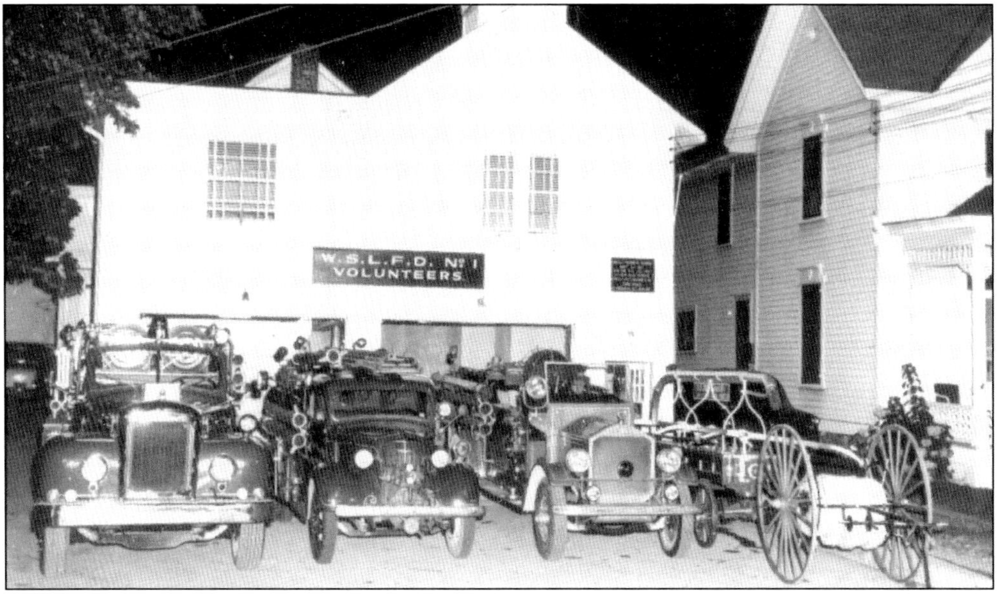

WEST SAND LAKE VOLUNTEER FIRE COMPANY NO. 1. Seen here in front of the first firehouse are, from left to right, the 1957 Mack pumper, the 1937 Chevrolet truck and equipment purchased in 1944, the 1926 Sanford pumper, the 1830 hand pumper nicknamed "Old Joe," and the hose cart purchased in 1874. Current plans for this building include space for memorabilia. The hall in the back, with a new roof and wall supports, has been redecorated for rental occasions. (SLHSC.)

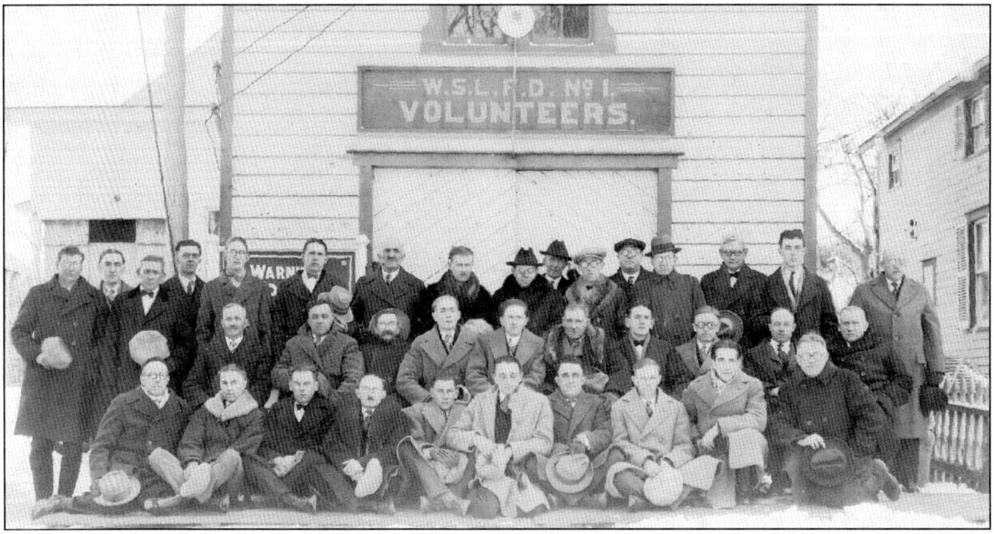

WEST SAND LAKE VOLUNTEER FIRE COMPANY MEMBERS, 1926. Seen here are, from left to right, (first row) Warren King, unidentified, Herbert Wehnau, Charles E. Brookner, three unidentified, Walter Hitchcock, Harold Hogle, and J. Elwin DeGraaf; (second row) Willard B. Schants, unidentified, Joel P. Hitchcock, Glenn Hitchcock, chief Allan J. Hitchcock, Arthur Ferguson, Harry G. Werger, Nelson Brookner, Edward Berrigan, and unidentified; (third row) Walter Lerch, Emmor Middleton, unidentified, Robert Hastings, Joseph Werger, unidentified, George W. Fredenburgh, George Cipperley, Leslie King, charter member John Schumann, Shirley Swike, Wilbur J. Bower, Clarence Bame, Harry C. Werger, unidentified, and Fayette Thomas. (JB.)

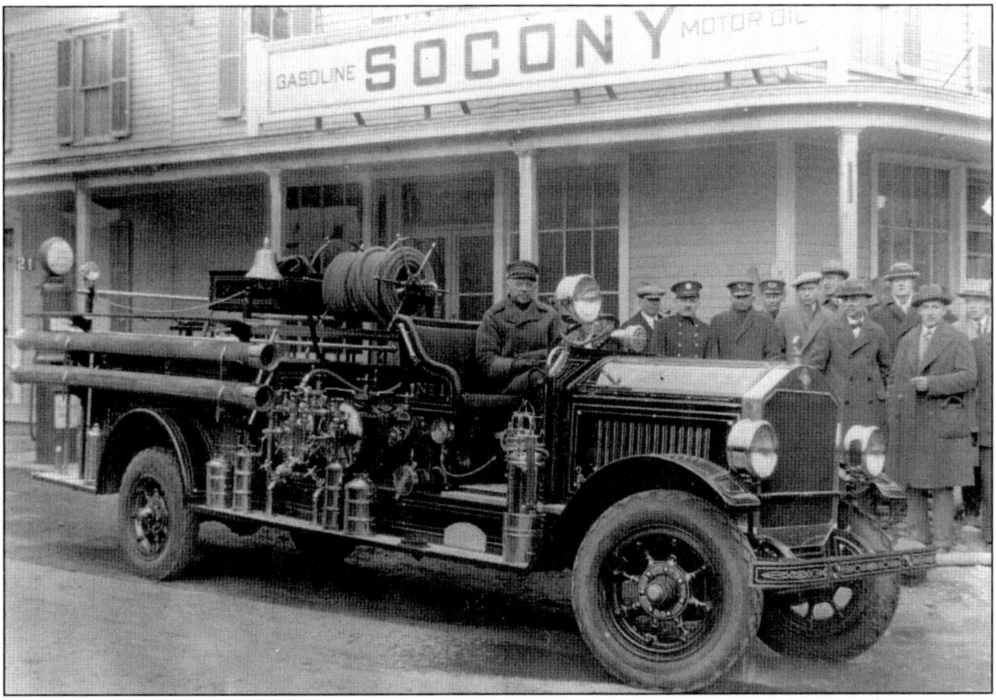

WEST SAND LAKE VOLUNTEER FIRE COMPANY NO. 1. The West Sand Lake Fire Company retired "Old Joe" when it raised $6,035 and purchased this 1926 Sanford pumper. The company now had motorized equipment. (CV.)

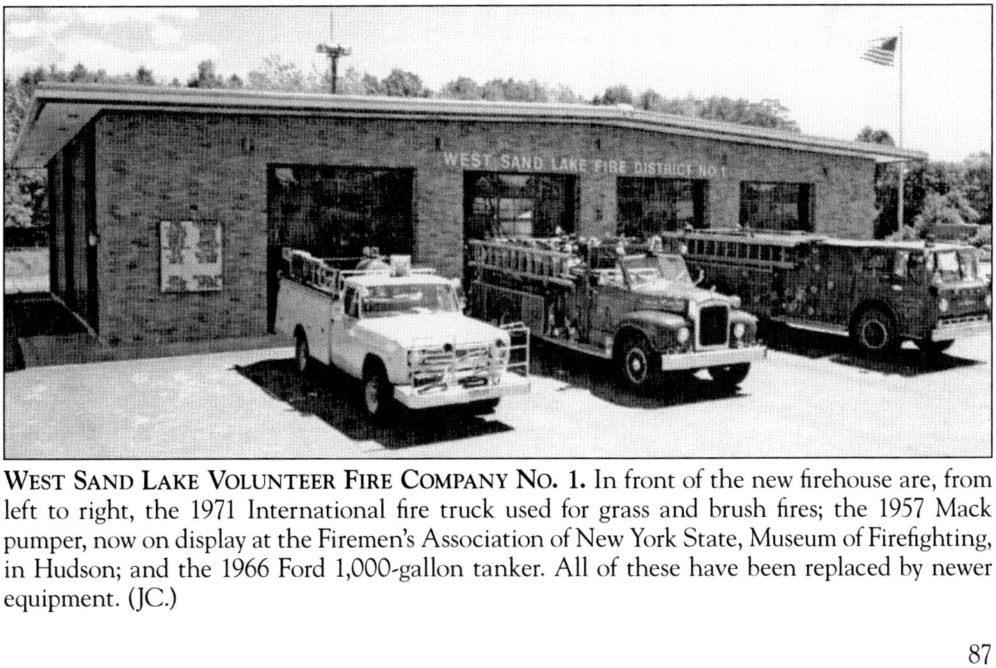

WEST SAND LAKE VOLUNTEER FIRE COMPANY NO. 1. In front of the new firehouse are, from left to right, the 1971 International fire truck used for grass and brush fires; the 1957 Mack pumper, now on display at the Firemen's Association of New York State, Museum of Firefighting, in Hudson; and the 1966 Ford 1,000-gallon tanker. All of these have been replaced by newer equipment. (JC.)

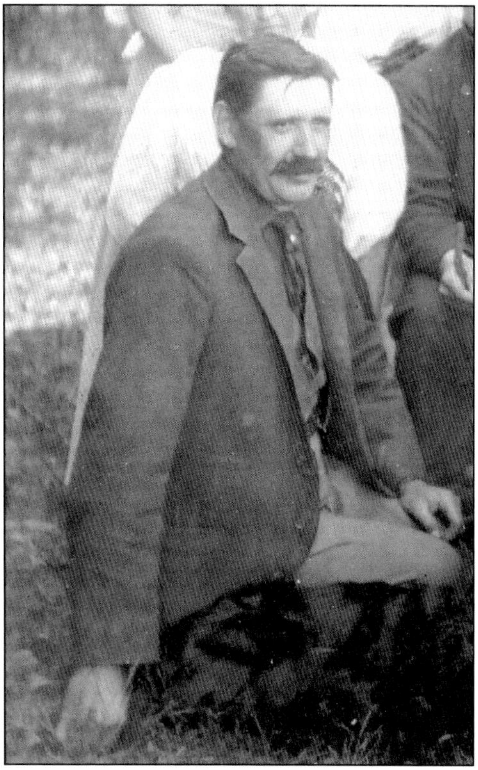

Dr. Elmer E. Reichard. Dr. Elmer E. Reichard was a family doctor from 1896 until 1941 when Dr. Frank Davenport took over his practice. Known as an uncanny diagnostician, after retirement Reichard was called on a case thought to be small pox. Standing at the foot of the bed, he pronounced, "All that boy has is both chicken pox and scarlet fever. He'll be fine in a couple of days." And he was. (TSLC.)

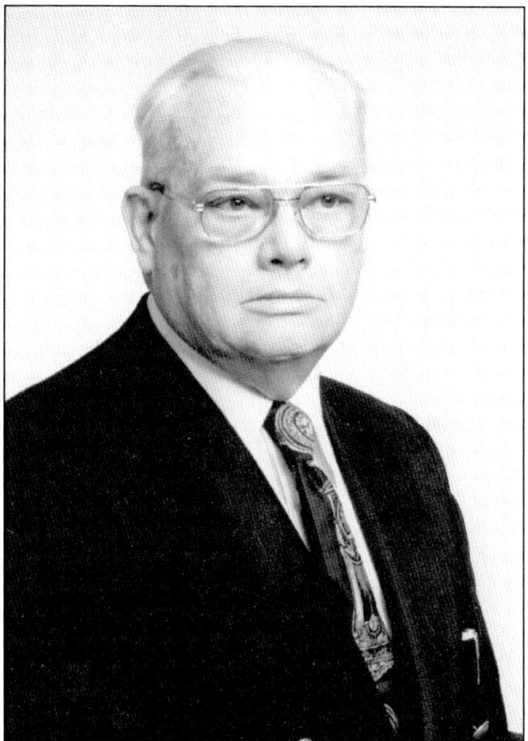

Dr. John Reid. Dr. John Reid had his office at the junction of Eastern Union Turnpike and Johnnycake Lane from 1954 to 1986 (see page 121). He was Rensselaer County commissioner of health from January 1, 1972, to January 1, 1983, and Rensselaer County medical consultant from January 1, 1983, to November 2, 1984. (MR, *Troy Record* photograph.)

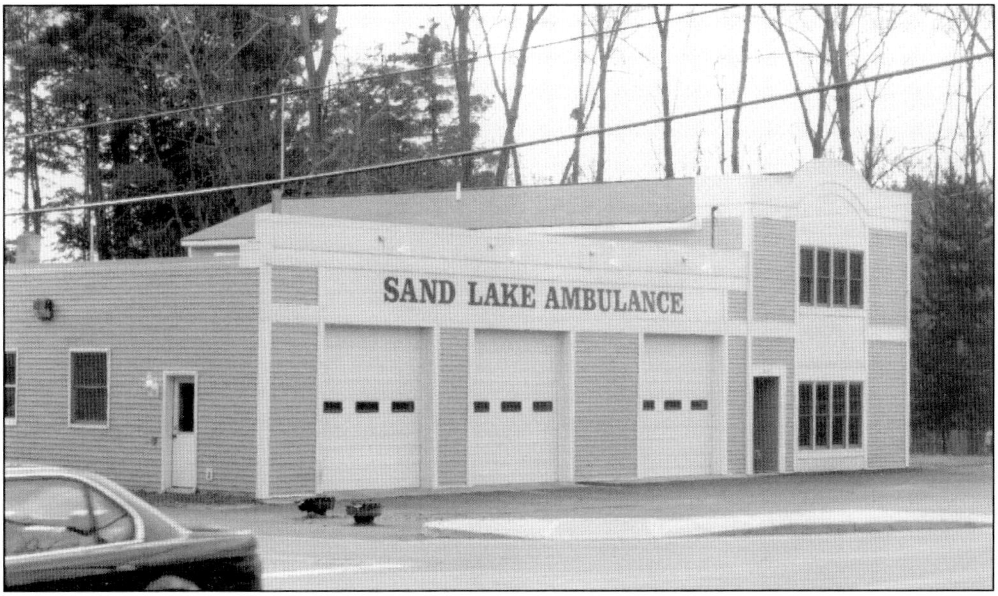

Sand Lake Ambulance. Founders for the Sand Lake Ambulance in 1959 were Robert McNaney, Carl Wicks, Ralph Wehnau, Clyde Sherwin, and Rev. Roy Severance. There were 41 charter members. The Rensselaer County Ambulance and Rescue Association trains volunteers as emergency medical technicians. Until the late 1990s, the ambulance service was supported totally by volunteers and donations. Now there is a charge for transportation and paramedic support service. (SLHSC.)

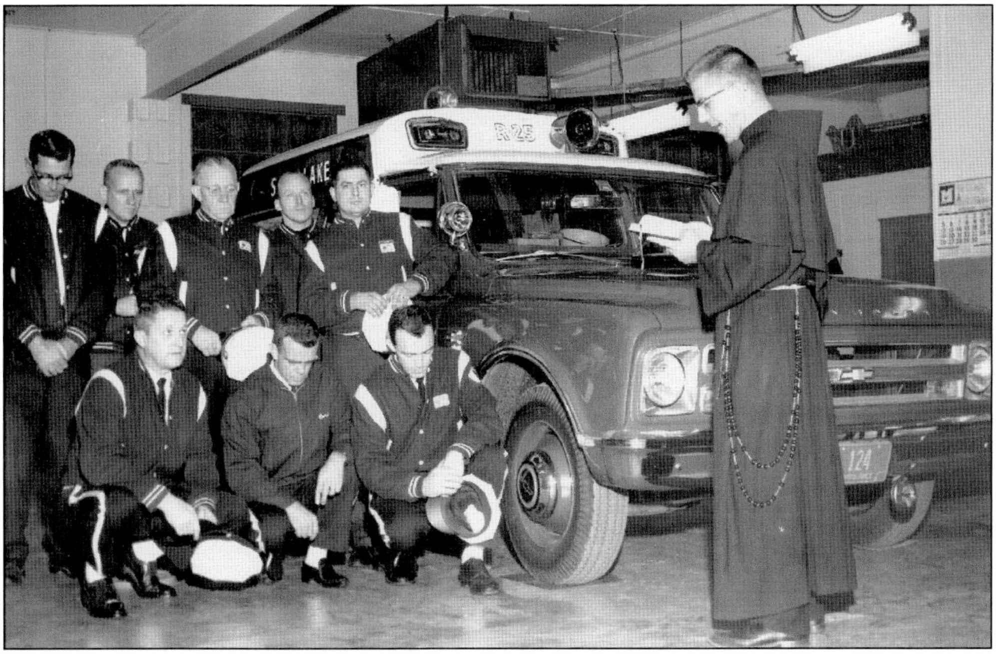

Blessing the Sand Lake Ambulance. In November 1967, Fr. Sylvester Thomas Kardos blesses the new Sand Lake ambulance and the crew. Seen here are, from left to right, (first row) John Donahue, Orin Galbraith, and Robert McNaney; (second row) Thomas Caufield, Lawrence Malone, Clyde Sherwin, Arthur Ferguson, and James Hart. (LM, Gene Baxter photograph.)

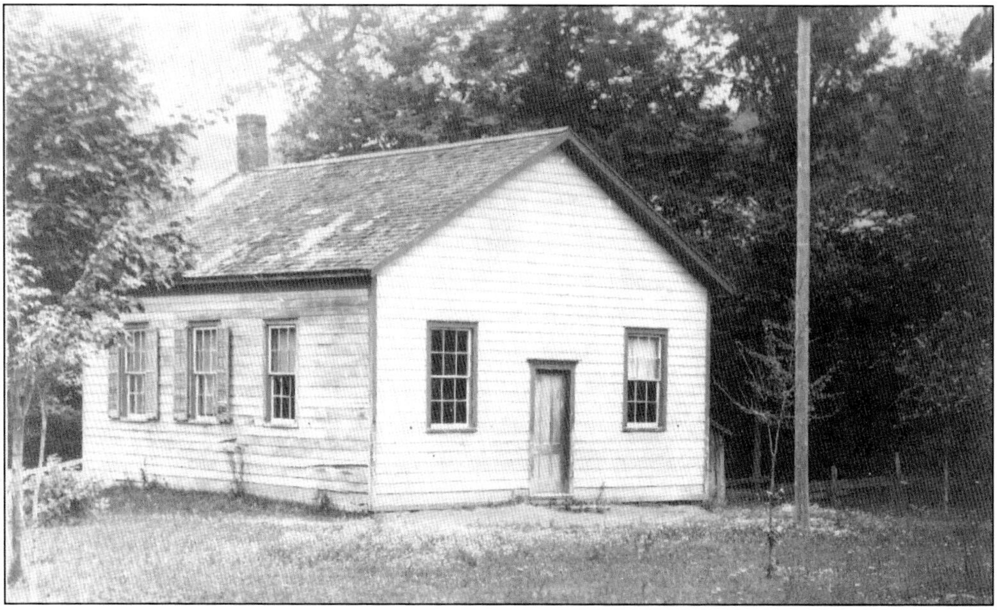

DISTRICT NO. 3 SCHOOL POSTCARD. Written on the reverse side is, "Miss Josephine Middleton / Merry Christmas / Mrs. Charles R. Miller." Miller was Middleton's schoolteacher (see page 91). District No. 3 School was located in the southwest corner of town. (BLT.)

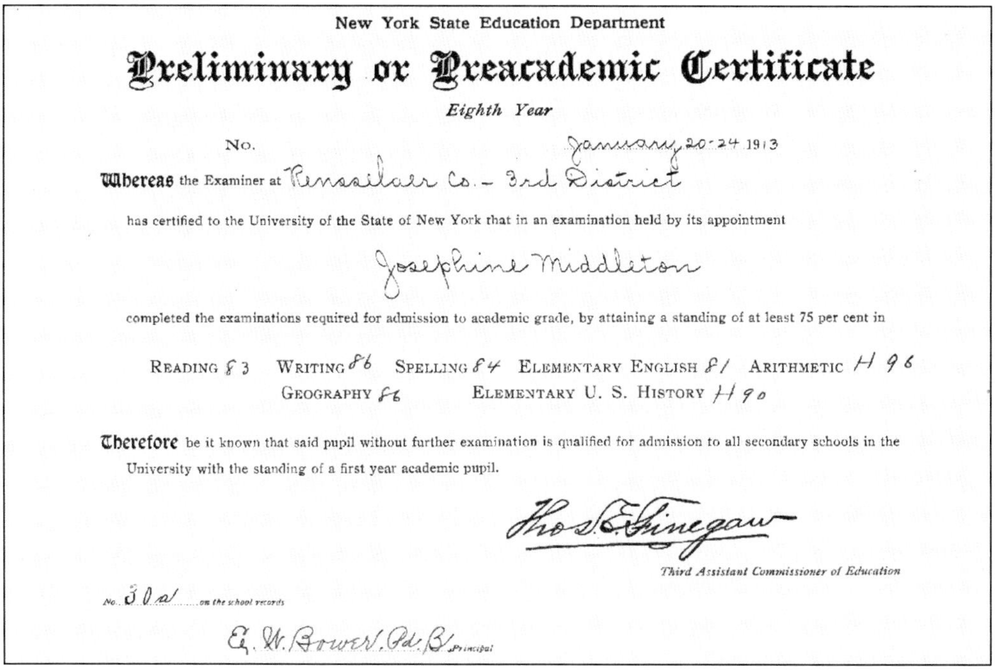

New York State Education Department

Preliminary or Preacademic Certificate

Eighth Year

No. January 20-24 1913

Whereas the Examiner at Rensselaer Co. - 3rd District

has certified to the University of the State of New York that in an examination held by its appointment

Josephine Middleton

completed the examinations required for admission to academic grade, by attaining a standing of at least 75 per cent in

READING 83 WRITING 86 SPELLING 84 ELEMENTARY ENGLISH 81 ARITHMETIC H 96
GEOGRAPHY 86 ELEMENTARY U. S. HISTORY H 90

Therefore be it known that said pupil without further examination is qualified for admission to all secondary schools in the University with the standing of a first year academic pupil.

Thos. E. Finegan
Third Assistant Commissioner of Education

No. 30a on the school records

E. W. Bower, Pd. B. Principal

EIGHTH-GRADE EXAMINATON CERTIFICATE. Middleton satisfactorily completed the examinations for eighth grade on January 20–24, 1913, and would be eligible to begin secondary education. (BLT.)

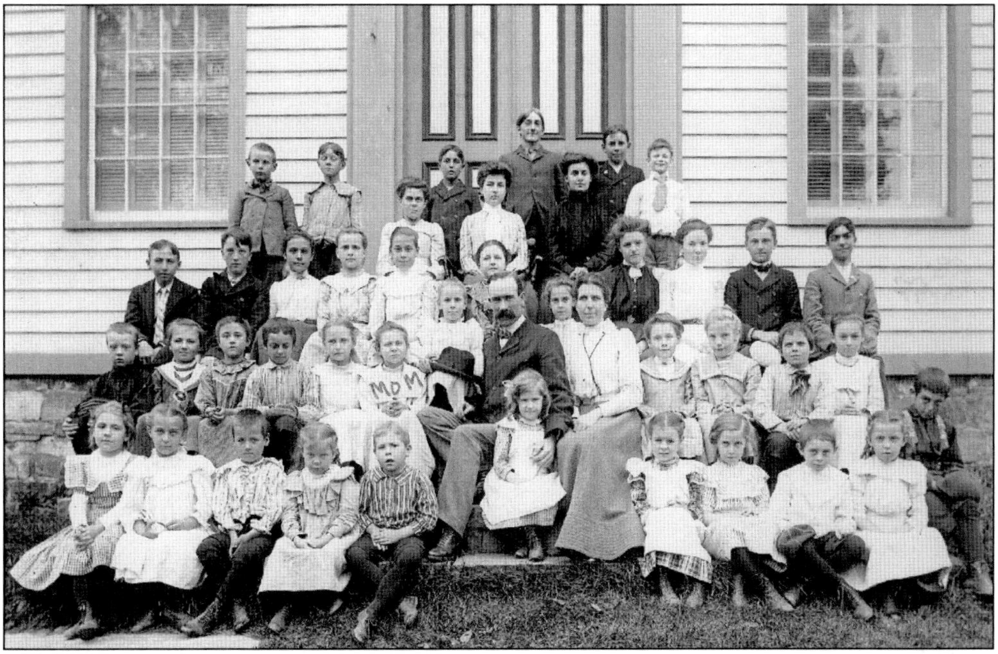

WEST SAND LAKE DISTRICT NO. 4 SCHOOL. Marion Bame Smauder's mother, Mabel McPherson (Bame), is on the right of Charles and Ida Miller and has "Mom" on her blouse. The Millers were principal and teachers from 1891 to 1909. District No. 4 School was located next to the Salem Evangelical United Brethren Church on Route 150. (SLHSC.)

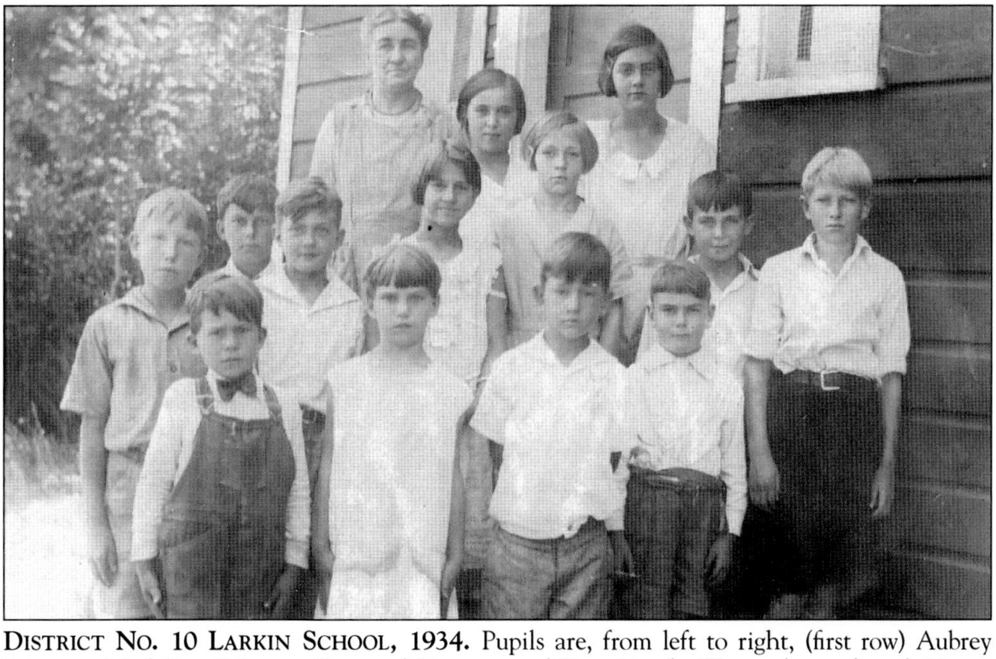

DISTRICT NO. 10 LARKIN SCHOOL, 1934. Pupils are, from left to right, (first row) Aubrey Primeau, Madeline Primeau, Ramond Engwer, and Bart Vande Water; (second row) Henry Engwer, Eric Muellecker, Ted Vande Water, Olive Engwer, Viola Wagner, Joseph Obert, and Carl Anderson; (third row) teacher Ruby Coon, ? Vande Water, and Marion Obert. This school was located on Momrow Road. (AP.)

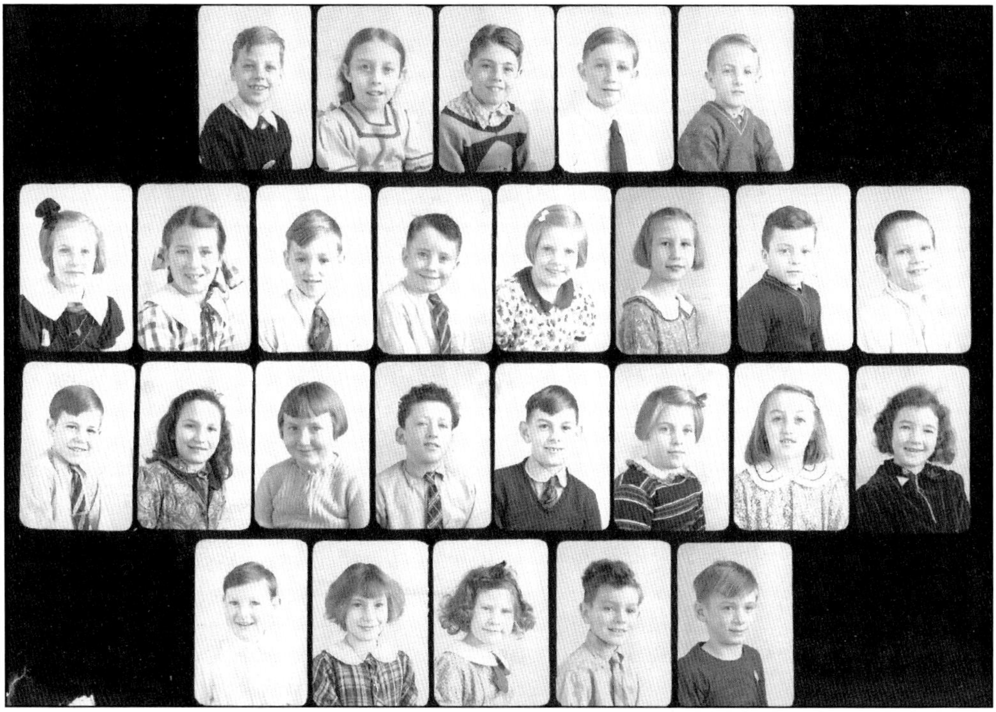

WEST SAND LAKE ELEMENTARY SCHOOL CLASS, 1935. Seen here are, from left to right, (top row) Robert Parslow, Eleanor Waterbury, Raymond Lape, Richard Clark, and Walter Wehnau; (second row) Norma Bailey, Shirley Sisson, James Platt, William Mambert, Kathryn Knapp, Edna Malik, Ralph Wehnau, and Steven Malik; (third row) Irving Sewell, Frances Konopka, Betty Harrington, Arthur Ferguson, Raymond Barnes, Doris Hogle, Janet Reid, and Lois Rescott; (fourth row) Clyde Rescott, Dorothy Samjohn, Ann Mambert, William Collins, and Albert Goodwin. (IS.)

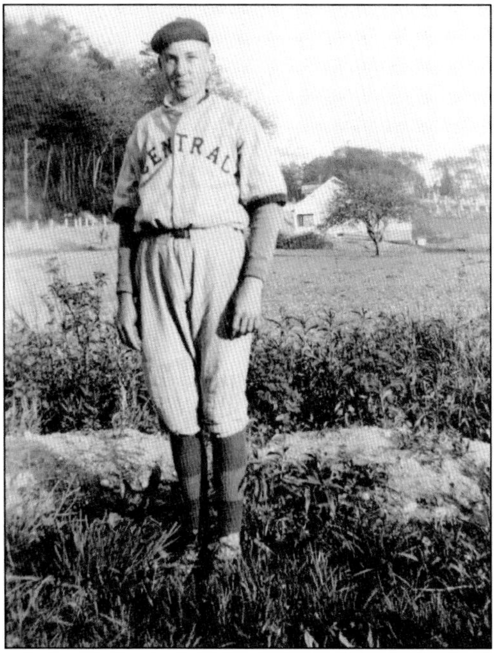

HOWARD LERCH. Howard Lerch, in his high school baseball uniform around 1930, is standing in his parents' yard looking south along Route 150 in West Sand Lake. The Elmwood Cemetery is visible in the background. In the field behind him would later be the sawmill he operated with his father, Edward (see page 47). (BLT.)

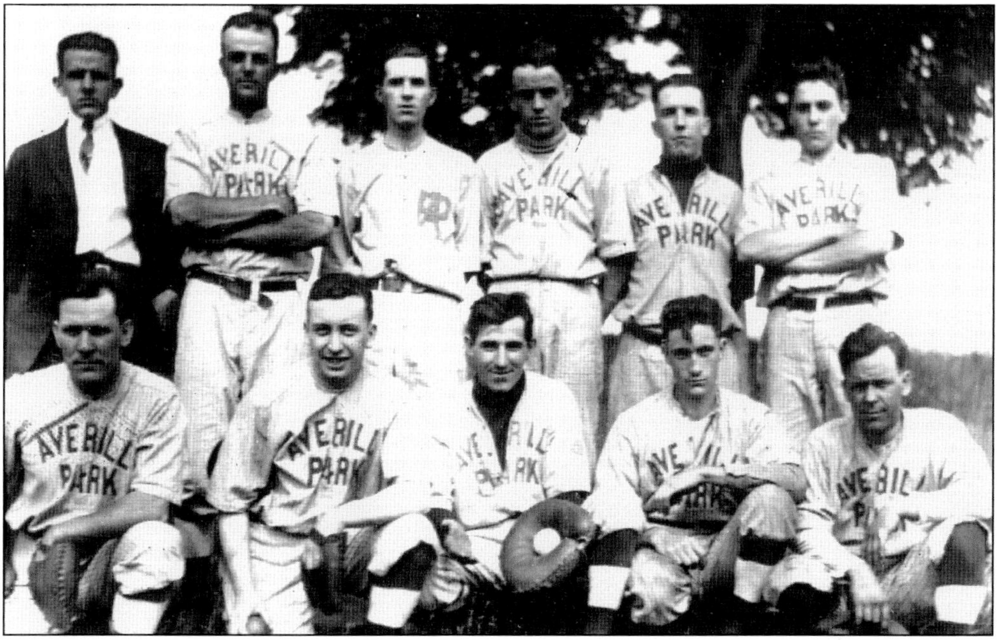

AVERILL PARK BASEBALL TEAM, C. 1923. Seen here are, from left to right, (first row) Norman Vickery, Collin Garstang, Frank Hack, Henry Dowd, and Edward McCarthy; (second row) Leon Smith, Fred Graffunder, unidentified, Dennis Warren, George ?, and William Rendert. The Town of Sand Lake played other towns. Originally they could not play baseball on Sunday, but this was later changed. (SLHSC.)

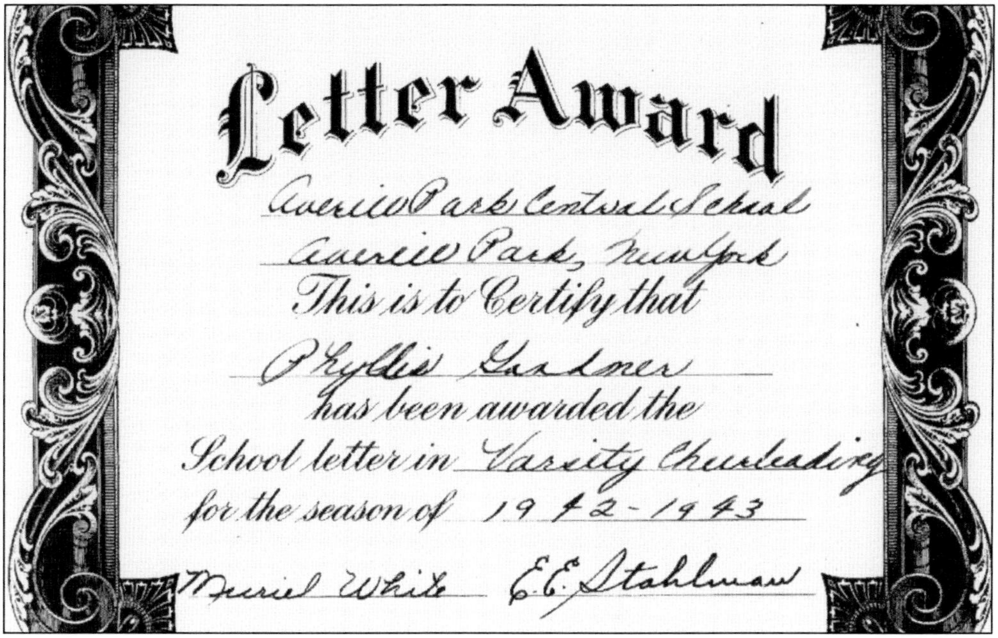

Letter Award

Averill Park Central School

Averill Park, New York

This is to Certify that

Phyllis Gardner

has been awarded the

School letter in Varsity Cheerleading

for the season of 1942-1943

Muriel White E.C. Stahlman

VARSITY CHEERLEADING LETTER AWARD. Phyllis Gardner received this certificate when she was awarded the school letter for the 1942–1943 varsity cheerleading season. The letter was C for Central School, which was the team's logo until it became *AP* for Averill Park Central School in 1948. (SLHSC.)

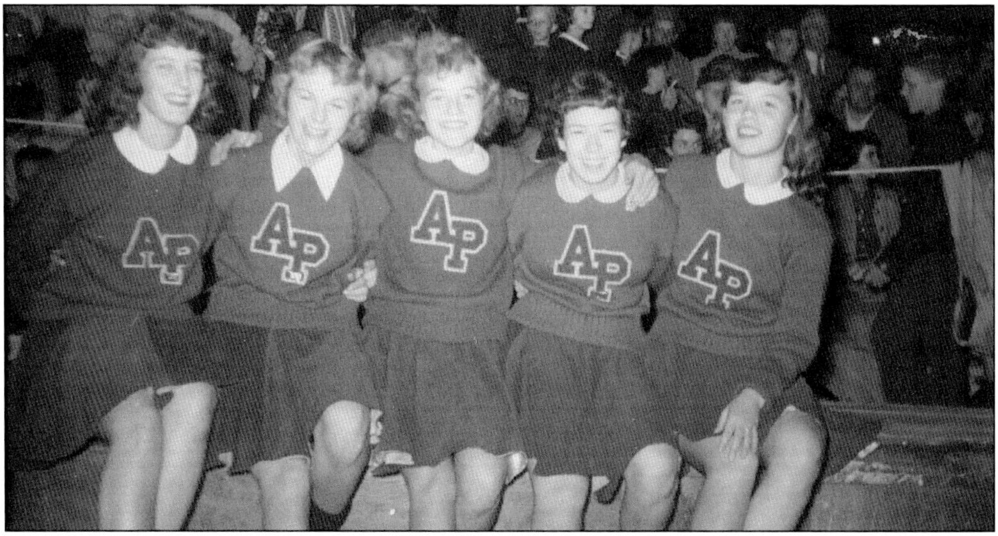

AVERILL PARK CHEERLEADERS. Seen here are, from left to right, Susan Hanchett, Janet Hoffay, Patricia Sewell, Ann Lampert and Janet Fetcher for the 1951 season. (IS.)

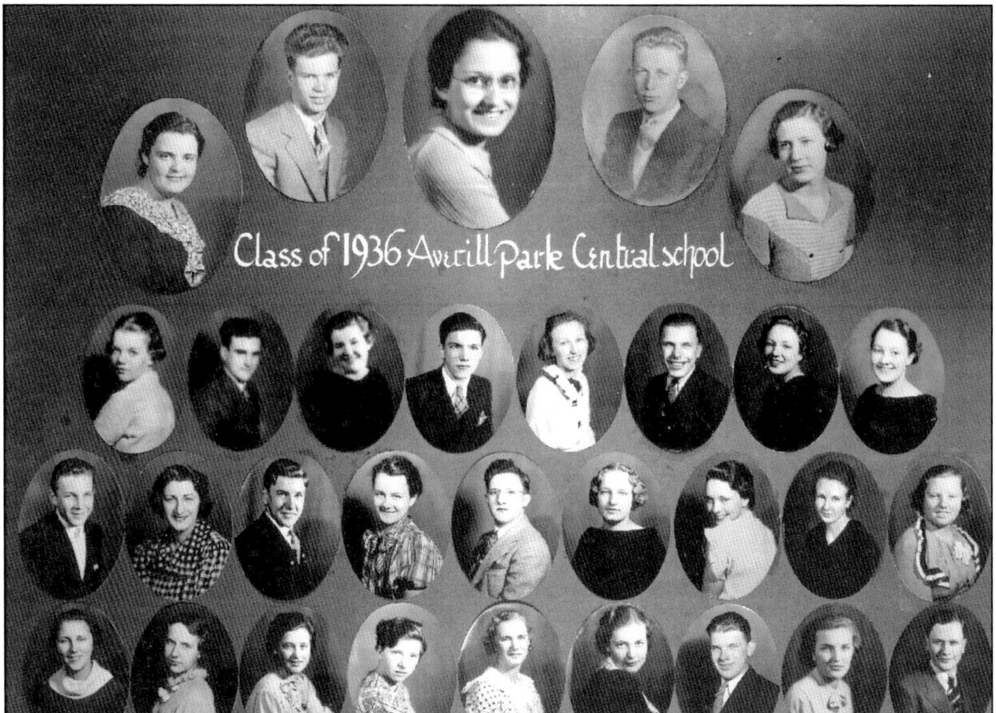

AVERILL PARK CENTRAL SCHOOL CLASS OF 1936. In this image are, from left to right, (top row) Evelyn Culver, John Shafer, Edna diDomenica, Charles Kowsky, and Iona Gundrum; (second row) Mary Butler, Oakley Bink, Helene Shafer, Fred Orr, Helen Rogers, Barney Motilage, Margaret McNary, and Dorothy Brown; (third row) Laddie Milkiewiez, Shirley Jasper, Howard Lerch, Albertine Brown, George Karl, Frances Stanis, Mildred Gardner, Grace Foster, and Elizabeth Griffin; (fourth row) Gertrude Vines, Frances Krause, Doris Gardner, Isabel Sowalski, Alma Robertson, Mary Helen Bethman, Stanley Motilage, Helen Milkiewiez, and John Capelle. (BLT.)

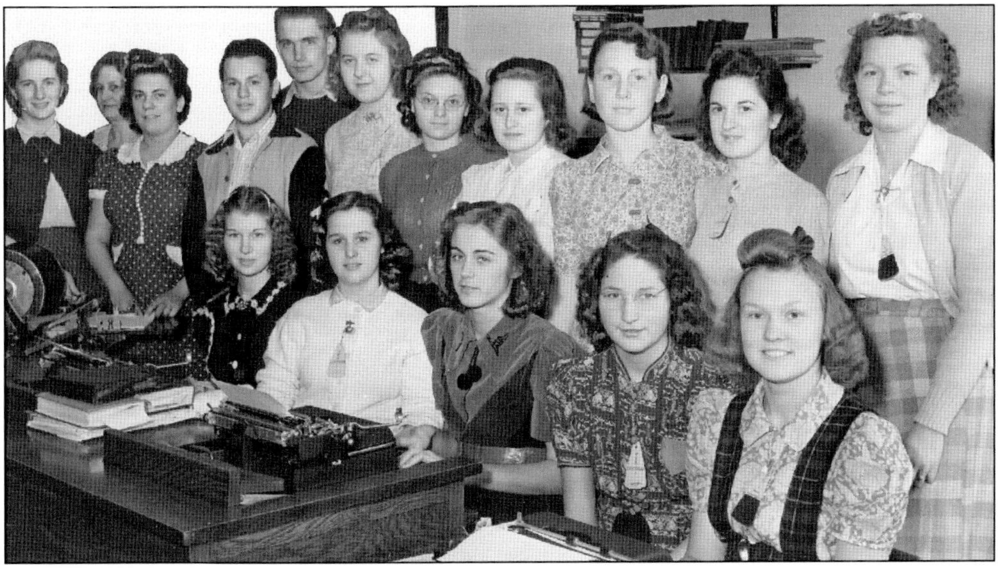

AVERILL PARK CENTRAL SCHOOL BUSINESS SERVICE CLUB, 1941. Seen here are, from left to right, (first row) Frieda Samjohn, Barbara Siegmund, Lois Wunderling, Ruth Brown, and Genevieve Stenowick; (second row) Jane Tayer, advisor Dorothy England, Evelyn Mizener, George Fader, Earl Hall, Mildred Anselment, business manager Elizabeth Kleiber, treasurer Evelyn Marbot, secretary Grace Hall, vice president Cora Bonesteel, and president Dorothy Karl. (TSLC.)

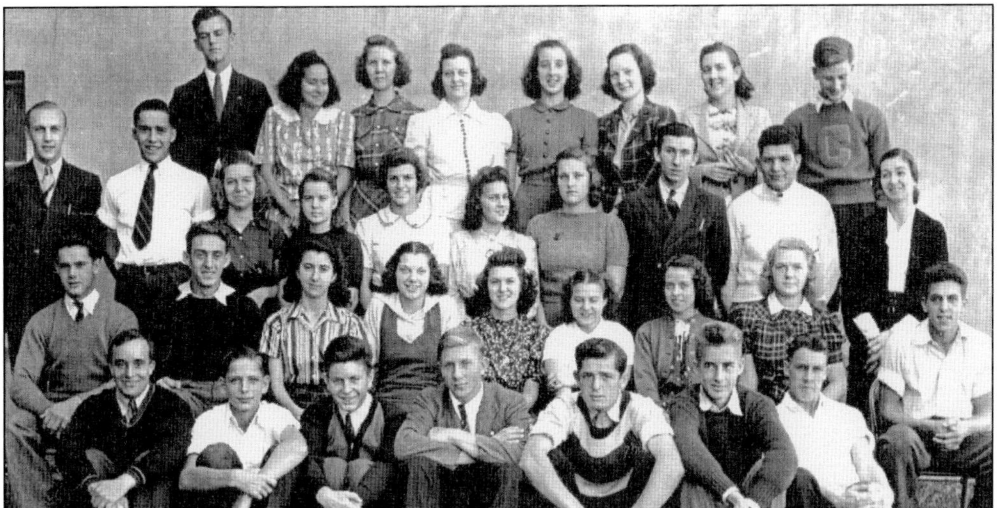

SENIOR CLASS TRIP TO WASHINGTON, D.C., 1940. This picture depicts, from left to right, (first row) Kenneth Floyd, John Udwary, Arnold Reide, president John Tomchick, Nicholas Karpiak, Burger Coons, and Robert Mielenz; (second row) Irving Edwards, vice president Walter Dankhoff, secretary Bernice Miller, Grace Sowalski, Martha Shrauder, Jeanne Bailey, Marie Hollingsworth, Ruth Bashford, and Warren Jones; (third row) Lawrence Barnum, John Prout, Kate Biittig, Helen Coons, Vivian Link, Betty Sorenson, Marjorie Teal, Stephen Luckow, Walter Nutt, and faculty advisor Marcelle Gehle; (fourth row) John Conway, Ruth L. Schillinger, Marion Carlson, Genevieve Shorey, Frances Hidley, Helen Trumble, Ruth E. Schillinger, and Perry Williams. (SLHSC.)

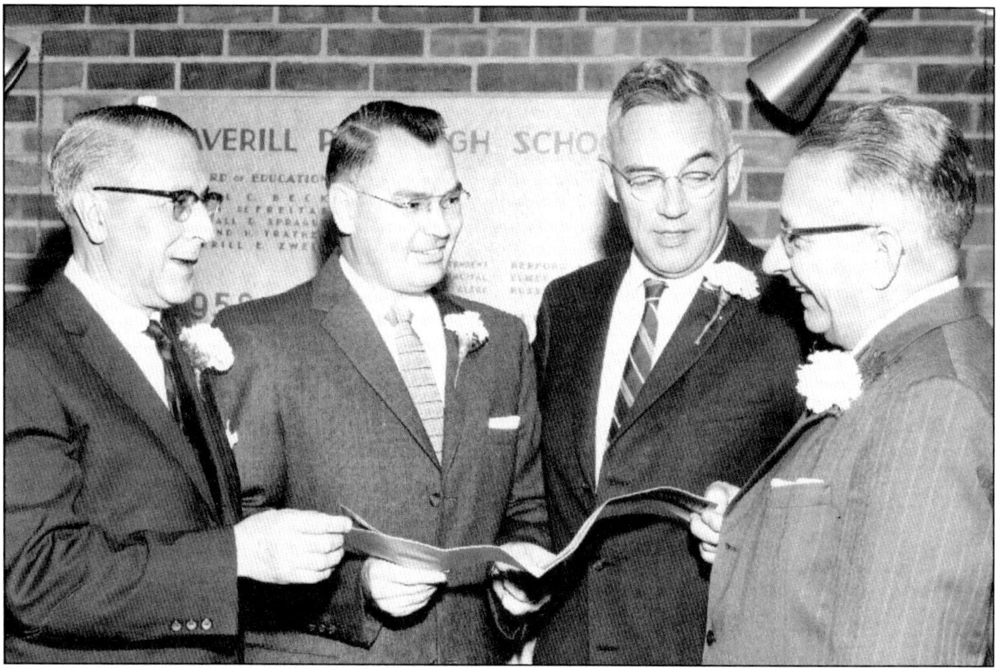

AVERILL PARK HIGH SCHOOL DEDICATION. Seen here are, from left to right, John deFreitas, president of the board of education; Howard K. Fuller, high school principal; Dr. Richard Folsom, president of Rensselaer Polytechnic Institute; and Hereford A. Smith, superintendent of third supervising district, at the formal dedication of Averill Park High School on October 24, 1958. (MSt.G.)

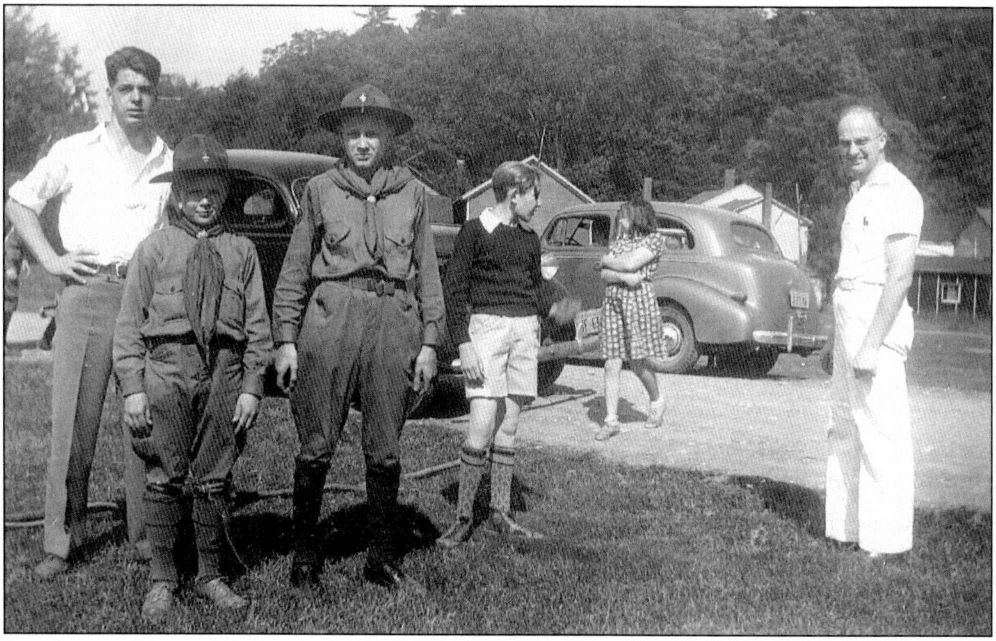

BOY SCOUT TROOP 25. On the left is Robert B. Kachadurian, who was with Boy Scout Troop 25 in West Sand Lake. The project on this day, June 2, 1939, was to plant trees on Route 150. The ones in full-dress Scout uniforms contrast with the summer garb of others in the scene. (BD-M.)

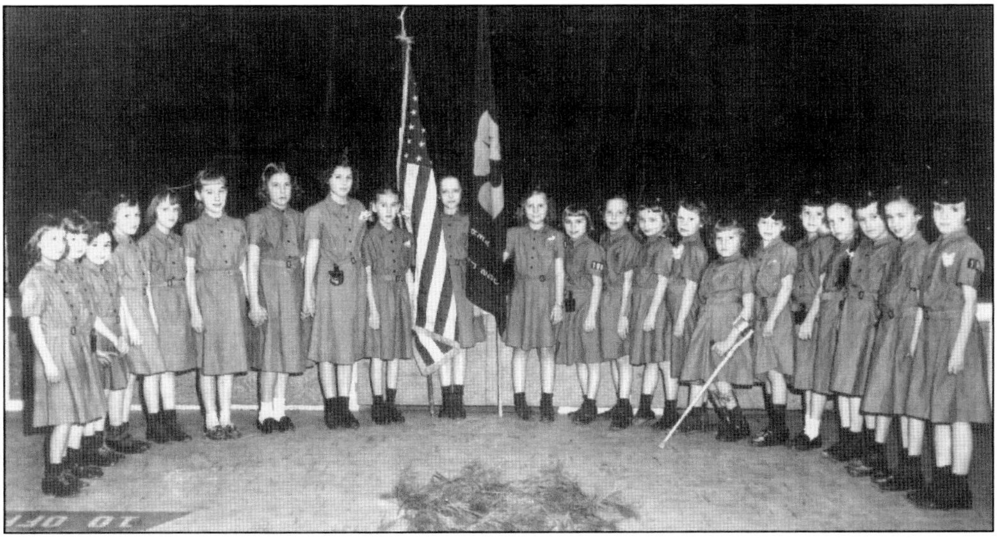

WEST SAND LAKE BROWNIE SCOUT TROOP, 1955. Pictured from left to right at the West Sand Lake Methodist Church hall are Patricia Bashford, Gertrude Cook, Eunice Rescott, Susan Service, Anna Hoffay, Sharon Miller, Barbara Lerch, Jane Robinson, Nancy Spence, Dorothy Halligan, Susan Coulter, unidentified, Jill Morlock, Joyce Hitchcock, Sharon Shoemaker, Linda Droste, Pamela Murdock, Marion Bort, and Cheryl Turner. Weekly meetings were held at the home of the troop's leader, a Mrs. Robinson. (BLT.)

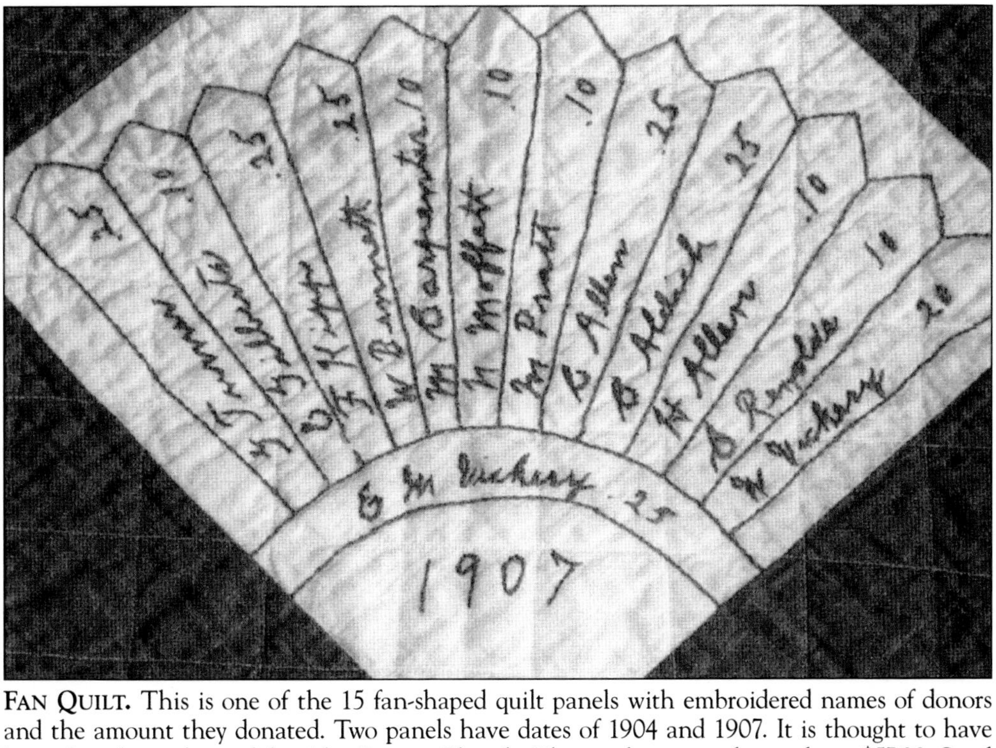

FAN QUILT. This is one of the 15 fan-shaped quilt panels with embroidered names of donors and the amount they donated. Two panels have dates of 1904 and 1907. It is thought to have been done by quilters of the Alps Baptist Church. The total amount donated was $57.20. Sand Lake residents included are "E.E. Reichard 50¢," "Arthur Peck 2.00," and "Mr. Henry Stanley. 25cts." (EG.)

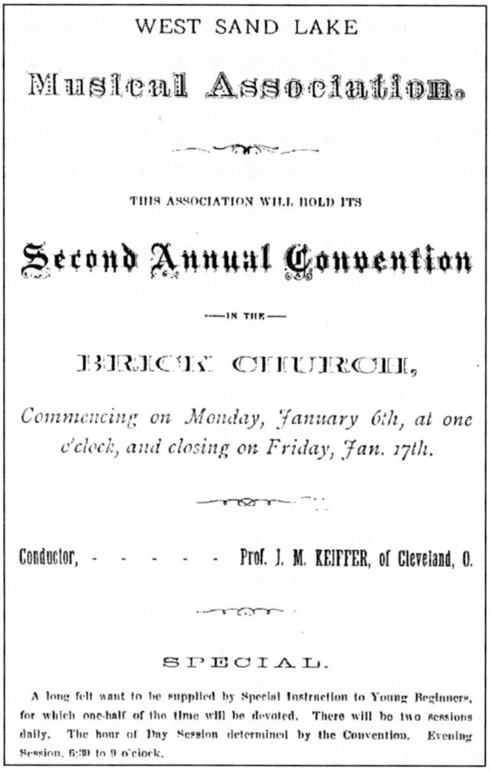

WEST SAND LAKE

Musical Association.

THIS ASSOCIATION WILL HOLD ITS

Second Annual Convention

—IN THE—

BRICK CHURCH,

Commencing on Monday, January 6th, at one o'clock, and closing on Friday, Jan. 17th.

Conductor, - - - - - - Prof. J. M. KEIFFER, of Cleveland, O.

SPECIAL.

A long felt want to be supplied by Special Instruction to Young Beginners, for which one-half of the time will be devoted. There will be two sessions daily. The hour of Day Session determined by the Convention. Evening Session, 6:30 to 9 o'clock.

WEST SAND LAKE MUSICAL ASSOCIATION. Shown is the front program page of second annual convention of the West Sand Lake Musical Association with the conductor from Cleveland at the Brick Church. The Second Evangelical Lutheran Church on Route 43 was often referred to as the "Brick Church." The convention lasted 11 days. (TSLC.)

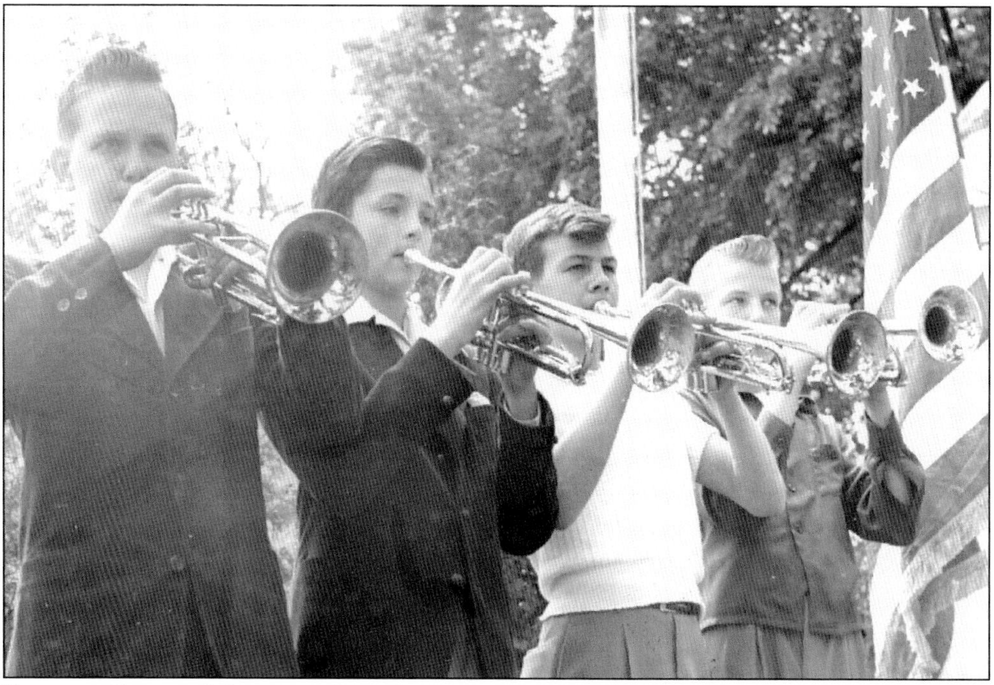

PLAYING TAPS AT MEMORIAL DAY CELEBRATION. Seen here are, from left to right, Donald Stiles, Joseph Connors Jr., unidentified, and Harold Foster, playing taps at the West Sand Lake veterans monument at a Memorial Day celebration around 1951. (JC.)

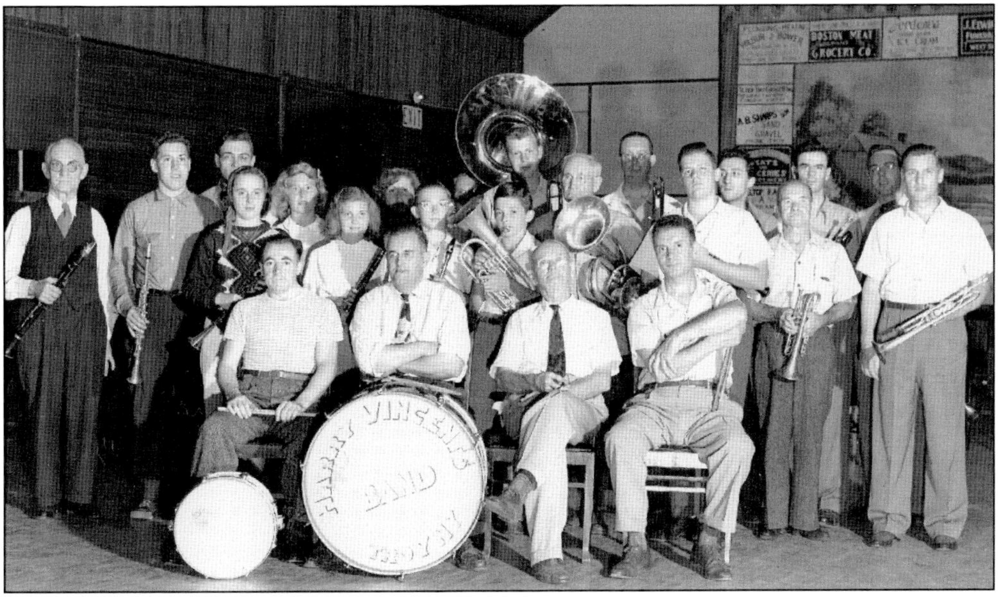

HARRY VINCENT'S BAND. Members of the band are practicing at the West Sand Lake fire hall around 1947. They also practiced at the Grange hall. In the front row, third from the left is Harry Vincent; in the second row, beginning third from the left, are Lewis McCaw, Joseph Connors Jr., ? Ferguson, and Kenneth McCaw; and in the third row, beginning second from the left, are Charles McAllister and Fred Rapp. They played at local social events throughout the town. (SLHSC.)

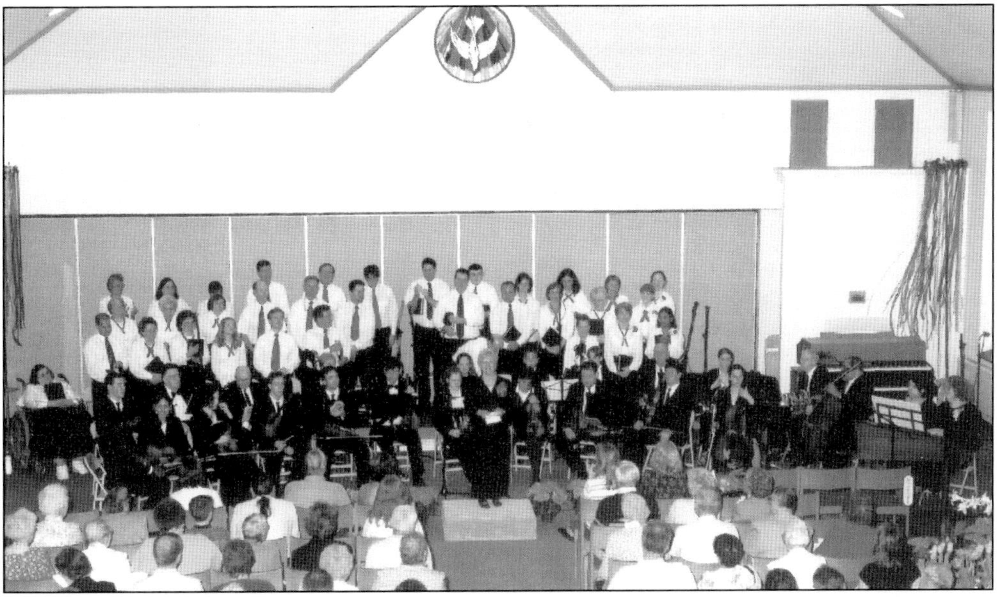

AVERILL PARK STRINGS AND WINDS ORCHESTRA AND SAND LAKE CHORALE. Janine T. Budesheim, founder and conductor of the Averill Park Strings and Winds Orchestra in 1995 and Sand Lake Chorale in 2001, has given many students and adults who sing and/or play instruments an opportunity to be a part of these two groups and to bring the joy of their performances to community events and holiday celebrations. The two groups have joined in performing *The Messiah* at St. Henry's Church. (JTB.)

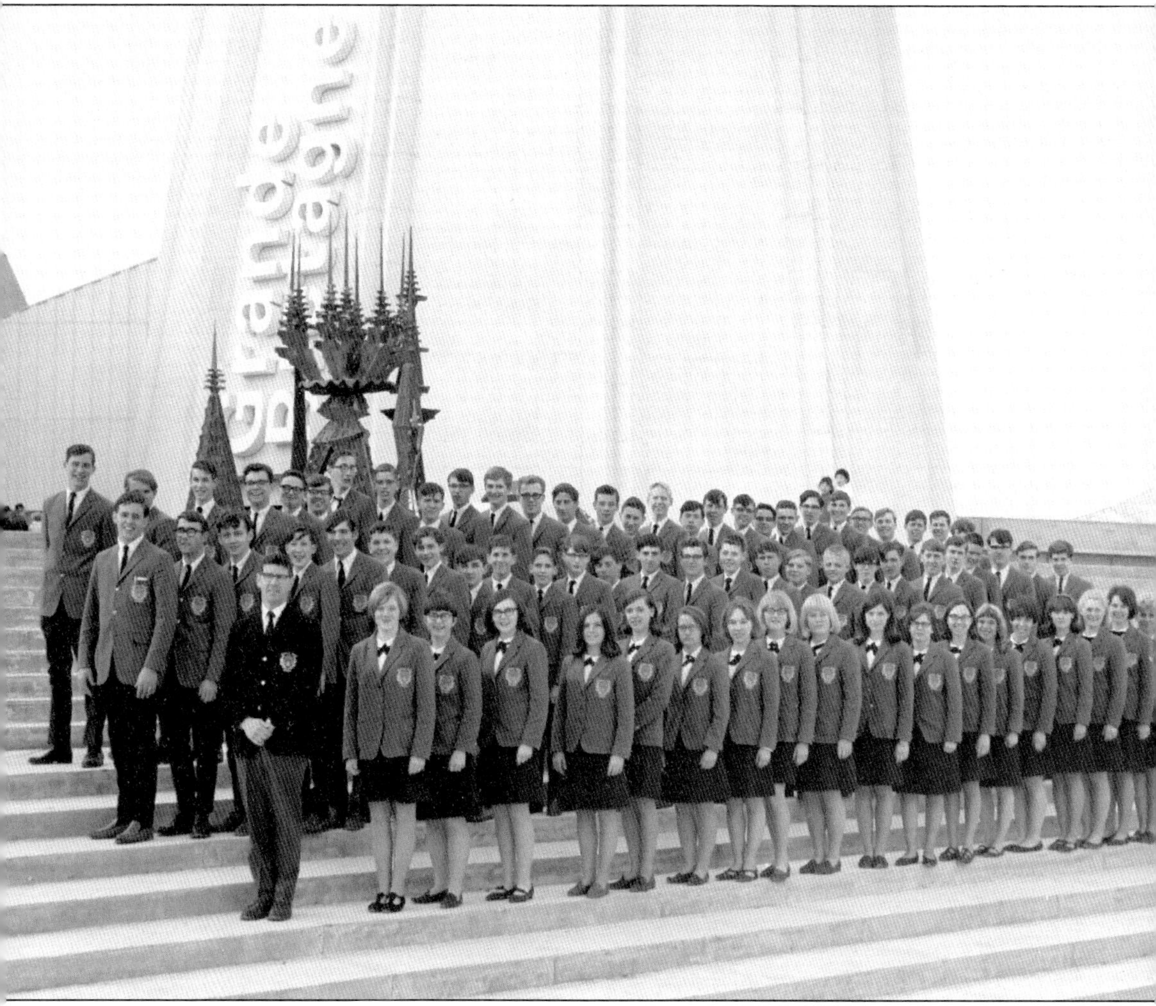

AVERILL PARK HIGH SCHOOL BAND TOUR. In 1967, the Averill Park High School band tour went north, culminating in concerts at Expo 67 (Terre des Hommes), the world's fair in Montreal. Here the band poses in front of the Great Britain pavilion. They are, from left to right, (first row) band director Richard Knipes, Chris Asher, Susan Jewell, Sally Spence, Carol Asher, Sylvia O'Donnell, Vicki Heffner, Pat Robinson, Ann Rugh, Jean Ansonia, Martha Whelden, Wanda Flint, Evelyn Harris, Constance Cooke, Marilyn Brown, Susan Bryan, Sandra Debus, Jane Crowley, Virginia "Dee Dee" Pierce, and Deanna Gardner; (second row) Daniel Crowley, Michael Heffner, Neil Bonesteel, Tom Cassavaugh, Jonathan Schwam, Francis "Corky" Bonesteel, Keith Reynolds, Andrew Mace, Ralph Slighter, John Udwary, Glenn Snyder, Ole Heggen, Kenneth Coonrad, Charlie Heffner, Tom Gerard, David Rogers, Billy Ilves, Trig Tomlinson, Jon Plant, Mark Heffner, Donald Ackner, Bill McKee, Dennis Buck, John Abbott, Ronald McKee, and David Reynolds; (third row) Mark Flanagan, James Wilkins, Robert Pawlson, John Miadzielec, David Snyder, James Miller, Donald Hoffman, unidentified, Dennis Noonan, Gary Hack, David Lance, Thomas Coffey, Thomas Smith, Dan Driggs, Ken Kinne, Jeff Debus, Greg Horine, Ed Barlow, Duane Campbell, Albert Tinker, Glenn Hankle, Kevin McCarthy, Jeff Bashford, Bob LaFleur, Jeff House, John Shelgren, Donn Bleau, and unidentified. (AM.)

Five

CHURCHES AND CEMETERIES

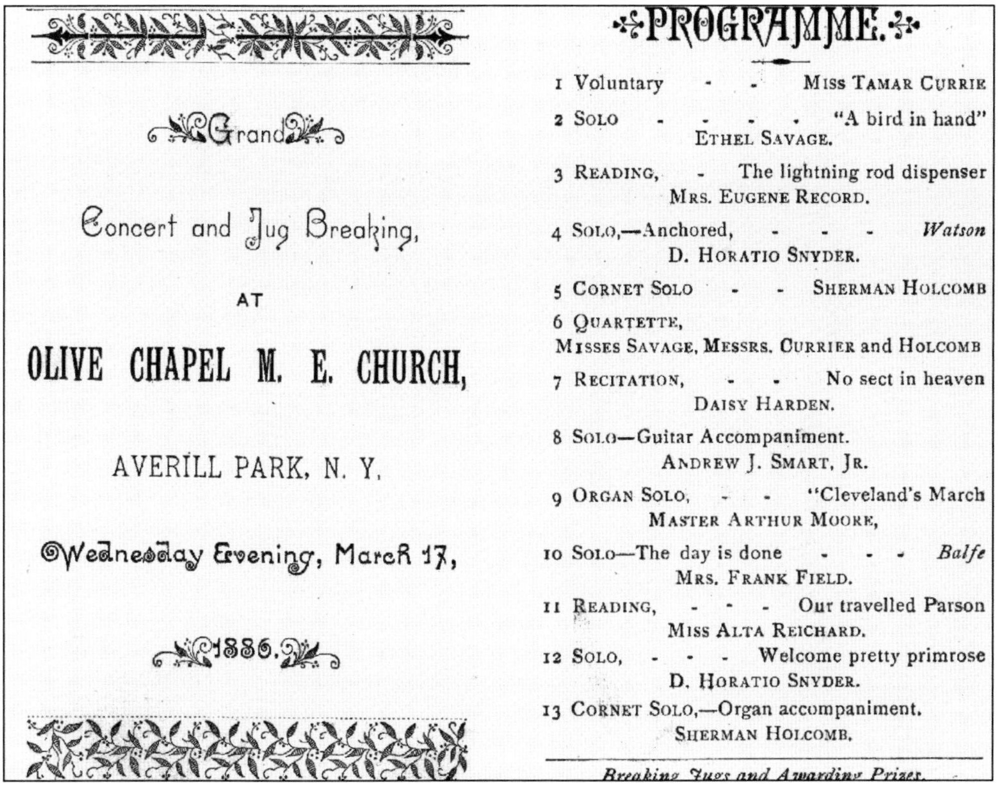

Grand

Concert and Jug Breaking,

AT

OLIVE CHAPEL M. E. CHURCH,

AVERILL PARK, N. Y.

Wednesday Evening, March 17,

1886.

PROGRAMME.

1 Voluntary - - MISS TAMAR CURRIE

2 SOLO - - - - "A bird in hand"
ETHEL SAVAGE.

3 READING, - The lightning rod dispenser
MRS. EUGENE RECORD.

4 SOLO,—Anchored, - - - *Watson*
D. HORATIO SNYDER.

5 CORNET SOLO - - SHERMAN HOLCOMB

6 QUARTETTE,
MISSES SAVAGE, MESSRS. CURRIER and HOLCOMB

7 RECITATION, - - No sect in heaven
DAISY HARDEN.

8 SOLO—Guitar Accompaniment.
ANDREW J. SMART, JR.

9 ORGAN SOLO, - - "Cleveland's March
MASTER ARTHUR MOORE,

10 SOLO—The day is done - - - *Balfe*
MRS. FRANK FIELD.

11 READING, - - - Our travelled Parson
MISS ALTA REICHARD.

12 SOLO, - - - Welcome pretty primrose
D. HORATIO SNYDER.

13 CORNET SOLO,—Organ accompaniment.
SHERMAN HOLCOMB.

Breaking Jugs and Awarding Prizes.

METHODIST JUG BREAKING. At the end of the grand concert on March 17, 1886, there was jug breaking and awarding of prizes. A reference was found of a jug-breaking custom in a Methodist church in the early 1900s. Jugs were used to collect money; at a ceremony they were broken and the money counted for missionary projects. Possibly this was a similar affair. (A&WM.)

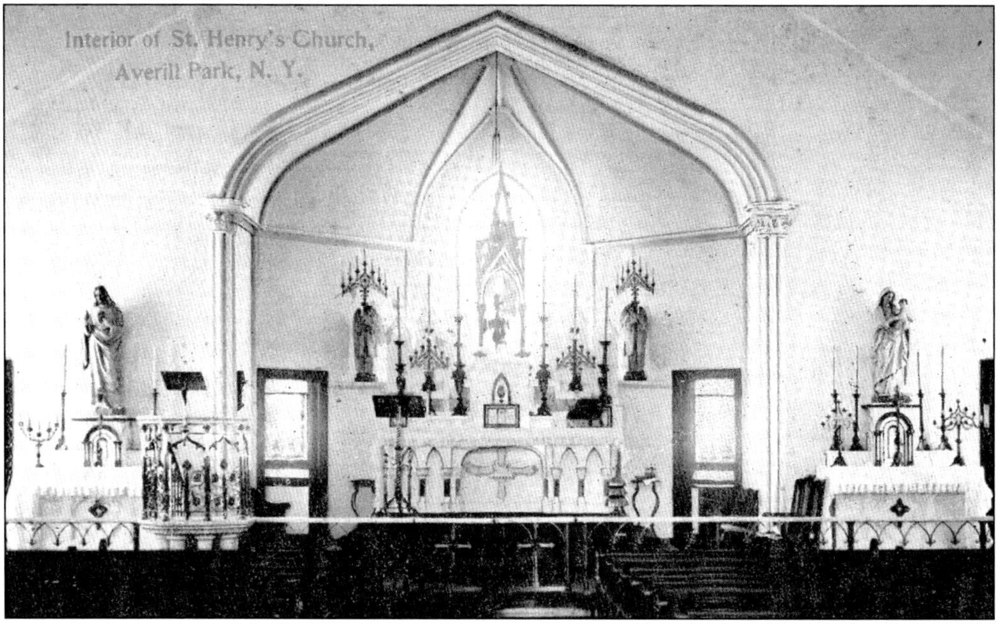

ST. HENRY'S CHURCH INTERIOR. The congregation of St. Henry's Church was familiar with its sanctuary having this appearance from 1902 until it became necessary to expand and renovate it in 1983 to accommodate the increase in parishioners. (AT.)

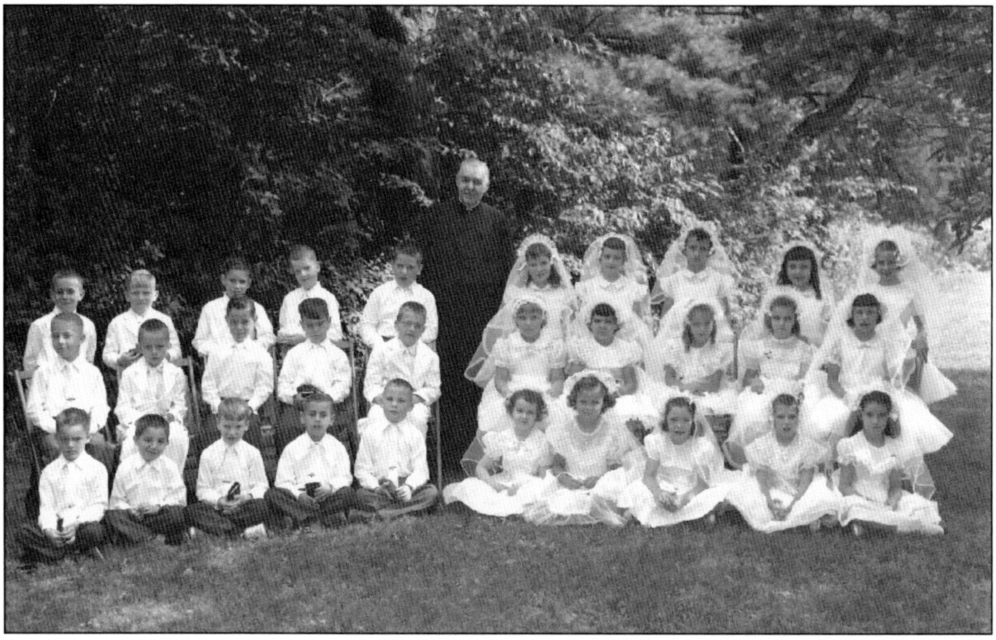

ST. HENRY'S FIRST COMMUNION, MAY 1957. Shown here with Fr. Francis P. Anthus, the boys are, from left to right, (first row) unidentified, Kenneth Coonrad, Michael St. Germain, Louis Ronzetti, and unidentified; (second row) Anthony Covert, John Griswold, unidentified, Michael Robideau, and Robert Weekly; (third row) unidentified, Kenneth O'Brien, Anthony Valente, Martin Gibbons, and unidentified. Girls identified are, from left to right in the second row, Stephanie Kronau and Madeline Sheppis. (MSt.G.)

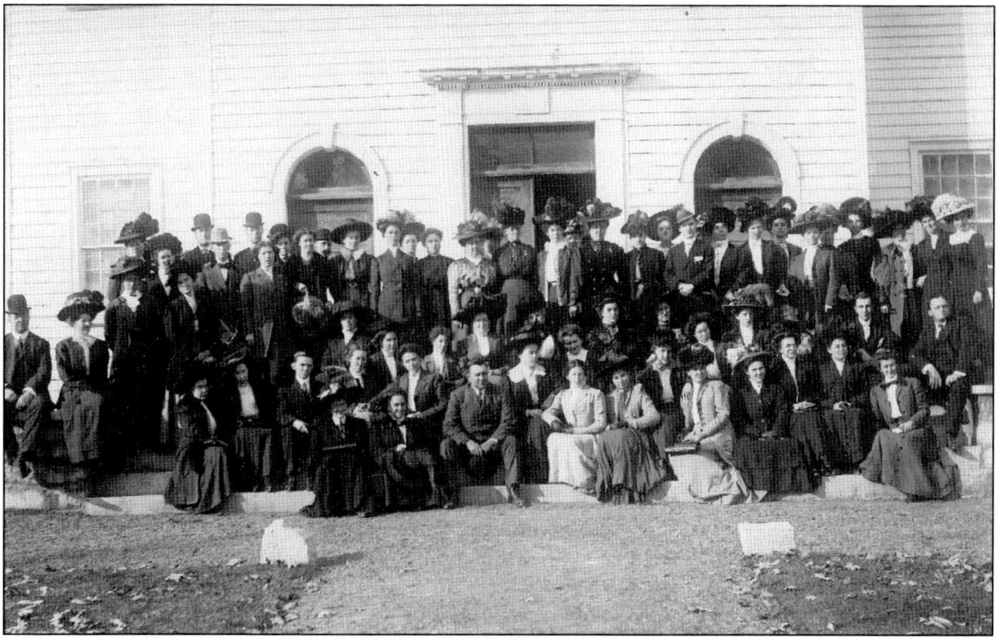

Sand Lake Baptist Church Congregation. This congregational picture was taken prior to 1911, when the stained-glass windows were installed in the church. During the pastorate of Elder Abel Brown from May 5, 1841, to April 3, 1842, the church had noted involvement in the Underground Railroad. (LH.)

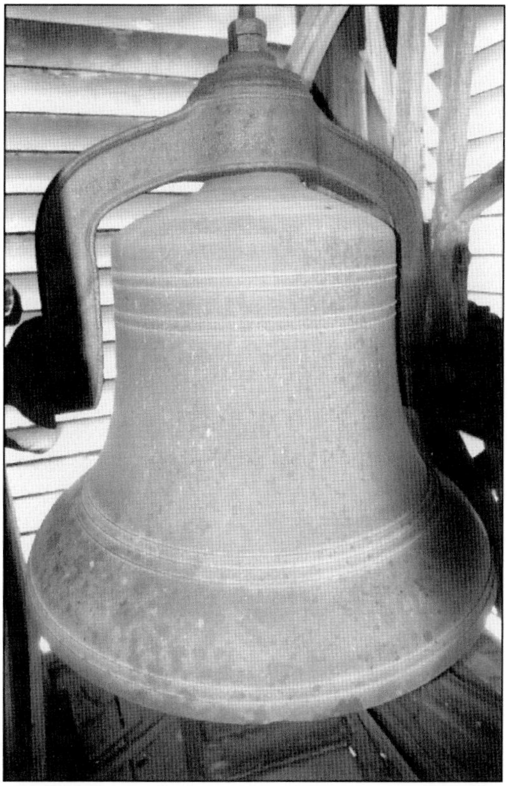

Sand Lake Baptist Church Bell. Several bells in town bear the Meneely Bell Companies' inscriptions. The Sand Lake Baptist Church bell is an 1890 Clinton Meneely Bell Company (Troy) bell and has the following Latin inscriptions: *Laudo deum verum* (I praise the true God), *Plebem voco* (I call the people), *Defunctos ploro* (I mourn the dead), *Festa decoro* (I honor the feasts), *Sabbata pango* (I sing the Sabbaths), and *Excito lentos* (I wake up the sluggish). (JC.)

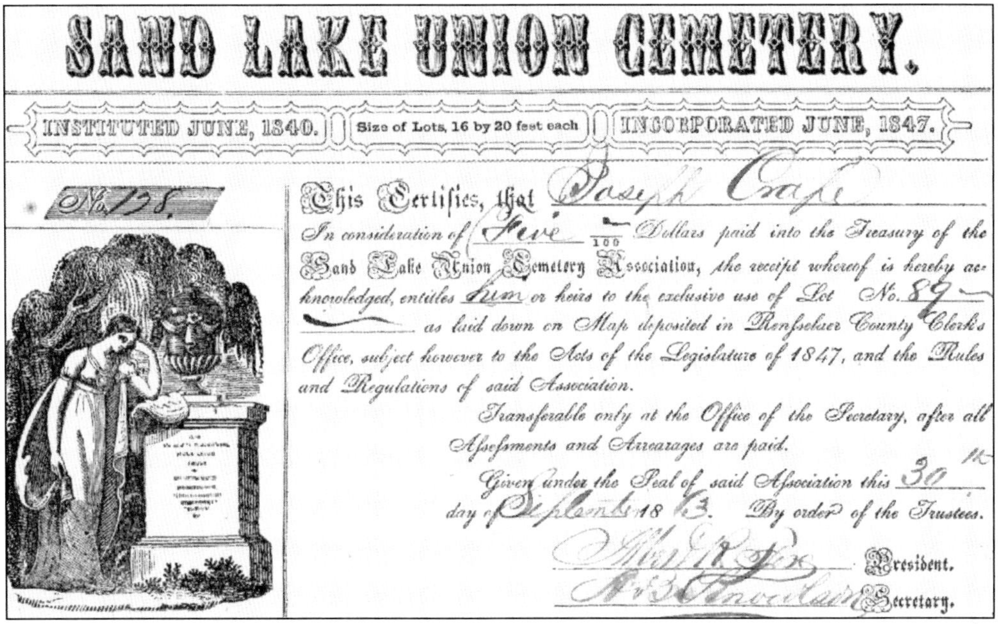

SAND LAKE UNION CEMETERY.

INSTITUTED JUNE, 1840. | Size of Lots, 16 by 20 feet each | INCORPORATED JUNE, 1847.

No. 138.

This Certifies, that Joseph Crape

In consideration of Five $\frac{}{100}$ Dollars paid into the Treasury of the Sand Lake Union Cemetery Association, the receipt whereof is hereby acknowledged, entitles him or heirs to the exclusive use of Lot No. 89 as laid down on Map deposited in Rensselaer County Clerk's Office, subject however to the Acts of the Legislature of 1847, and the Rules and Regulations of said Association.

Transferable only at the Office of the Secretary, after all Assessments and Arrearages are paid.

Given under the Seal of said Association this 30th day of September 1863. By order of the Trustees.

President.

Secretary.

CEMETERY RECEIPT. Joseph Crape purchased lot No. 89 in Sand Lake Union Cemetery for $5 on September 30, 1863. The receipt is signed by president Albert R. Fox and secretary A. B. Knowlson. (aG.)

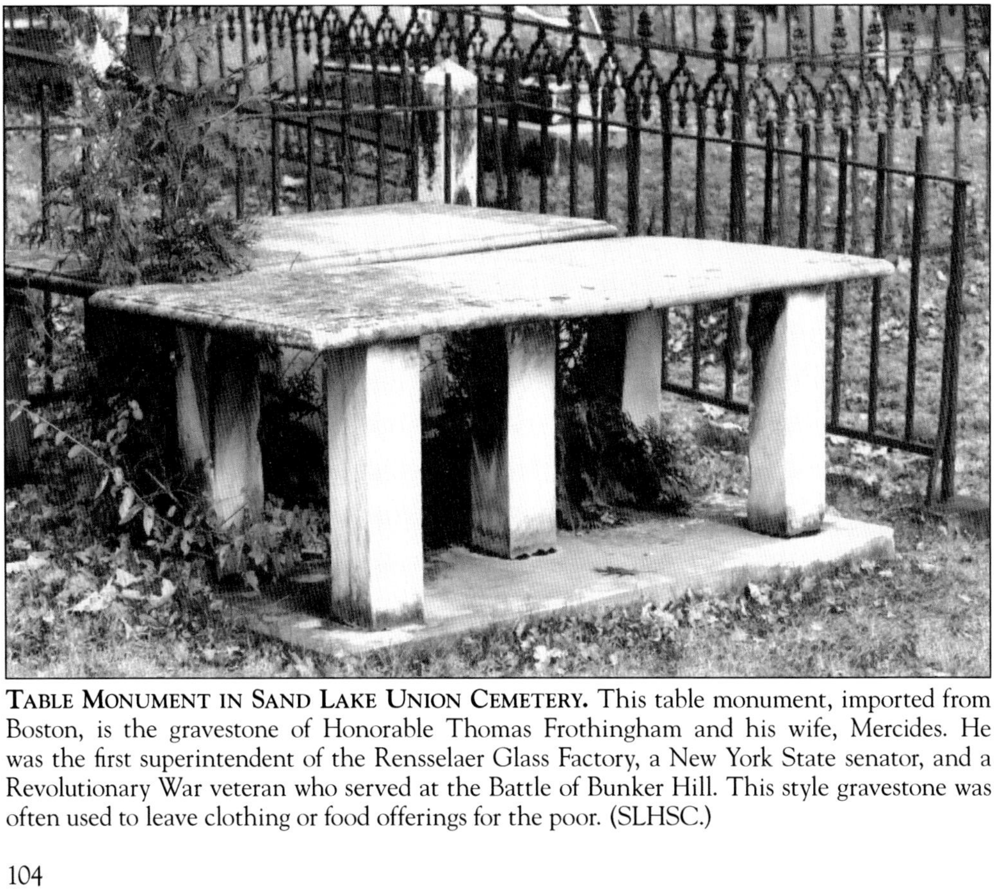

TABLE MONUMENT IN SAND LAKE UNION CEMETERY. This table monument, imported from Boston, is the gravestone of Honorable Thomas Frothingham and his wife, Mercides. He was the first superintendent of the Rensselaer Glass Factory, a New York State senator, and a Revolutionary War veteran who served at the Battle of Bunker Hill. This style gravestone was often used to leave clothing or food offerings for the poor. (SLHSC.)

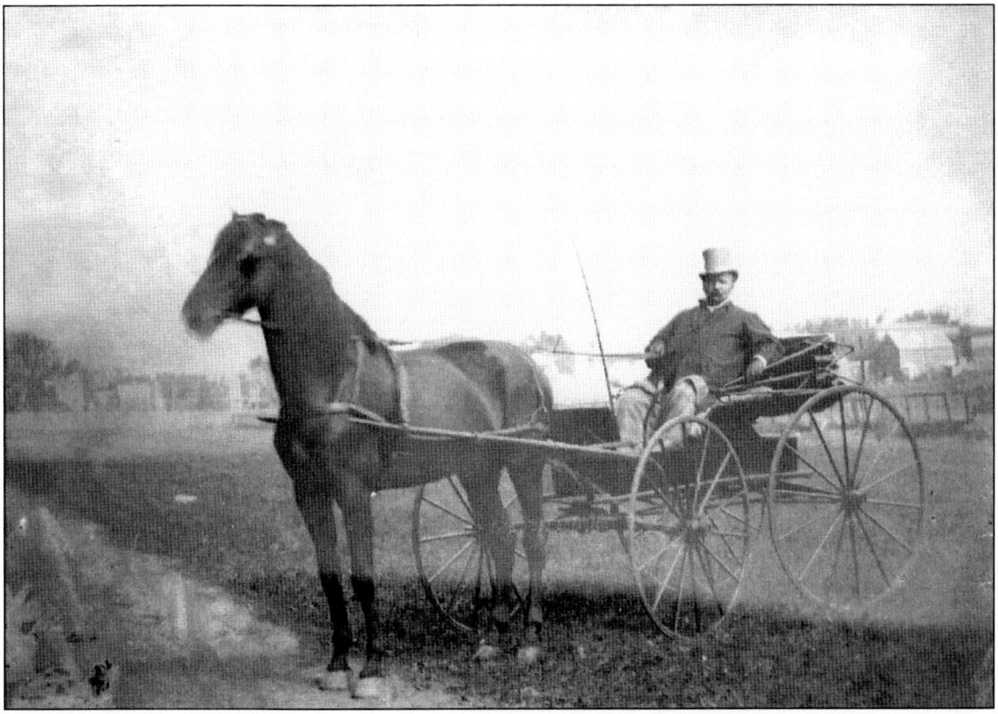

JAMES AVERILL AND MOSCOW. Shown here is James Knox Averill with Moscow, an equine veteran of the Civil War. The original tintype was defective, giving Moscow no ears. (TSLC.)

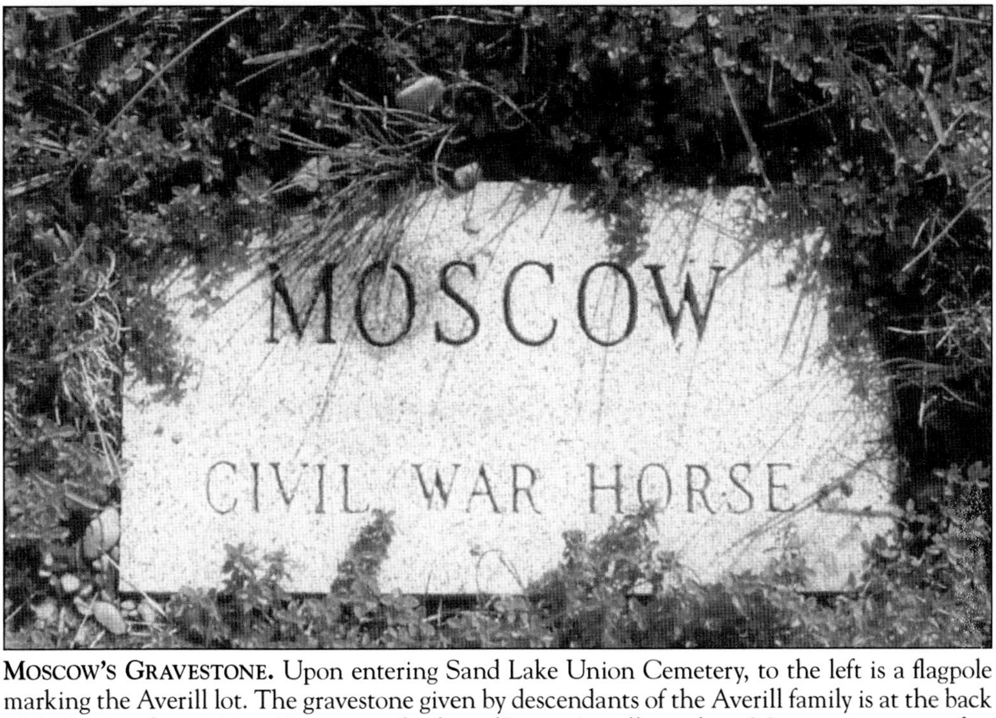

MOSCOW'S GRAVESTONE. Upon entering Sand Lake Union Cemetery, to the left is a flagpole marking the Averill lot. The gravestone given by descendants of the Averill family is at the back of the lot, marking Moscow's grave at the feet of James Averill, to whom Moscow was given after the Civil War. (TSLC.)

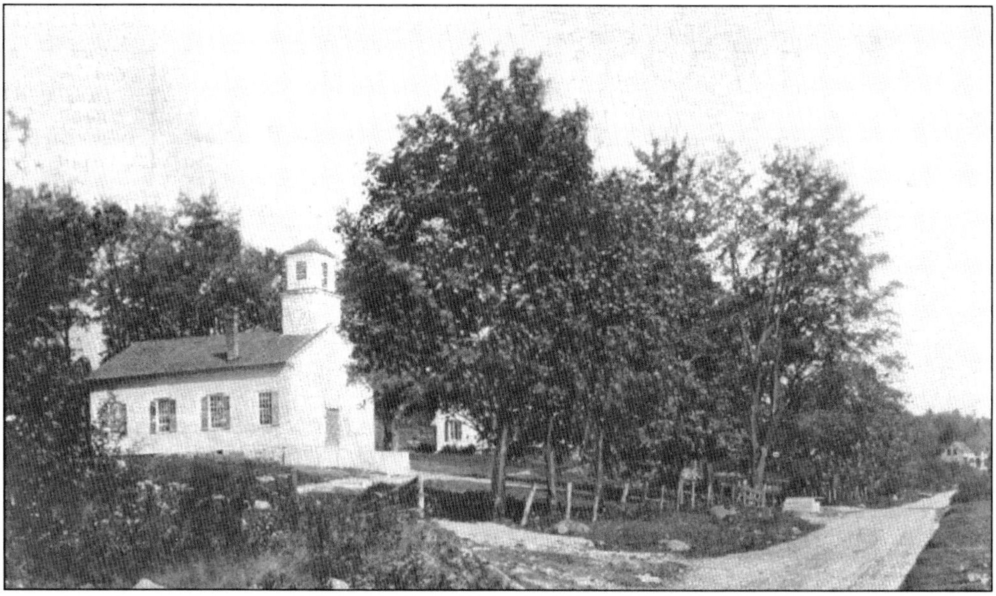

ZION'S UNITED CHURCH OF CHRIST OF TABORTON AND PARSONAGE. This picture shows the Zion's United Church of Christ of Taborton prior to 1907, before stained-glass windows were installed and with several trees in front. (LH.)

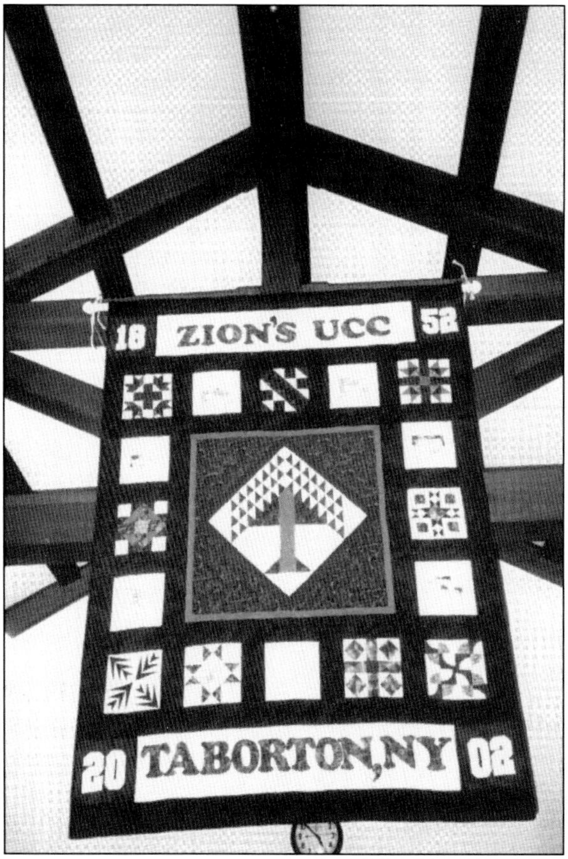

ZION'S UNITED CHURCH OF CHRIST OF TABORTON QUILT. This quilt, commemorating the 150th anniversary of the church, was designed with both historical and biblical references. Included are biblical sampler blocks and pictures of the church and surrounding buildings throughout the church's existence. The middle block in the bottom row has the Lord's Prayer in German, the language of the worship service from 1852 until 1917. (TSLC.)

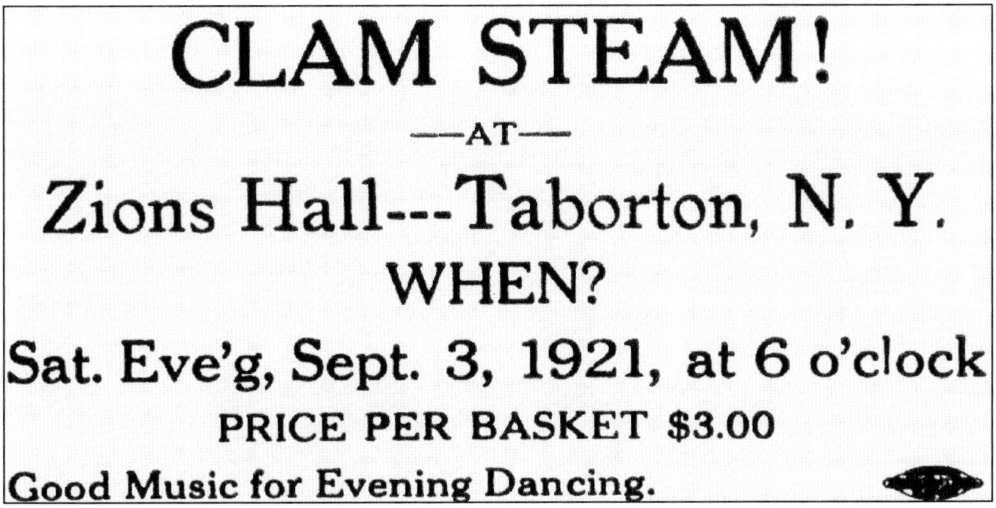
CLAM STEAM!

—AT—

Zions Hall---Taborton, N. Y.

WHEN?

Sat. Eve'g, Sept. 3, 1921, at 6 o'clock

PRICE PER BASKET $3.00

Good Music for Evening Dancing.

TABORTON CLAM STEAM. This September 3, 1921, ticket is for a clam steam would have been held in the new church hall, which was completed in 1921. The upper story afforded a place to dance and would become very popular for dancing over the ensuing years. (BB.)

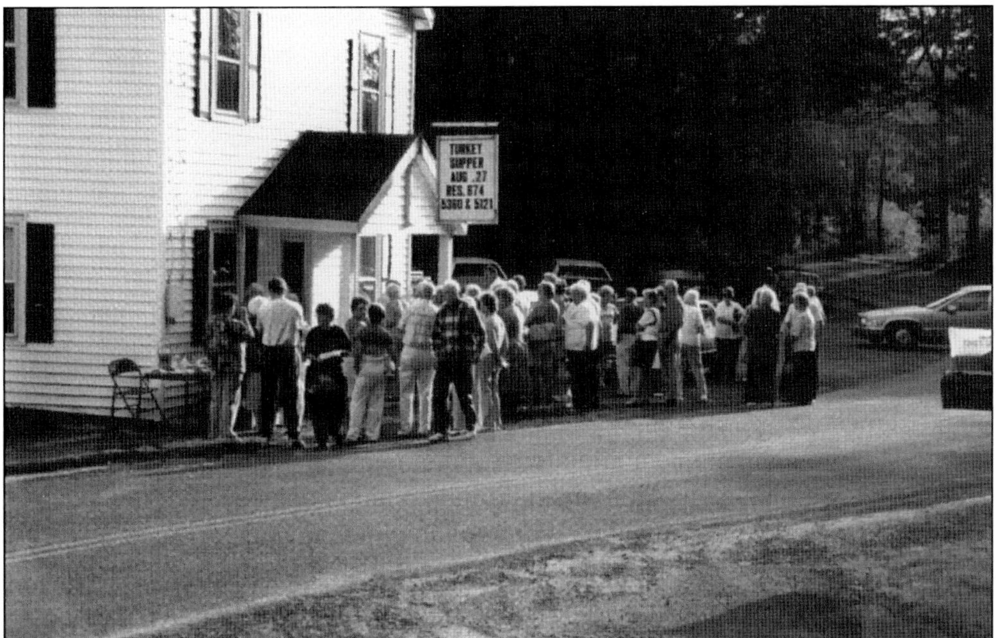

TURKEY SUPPER. The crowd has gathered outside the church hall at Zion's United Church of Christ of Taborton for the next seating of the turkey dinner in August 1994. This popular event draws over 100 people for two full sittings and a partial third sitting. Menu favorites besides the roasted turkey were the homemade dressing and pies. People now wait in the renovated horse sheds, which have been moved back from the road. (TSLC.)

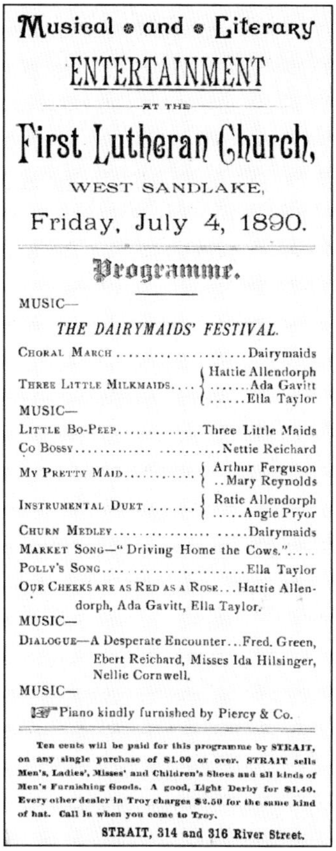

Musical and Literary
ENTERTAINMENT
AT THE
First Lutheran Church,
WEST SANDLAKE,
Friday, July 4, 1890.

Programme.

MUSIC—

THE DAIRYMAIDS' FESTIVAL.

Choral March .... Dairymaids
Three Little Milkmaids .... Hattie Allendorph .... Ada Gavitt ...... Ella Taylor
MUSIC—
Little Bo-Peep .... Three Little Maids
Co Bossy .... Nettie Reichard
My Pretty Maid .... Arthur Ferguson .. Mary Reynolds
Instrumental Duet .... Ratie Allendorph ..... Angie Pryor
Churn Medley ....Dairymaids
Market Song—"Driving Home the Cows." .....
Polly's Song .... Ella Taylor
Our Cheeks are as Red as a Rose ... Hattie Allendorph, Ada Gavitt, Ella Taylor.
MUSIC—
Dialogue—A Desperate Encounter ... Fred. Green, Ebert Reichard, Misses Ida Hilsinger, Nellie Cornwell.
MUSIC—

☞ Piano kindly furnished by Piercy & Co.

Ten cents will be paid for this programme by STRAIT, on any single purchase of $1.00 or over. STRAIT sells Men's, Ladies', Misses' and Children's Shoes and all kinds of Men's Furnishing Goods. A good, Light Derby for $1.40. Every other dealer in Troy charges $2.50 for the same kind of hat. Call in when you come to Troy.

STRAIT, 314 and 316 River Street.

DAIRYMAIDS' FESTIVAL. This July 4, 1890, entertainment at the First Lutheran Church of West Sand Lake capitalized on the Dairymaids' theme. (aG.)

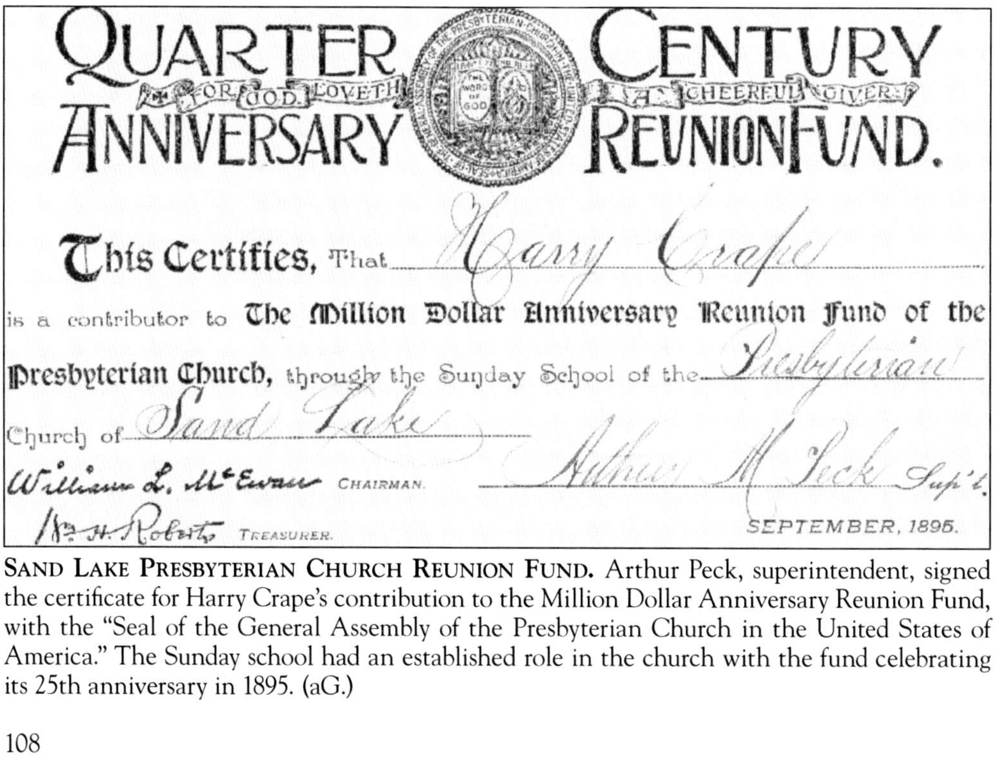

QUARTER CENTURY
FOR GOD LOVETH A CHEERFUL GIVER.
ANNIVERSARY REUNION FUND.

This Certifies, That Harry Crape
is a contributor to The Million Dollar Anniversary Reunion Fund of the Presbyterian Church, through the Sunday School of the Presbyterian Church of Sand Lake

William L. McEwan CHAIRMAN. Arthur M Peck Sup't.
Wm. H. Roberts TREASURER. SEPTEMBER, 1895.

SAND LAKE PRESBYTERIAN CHURCH REUNION FUND. Arthur Peck, superintendent, signed the certificate for Harry Crape's contribution to the Million Dollar Anniversary Reunion Fund, with the "Seal of the General Assembly of the Presbyterian Church in the United States of America." The Sunday school had an established role in the church with the fund celebrating its 25th anniversary in 1895. (aG.)

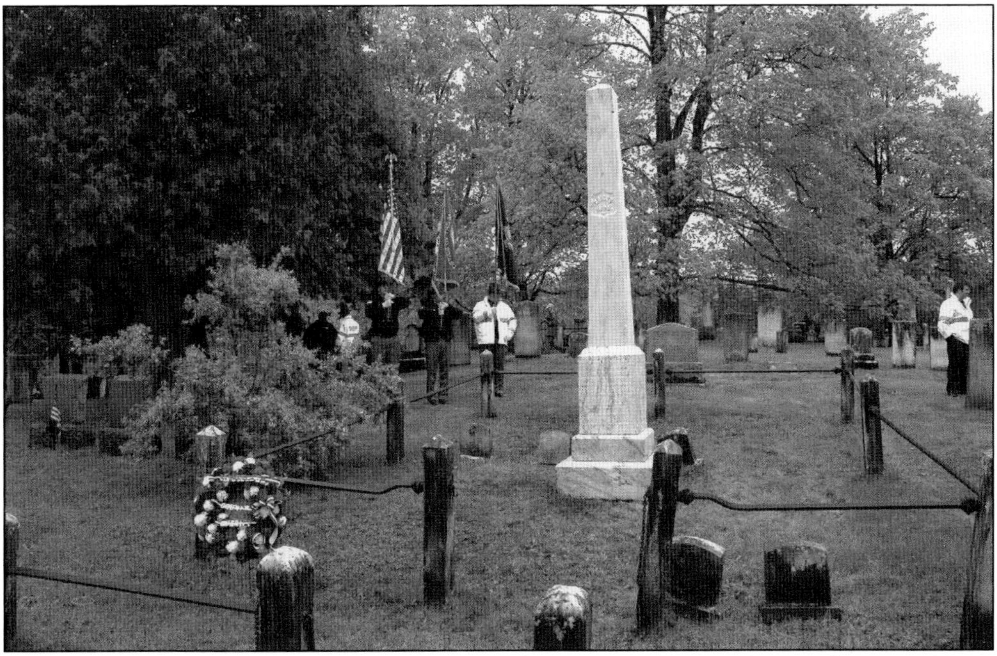

Willard Griggs Honored. "Lawman Honored 137 Years after Death" was the *Times Union* headline for the memorial service in Sand Lake Union Cemetery on May 19, 2006, at the grave of 19th-century deputy sheriff Willard Griggs. He was killed in the line of duty on July 31, 1869, when he went to evict William Witbeck from his farm for nonpayment of rent. The Anti-Rent War had grown violent. Those tried for his death were acquitted (see *Sand Lake*, page 119). (SLHSC.)

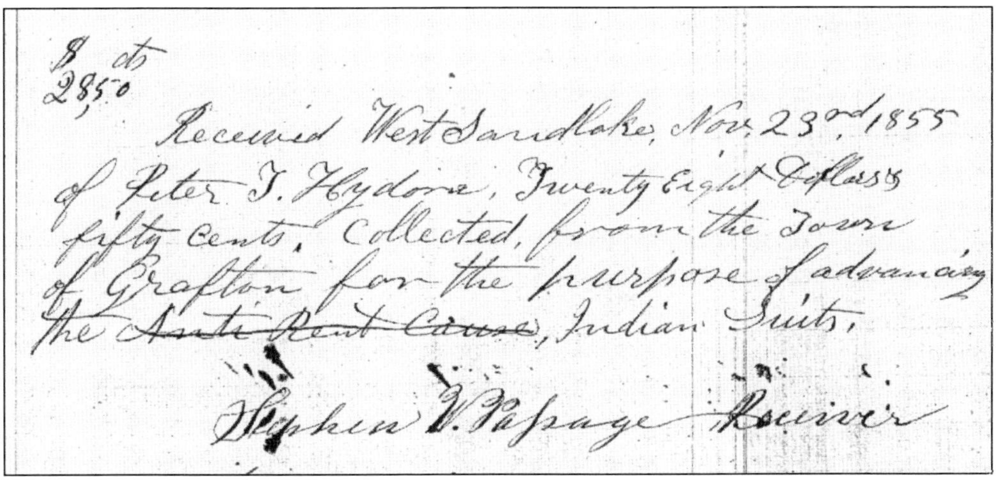

$ cts
28.50

Received West Sandlake, Nov. 23rd 1855
of Peter T. Hydorn, Twenty Eight dollars
fifty cents, collected from the Town
of Grafton for the purpose of advancing
the ~~Anti Rent Cause~~, Indian Suits,

Stephen W. Pepage Receiver

Anti-Rent Suits Receipt. The crossed out "Anti-Rent Cause" (see *Sand Lake*, page 119) in the receipt for "Indian Suits," gave credence of the efforts to disguise the identity of persons engaged in actions to keep the Van Rensselaer landlords on both sides of the Hudson River from collecting rent. (DC.)

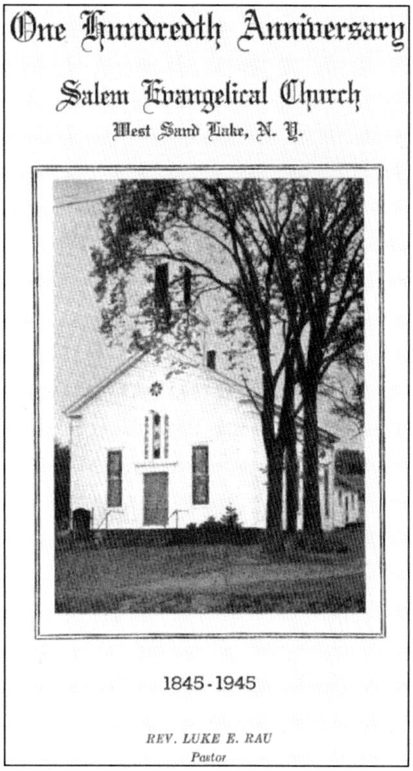

SALEM EVANGELICAL UNITED BRETHREN CHURCH 100TH ANNIVERSARY. In 1945, the Salem Evangelical United Brethren Church (the church's full name) celebrated its 100th anniversary. In 1968, the congregation merged with the West Sand Lake Methodist Church (see *Sand Lake*, pages 16 and 17). The new church became the Salem United Methodist Church. (TSLC.)

The Evangelical Youth Fellowship

In accordance with the plan drawn up by the General Board of Christian Education of the Evangelical Church, our young people's work is now merged into a new organization, "The Evangelical Youth Fellowship."

OFFICERS

Adult Counselor .... Mrs. Alfred Carner
President .... Mr. William Collen Jr.
Vice President .... Mr. Craig Kingsbury
Secretary .... Miss Elizabeth Harrington
Treasurer .... Miss Barbara Carner
Reporter .... Miss Norma Bailey
Chairman of Spiritual Life Commission .... Miss Phyllis Dixon
Chairman of Recreation Commission .... Mr. John Clark

★

CHURCH OFFICIARY

"Serve the Lord with all thy heart."

Bishop of the Eastern Epsicopal Area ....
Bishop J. S. Stamm, D.D., LL.D.
District Superintendent of N. Y. Conference .... Rev. M. E. Rickert
Minister .... Rev. L. E. Rau
Church Organist .... Mrs. Gladys Carner
Choir Director .... Mrs. William Smauder
Lay Member, Annual Conference (1945) .... Mrs. Clarence Bame
Trustees—
Mr. Clarence Bame, President — Mr. Warren King
Mr. Wilbur Bower, Rec. Sec. — Mr. Merrill Zweig
Mr. Christopher Van Gelder — *Mr. Clifford Kingbury
Stewards—
Mrs. Alfred Carner — Miss Sarah Werger
Mr. George Bame — Mrs. Warren King
Mrs. George Bame — Mr. Harold Harrington
*Mr. William Smauder
Church Treasurer .... Mr. George Bame
Recording Secretary .... Mrs. Clifford Kingsbury
Communion Steward .... Mrs. George Bame
Sexton .... Mr. George Bame

* Honorary Member.

— 12 —

SALEM EVANGELICAL UNITED BRETHREN OFFICERS. The inside of the 100th anniversary program gives the officers of the Evangelical Youth Fellowship and church officiary. (TSLC.)

Six

PEOPLE, PLACES, AND RESIDENCES

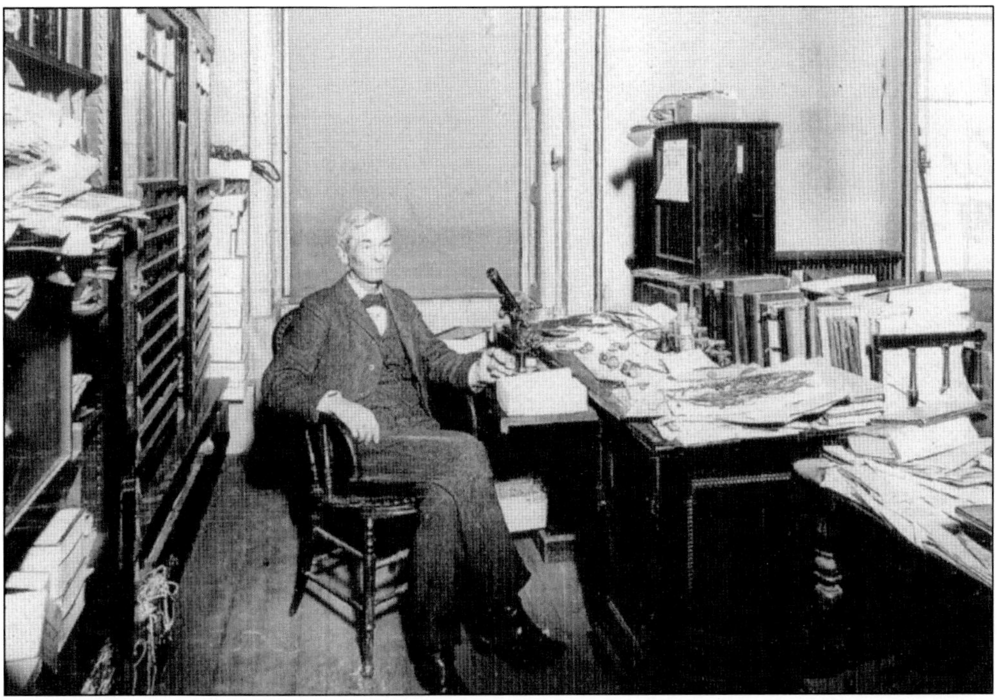

CHARLES PECK AT HIS MUSEUM OFFICE. Charles Peck, a brother of Arthur (see *Sand Lake*, page 110), was the first botanist at the New York State Museum, from 1868 to 1913. He never missed a chance to get more plant specimens. When his brother Marcus served in the Civil War, Charles's letter to him said, "As to moss gathering do your soldier duty first and dont [*sic*] bother with moss unless you have a convenient opportunity." (NSB, New York State Museum photograph.)

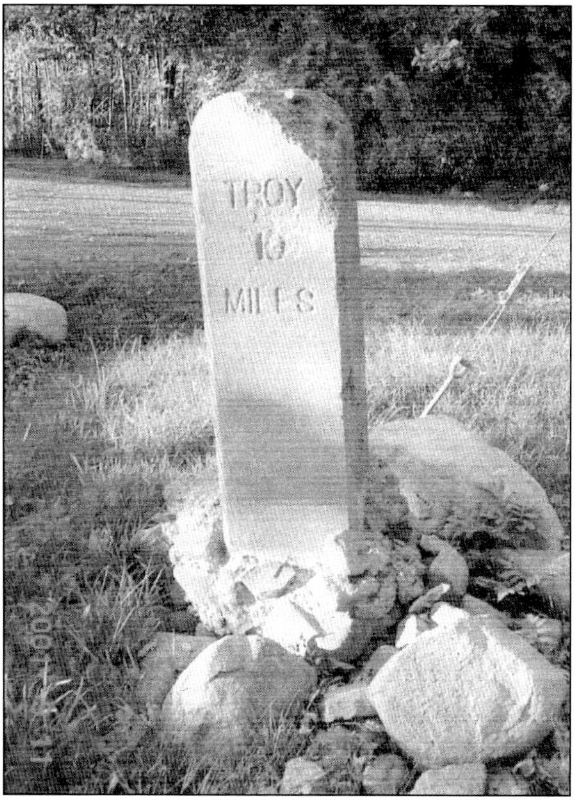

Mile Marker. When the mail stagecoach reached this point in the road near Crooked Lake House, the drivers knew it was 10 miles to Troy. (TSLC.)

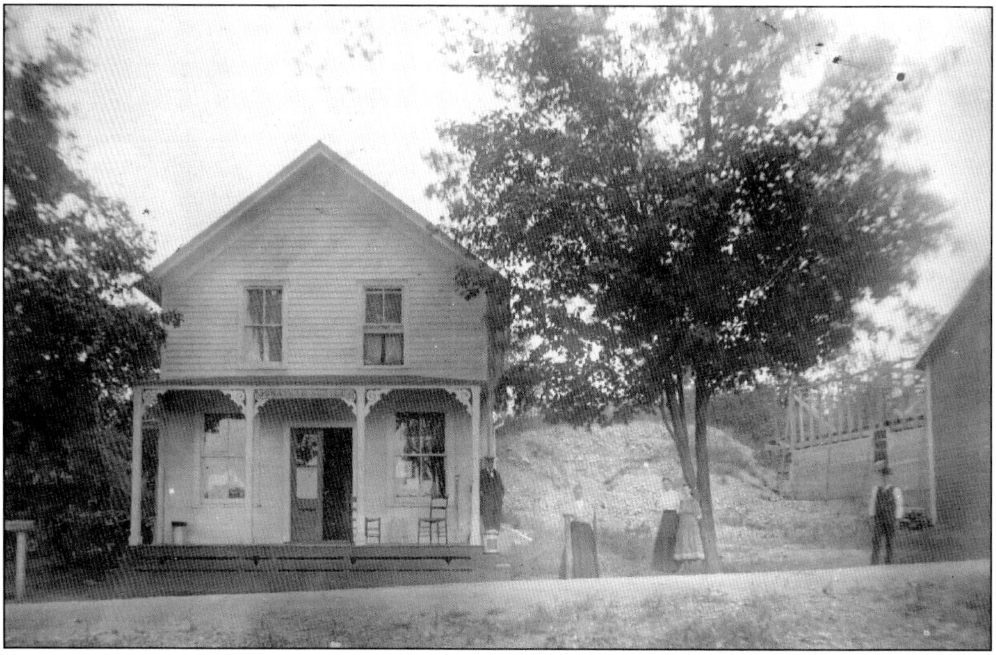

Huntley's Store. This store, converted to a house, was the home of Harriet and Earl Bailey. It is the first house on the left at the west end of Schumann Road and is now the home of Paul Murray. (DG.)

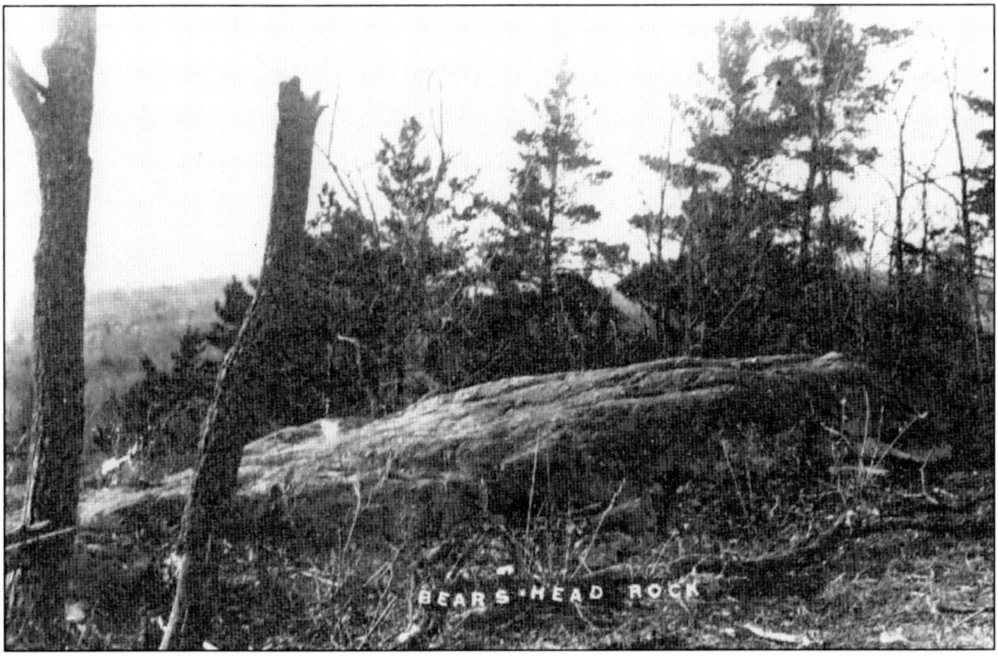

BEAR'S HEAD ROCK. From this vantage point, at a time when there was more clear land, Crooked, Glass, Crystal, Burden, and Reichard Lakes could be viewed. When he was vacationing at Crooked Lake and on a hunting trip, Gov. Theodore Roosevelt also went to Bear's Head. (AT.)

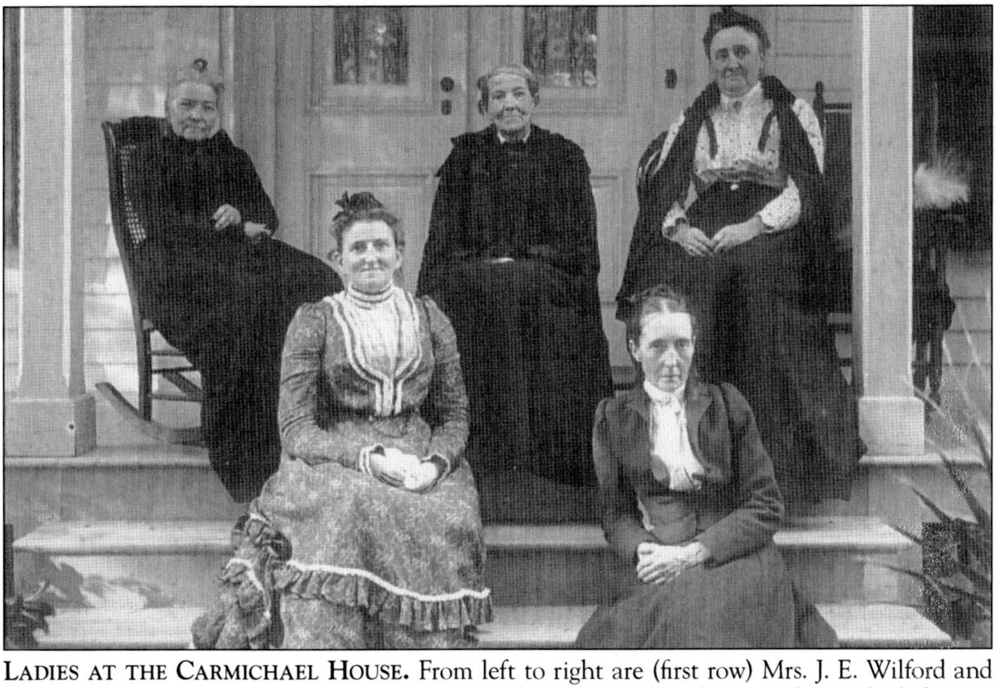

LADIES AT THE CARMICHAEL HOUSE. From left to right are (first row) Mrs. J. E. Wilford and Julia Lester; (second row) Mrs. D. W. Clark, Mrs. Philip Howard, and Mrs. Wiltsey. The ladies are visiting Lester at her home, often referred to as the Carmichael house. Lester was the daughter of Dr. Eber W. Carmichael, who was a member of the Rensselaer County Medical Association for many years. (TSLC.)

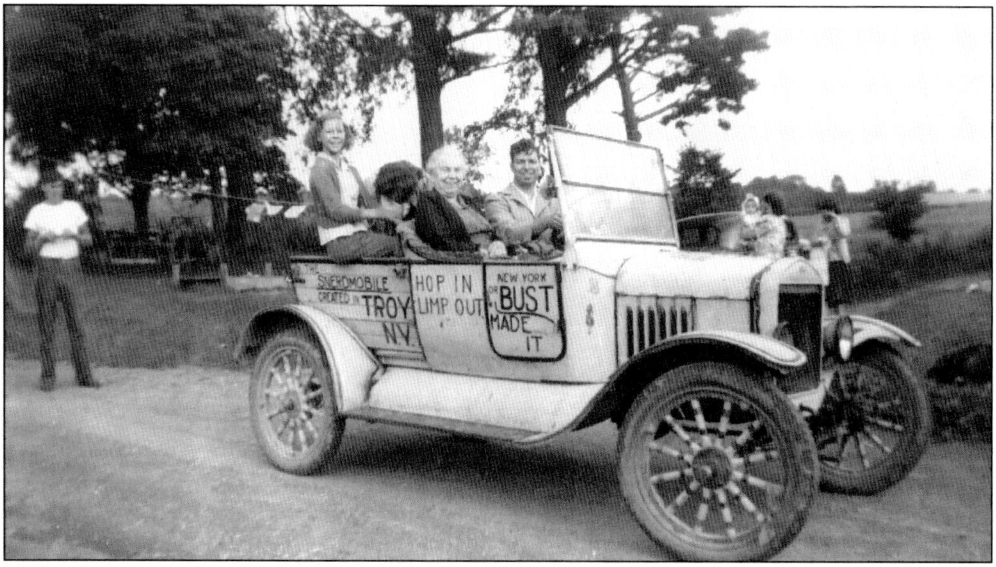

LELAND H. HILT'S FIRST CAR. On the left is 20-year-old Leland H. Hilt looking on as his father, Leland S. Hilt, takes Aunt Roxy Carey and Marilyn Bonesteel (seated on the back) for a ride in his son's first car of 1921 vintage. Hilt made it unique with his own decorations in this 1949 picture. (NHB.)

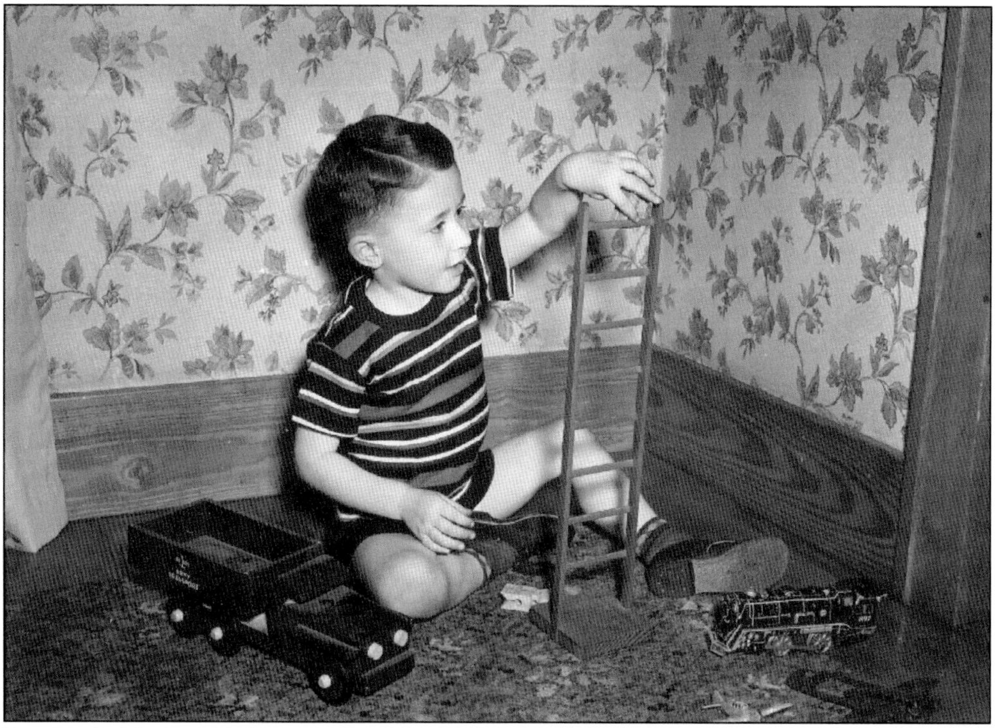

ROBERT I. MOORE. H. Irving Moore's son Robert was four years old in 1945. The wooden army truck says "Buddy L" and "Army Transport" on the side of its bed. Because of the war effort, metal was scarce and many toys were made from wood. Plastic had not come into general use yet. The metal train would have been prewar vintage. (RIM.)

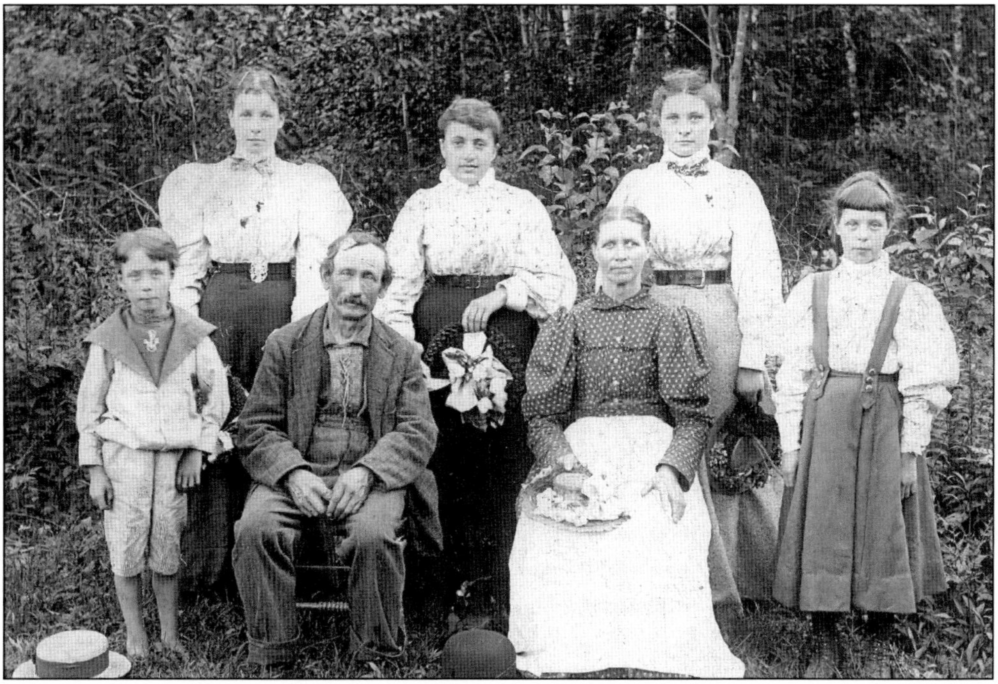

John Henry Meyers's Family, c. 1895. Seen here are, from left to right, (first row) August, father John Henry, mother Mary Elizabeth, and Emma; (second row) Louise, family friend Elizabeth Reinke, and Ann Meyers (see pages 76 and 77). Barbara Boughton, the great-great-granddaughter of John Henry and Mary Elizabeth, is now living in the Meyers home on the corner of Taborton and Lawson Roads. Her sons, Cole and August, began the sixth generation. (BB, Felix Willett photograph.)

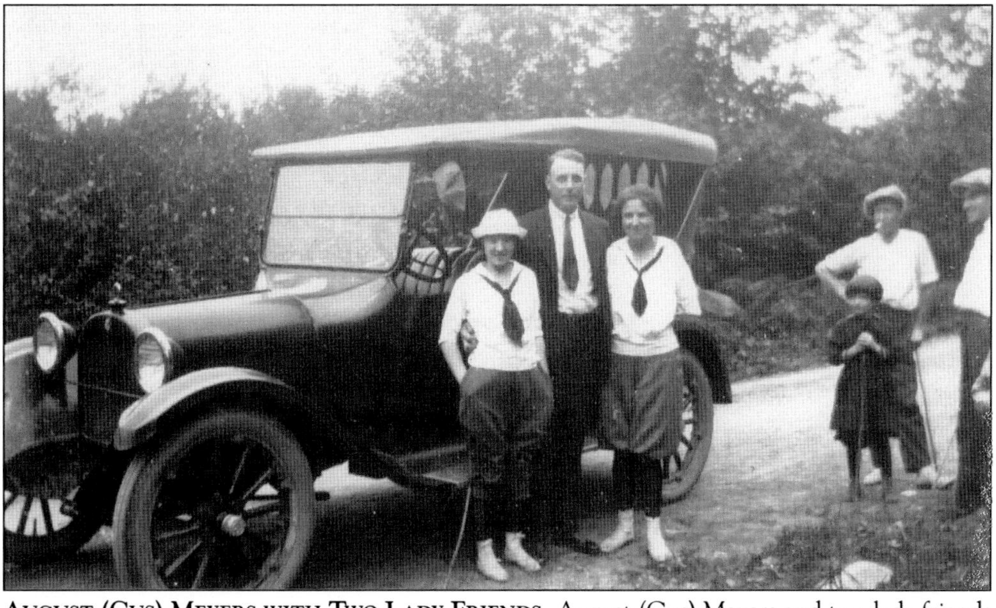

August (Gus) Meyers with Two Lady Friends. August (Gus) Meyers and two lady friends pose before taking a ride in Meyers's car, which appears to meet with the approval of the three persons looking on. Meyers lived his entire life on the Meyers homestead. (BB.)

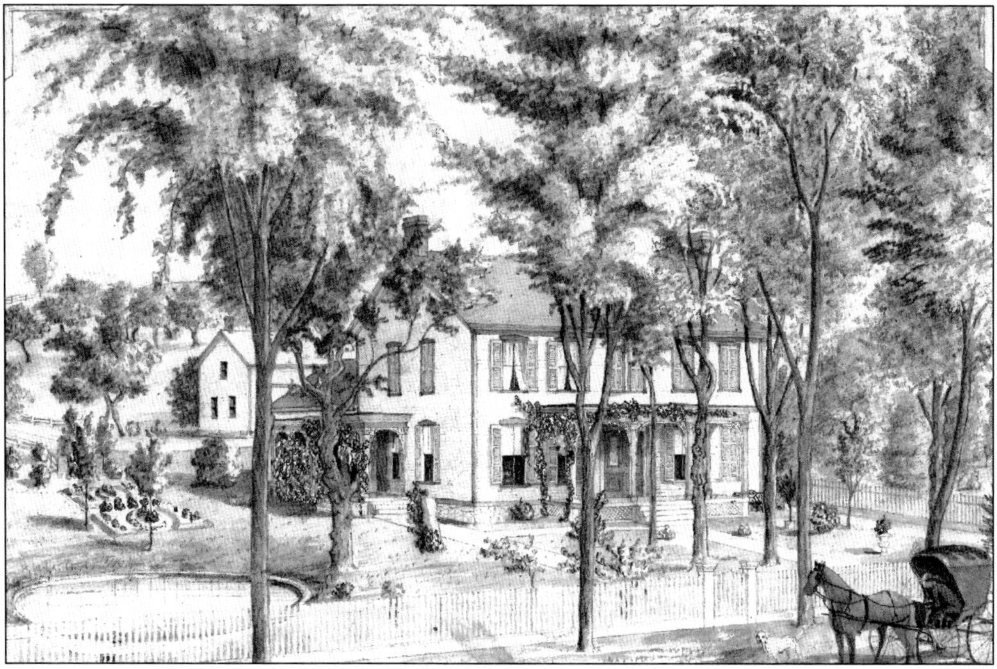

JOEL PECK HOUSE. This house of Joel Peck, father of Marcus, Charles, and Arthur, has been known as the Burroughs' house and the home of Helen Crape Guy. It is now the home of Dawn A. Vink. (NSB.)

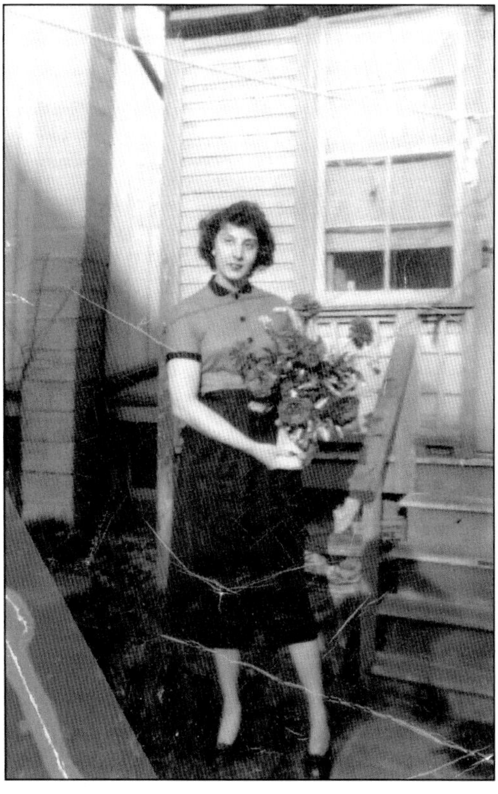

MARY HILT. Mary Hilt was the reporter for Sand Lake at the *Troy Record* for 30 years, from 1963 to 1993. She covered meetings, did feature articles, and had a humor column for the Sunday issue. Favorite stories are often recalled when Hilt's name is in the conversation. (NHB.)

HAROLD TIFFT. Harold Tifft was the first historian for the Town of Sand Lake, from 1954 until his death in 1959. In addition to his firearms collection, he collected postcards to illustrate the history of the town. (MSt.G, *Times Union* photograph.)

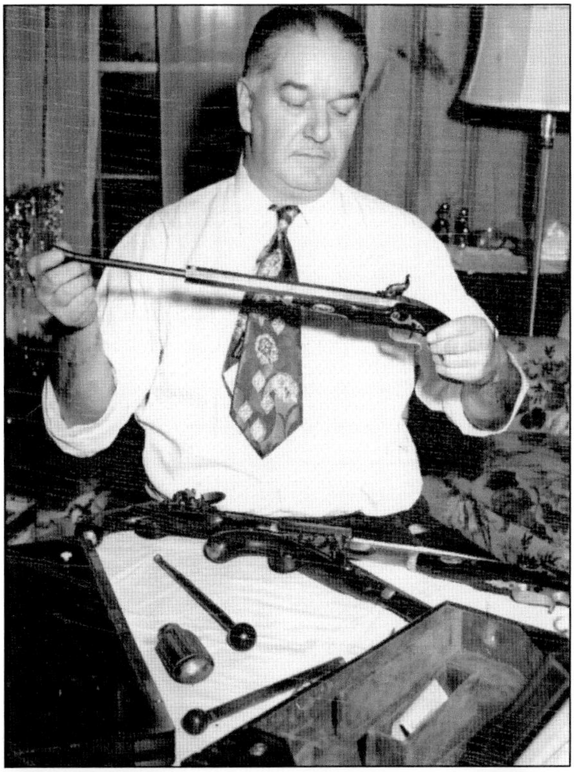

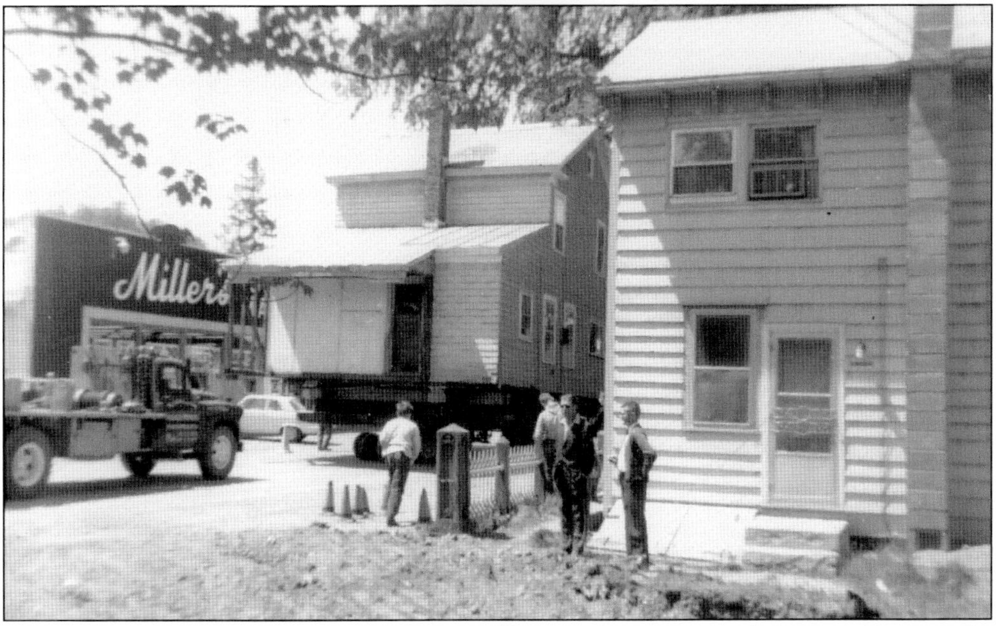

HOUSE BEING MOVED. This house next to Miller's Market was moved about 1965 across the road to space between the Second Evangelical Lutheran Church and Charles Werger's law office. All have since been razed. Another house, on the right of the old West Sand Lake Firehouse, was towed backward to the rear of Miller's parking lot on Firehouse Lane in 1975 to make room for the new firehouse. It is the home of Raymond Wheland. (MW.)

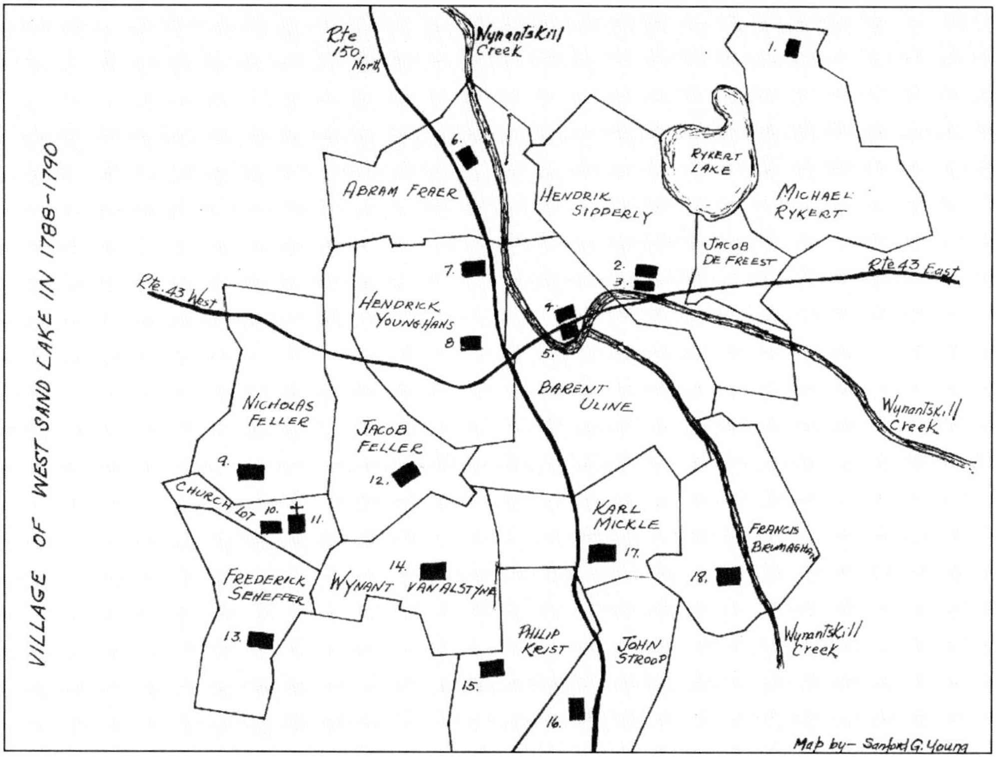

WEST SAND LAKE, 1788–1790. This map of West Sand Lake from 1788 to 1790 was done by Sanford G. Young from the John Van Alen Survey. For each area, Young included known information on the owner, members of the family, acreage, lease information, and the property owner in 1977. The booklet *Village of West Sand Lake 1788–1790* by Sanford Young was published posthumously by his friend Charles Viens. (SLHSC.)

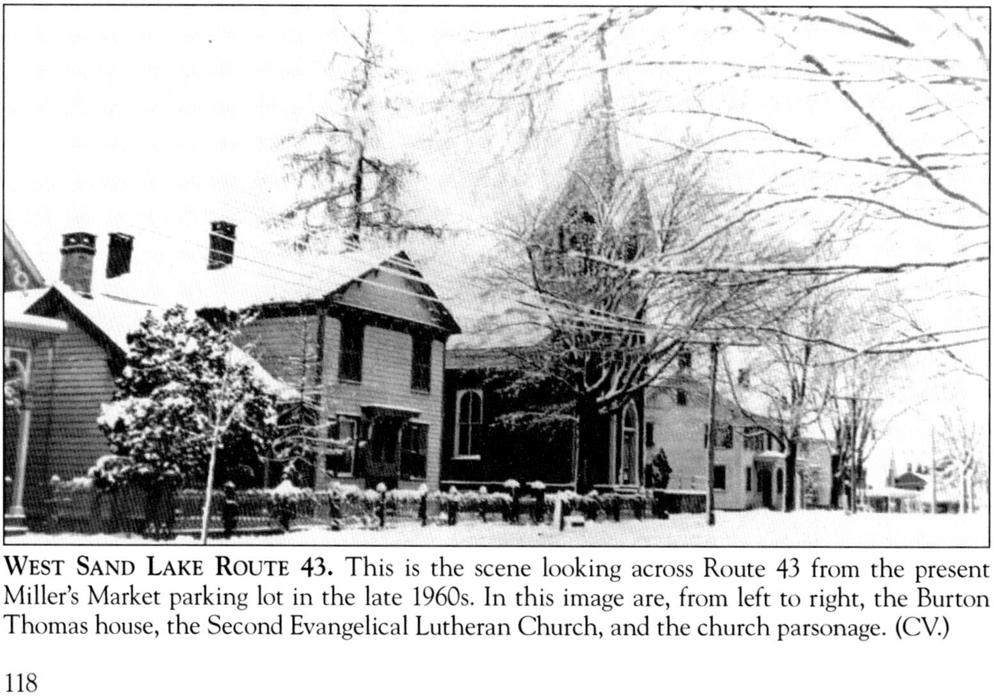

WEST SAND LAKE ROUTE 43. This is the scene looking across Route 43 from the present Miller's Market parking lot in the late 1960s. In this image are, from left to right, the Burton Thomas house, the Second Evangelical Lutheran Church, and the church parsonage. (CV.)

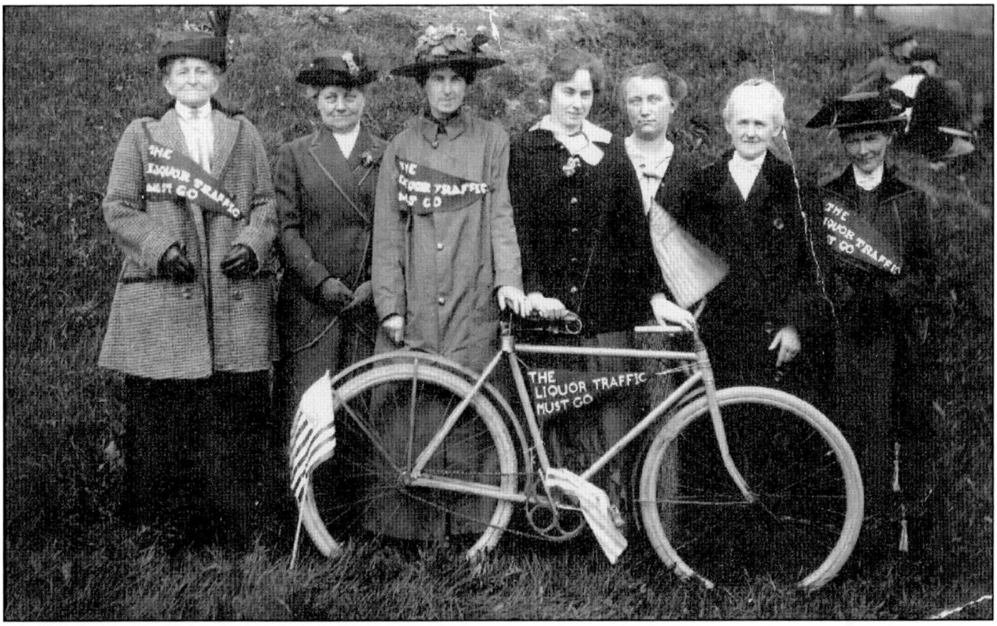

WIPE OUT LIQUOR. Among those identified are Mrs. Wilfarb, Miss Parsons, Mrs. Holser, Harriet Hayner, Annette Brown, and Mrs. "Mother Mother Brown" Hayner with their banners stating, "The liquor traffic must go." (TSLC.)

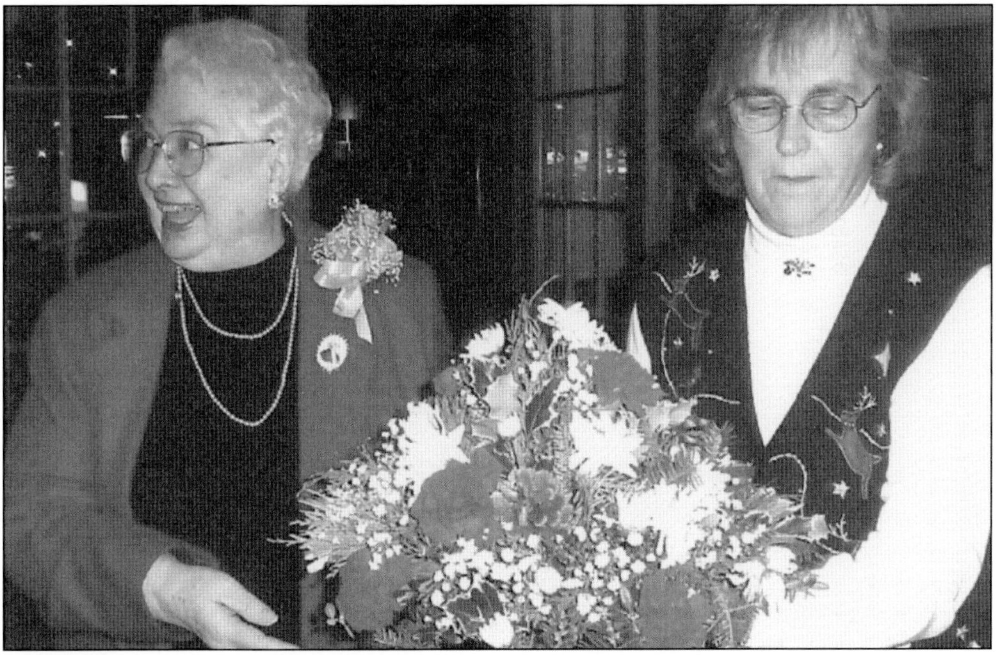

JUDY ROWE HONORED. In 2003, Bernice O'Neil (right), regent for the Daughters of the American Revolution, Fort Crailo Chapter, presented Judy Rowe with the National Society of the Daughters of the American Revolution Certificate Award for Women in American History for her years of service in historical research and genealogy. Since the position of Sand Lake town historian was created in 1975, Rowe was a continual source of assistance to the town historian and has held that position since 1998. (JR.)

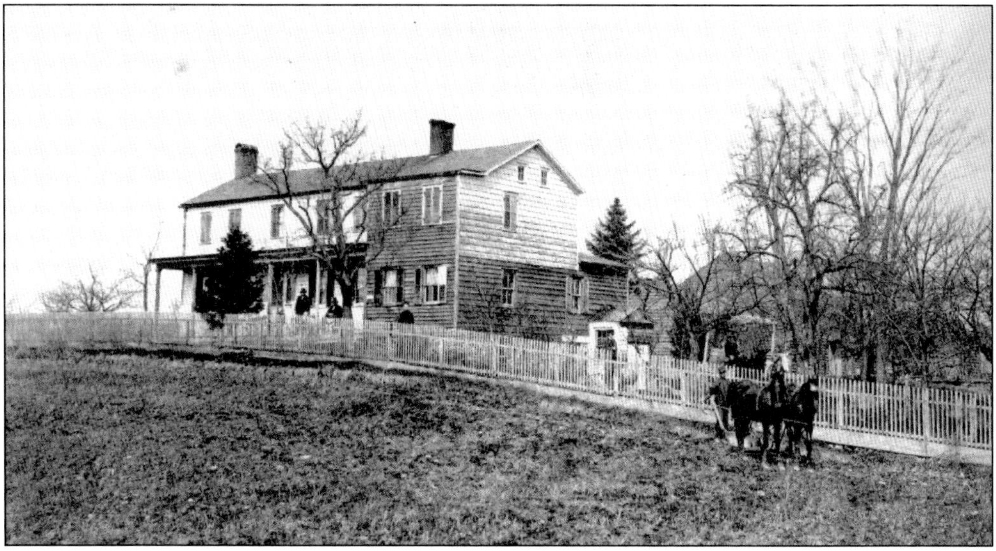

FARMHOUSE AT THE END OF SNYDER ROAD. This farmhouse was built in the 1790s and had several owners. When Kimball Sprague bought it in 1941, the deed included specific items for operating the farm along with "some 40,000 gladiolus bulbs." John Sprague Sr. lived in the house from 1975 until the early 1990s. After an electrical fire in 1979, restoration of the house revealed it had had several major additions in different eras. (TSLC.)

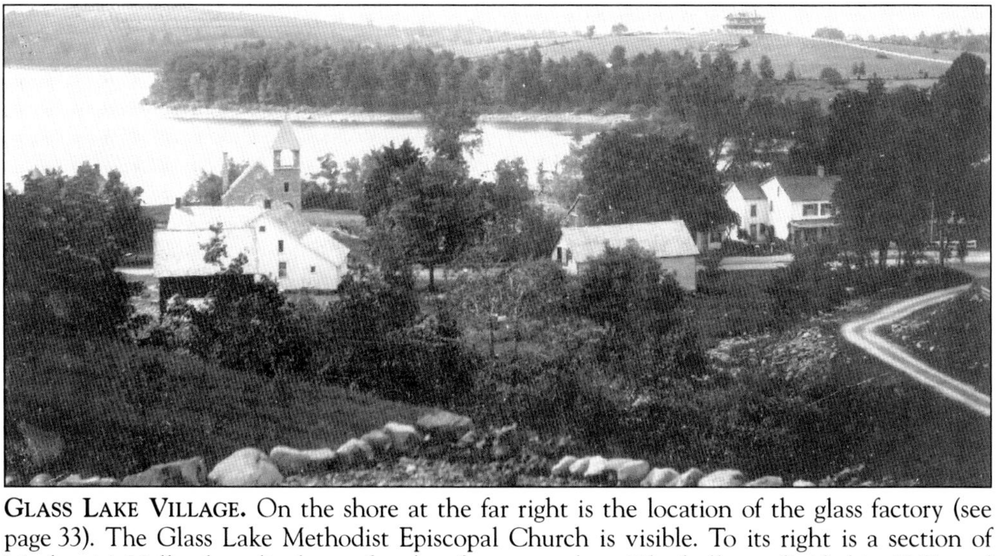

GLASS LAKE VILLAGE. On the shore at the far right is the location of the glass factory (see page 33). The Glass Lake Methodist Episcopal Church is visible. To its right is a section of Mechanic's Hall, a boardinghouse for glass factory workers. The hall was divided in 1866, and the second section became the Glass Lake Hotel. (JC.)

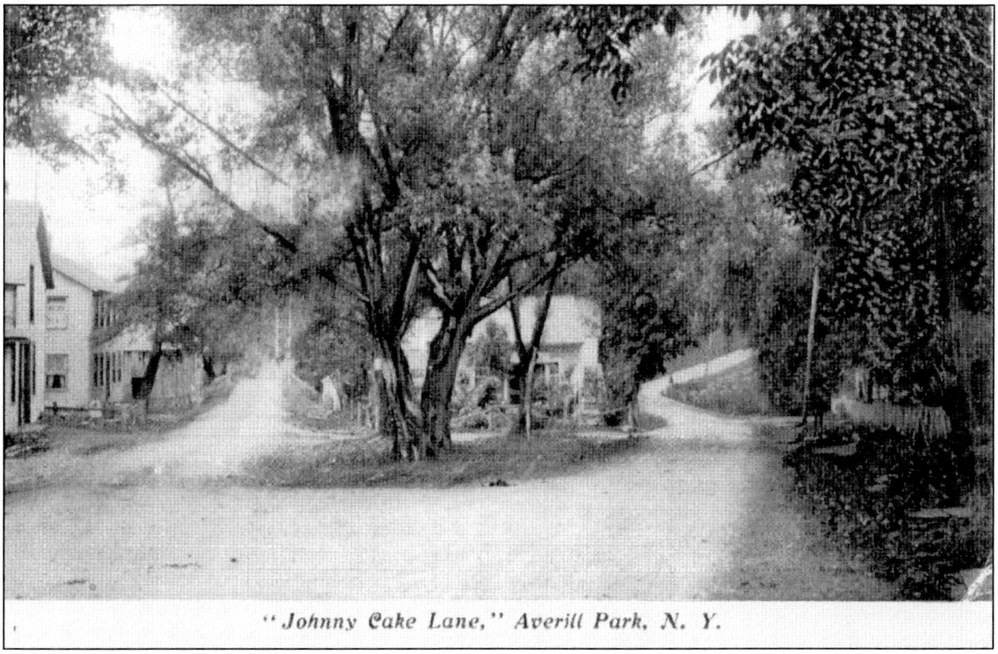

JOHNNYCAKE LANE. The building seen at the junction of Johnnycake Lane on the right and Eastern Union Turnpike on the left later became the location of a new building for the offices of Dr. John Reid from 1954 until 1986 (see page 88) and Dr. John Dunn from 1949 until 1987 (see page 77). (LH.)

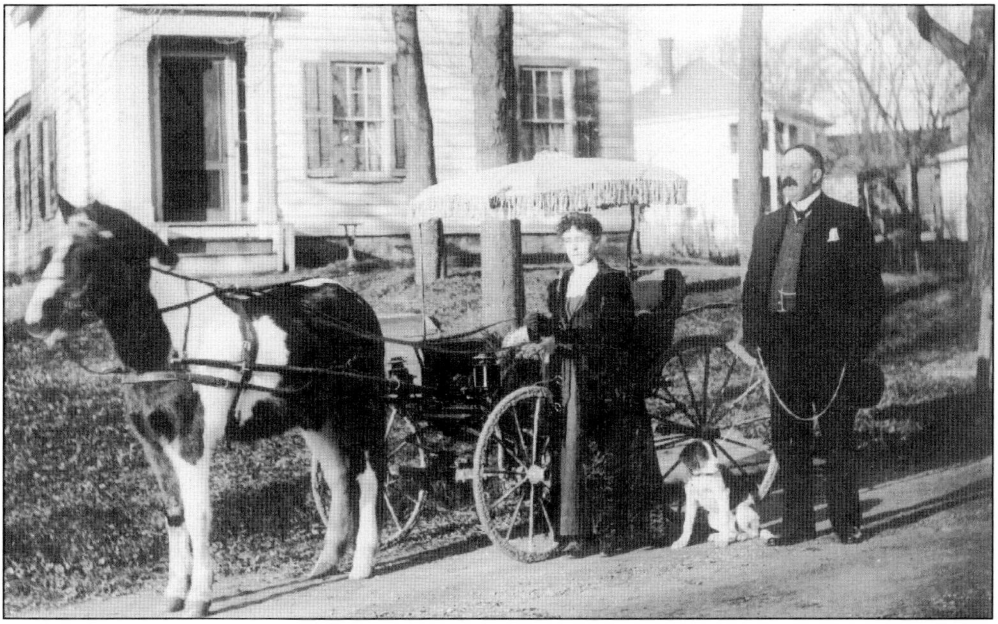

TAYLORS ON JOHNNYCAKE LANE. Cora and John Taylor, about to take a ride in their "surrey with the fringe on top," stand in front of their house on Johnnycake Lane, the third house on the right from the corner. In the background is the former Methodist parsonage. The Taylors' house is now owned by the Jason Grignon family, and the Methodist parsonage by Georgina Raus. (TSLC.)

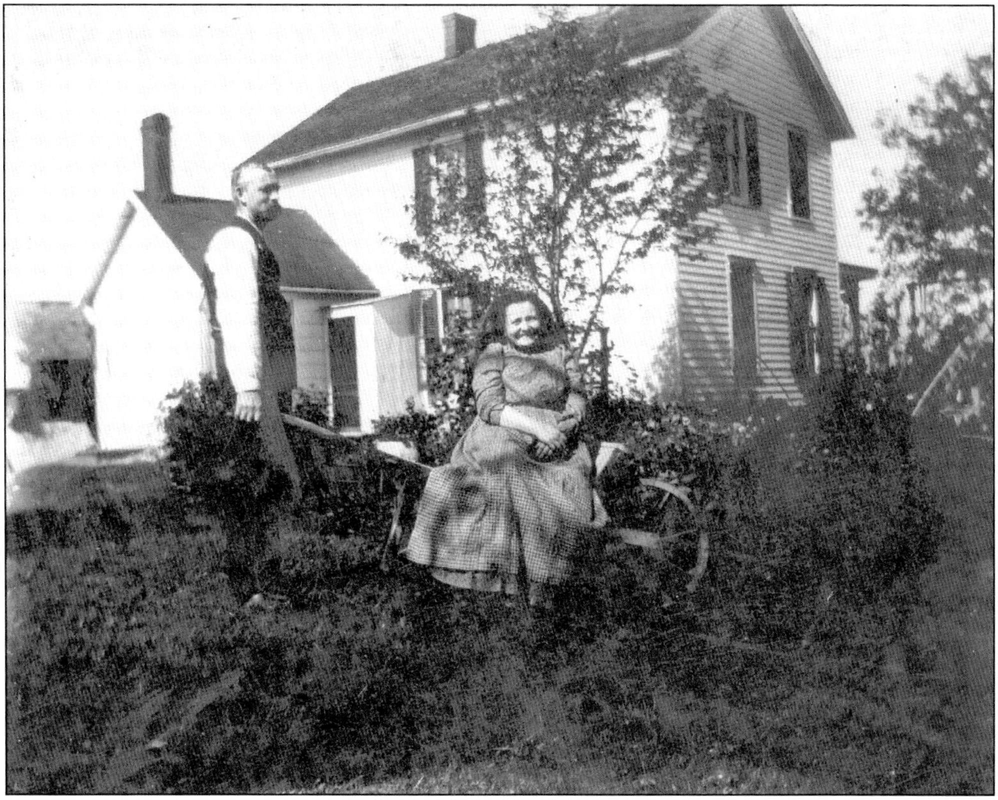

Gilbert Beebe's Home. Gilbert and Julia Wilkinson Beebe are in the backyard of their home on Johnnycake Lane. Gilbert had a blacksmith shop at this location (see *Sand Lake*, page 47). (TSLC.)

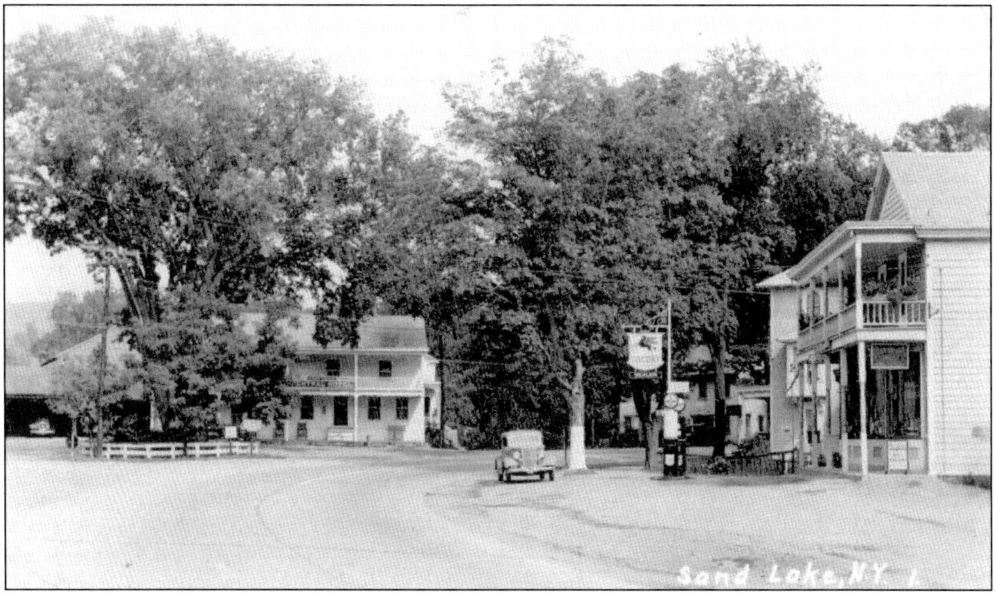

Sand Lake Corners. When the new state road was completed, the post office was relocated back from the corners for the expanded pavement. Gas pumps are now an added service. (SLHSC.)

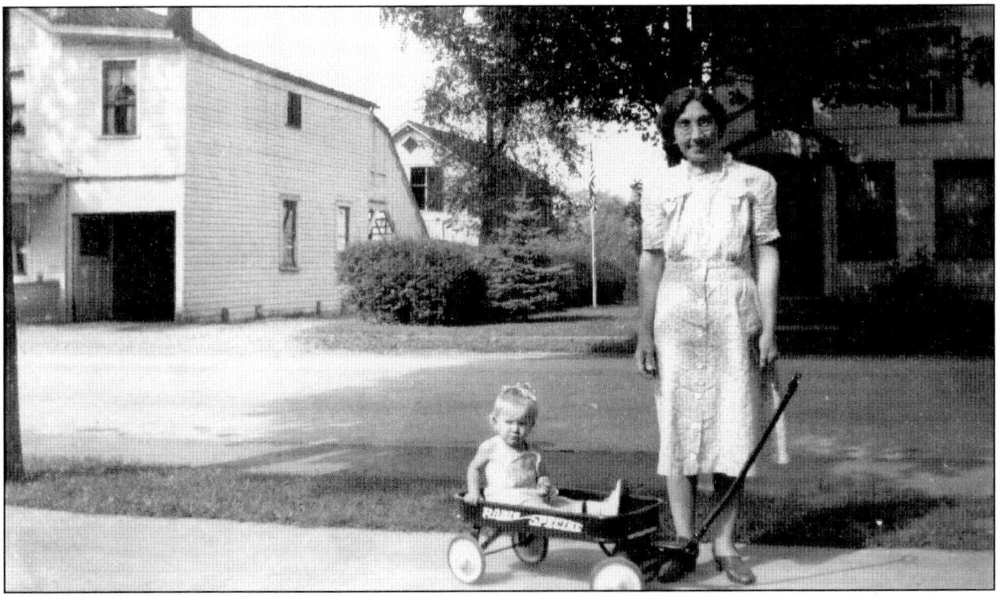

Josephine (Phenie) Lerch and Barbara Lerch. Barbara Lerch is getting a ride in her wagon from mother, Josephine (Phenie) Lerch (see page 11), on the sidewalk in front of the DeGraff residence in 1948. The West Sand Lake school yard is behind the properties. (BLT.)

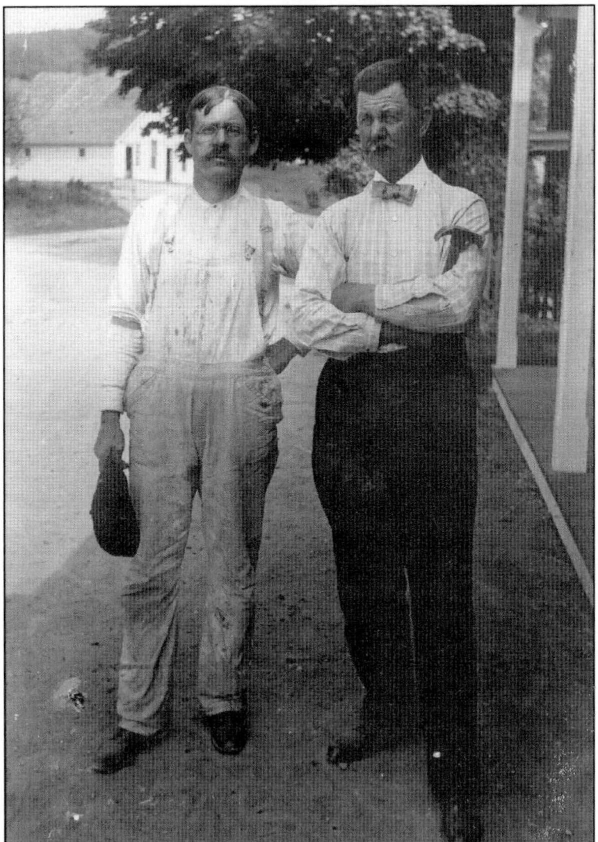

Charles McClellan and Steve Keeler at Glass Lake. Charles McClellan (right) was a conductor on the Troy and New England Railway. He also was the diver who verified there was a dugout canoe in Glass Lake. Diving again, he fastened a chain around it, and it was dragged to shore and was subsequently given to the New York State Museum, Albany (see *Sand Lake*, page 90). (A&WM.)

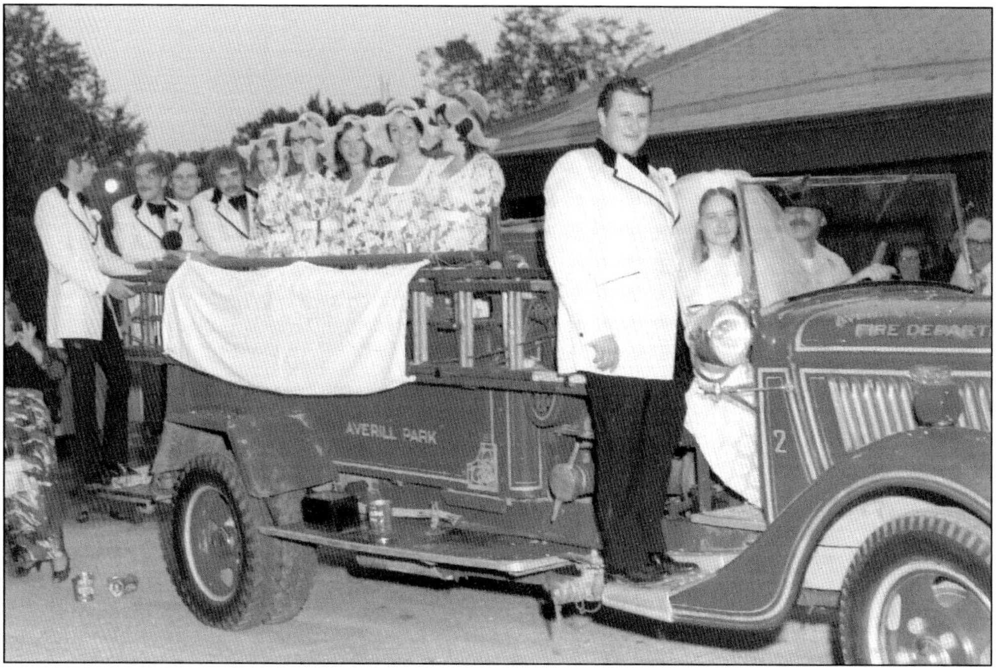

NEITZEL AND WAGNER WEDDING. On July 15, 1972, Brooke Neitzel Wagner and Robert Wagner were surprised to have a retired fire engine ready to transport them to their wedding reception. Seen here are, from left to right, (front seat) Robert Wagner, Brooke Wagner, and driver Arthur Ferguson; (back row) David Barnum, Barth Neitzel, Hal Shoemaker, Peter Neitzel, Samuel Samuels, Donna Samuels, Patricia Shoemaker, Susan Dansereau, Judy Neitzel, and Lena Barnum. (RW, *Troy Record* photograph.)

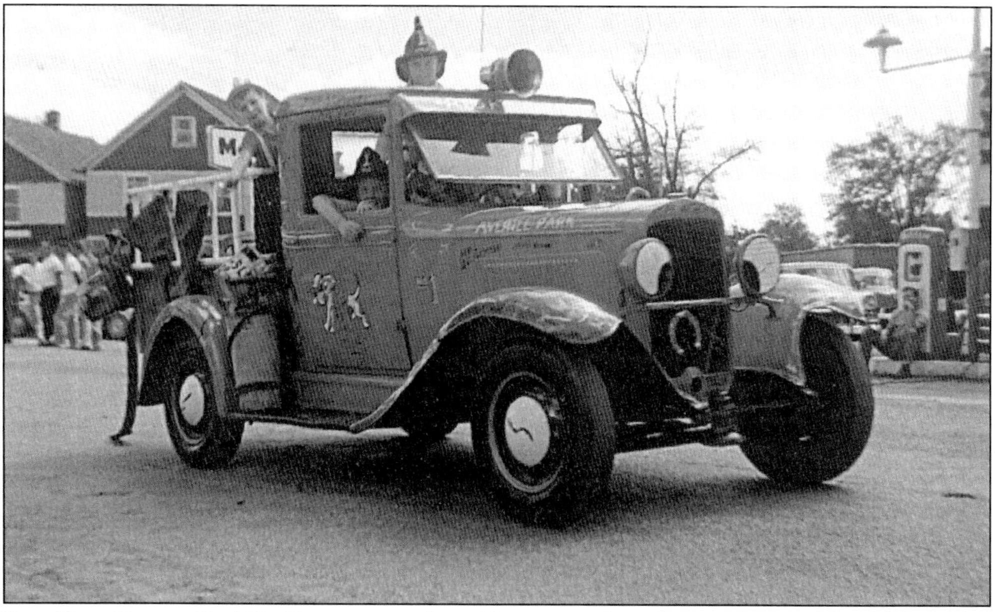

FUN FIRE TRUCK. Paul St. Germain got this old town truck and painted it up to look like a "fun fire truck" with the mascot dog on the side door and cross-eyed headlights for the Averill Park and Sand Lake Fire Company field day in 1957. (MSt.G.)

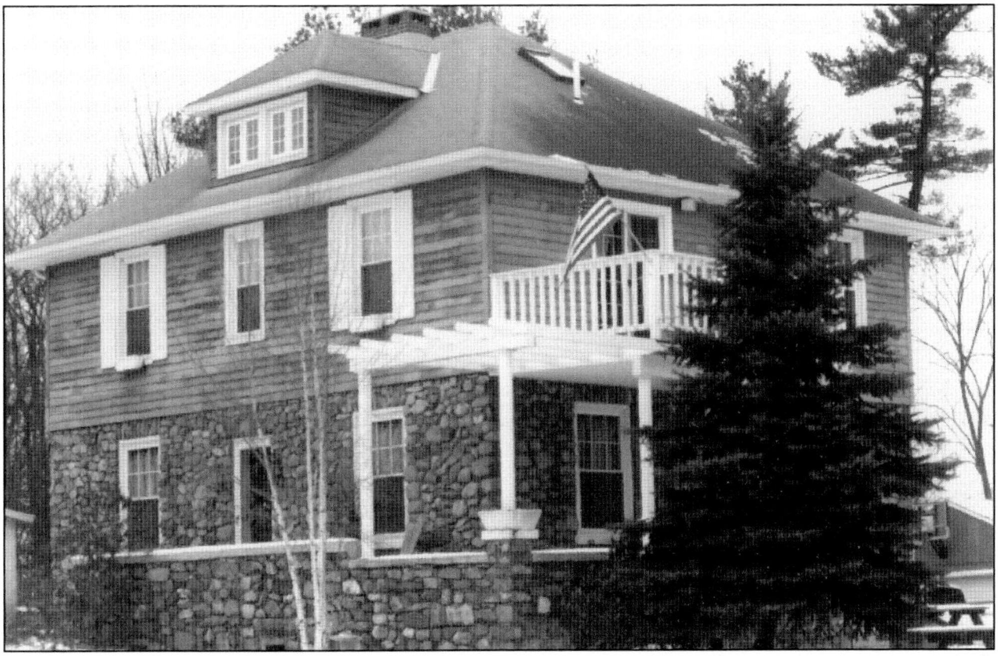

JACK "LEGS" DIAMOND'S "UNSAFE HOUSE." In the early 1930s, the notorious gangster Jack "Legs" Diamond used this house at the corner of Old Route 66 and Lake Avenue as a safe house. Law enforcement officers discovered this fact and conducted a raid. Bullet holes in a wall are evidence of activities in the house. (SLHSC.)

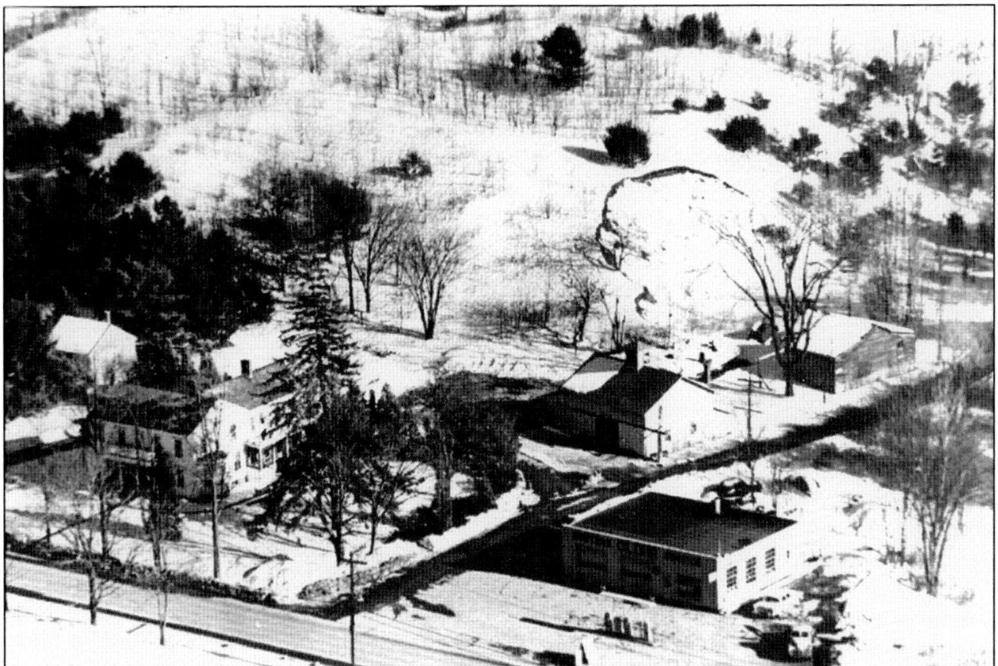

ROUTE 43 AND SPRINGER ROAD. This aerial view shows Foster's Garage, now the Sand Lake Ambulance building (see pages 38 and 89), in the lower right on the corner of Route 43 and Springer Road. The snow outlines the excavated gravel sites. (JB.)

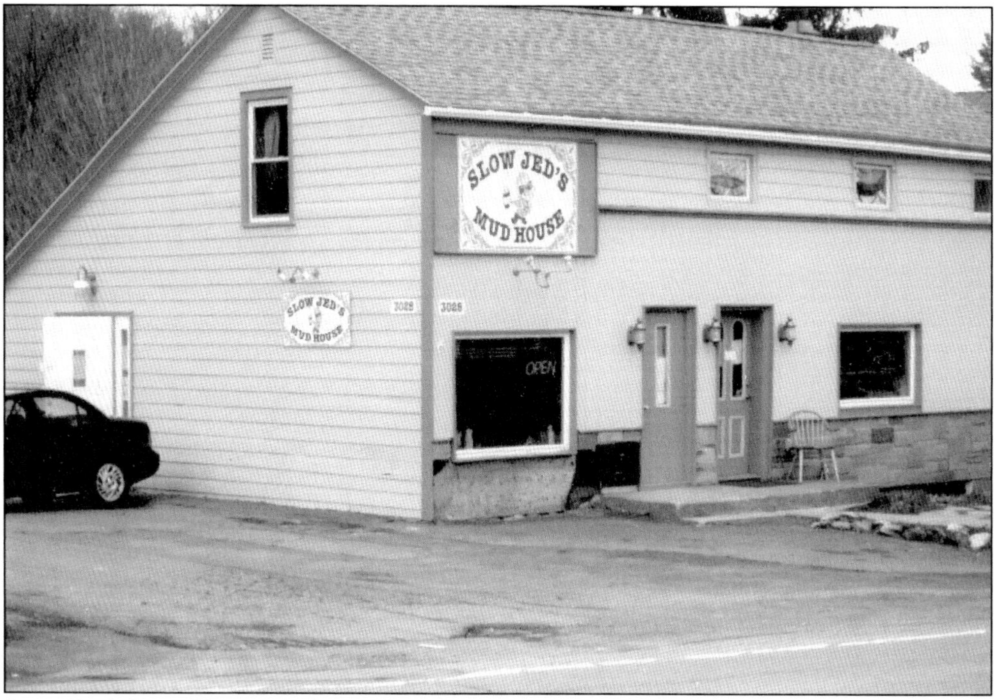

SLOW JED'S MUD HOUSE. Debra and Andy Dorr and Kristen Keough have restored the former O'Donnell's, and later Marty Ormsby's, liquor store and have opened it as Slow Jed's Mud House. The vegetarian coffeehouse serves light fare, pastries, and desserts. It has a lending library, a gallery for artist displays, and a stage to hold a three-piece band or for someone to do a reading. (SLHSC.)

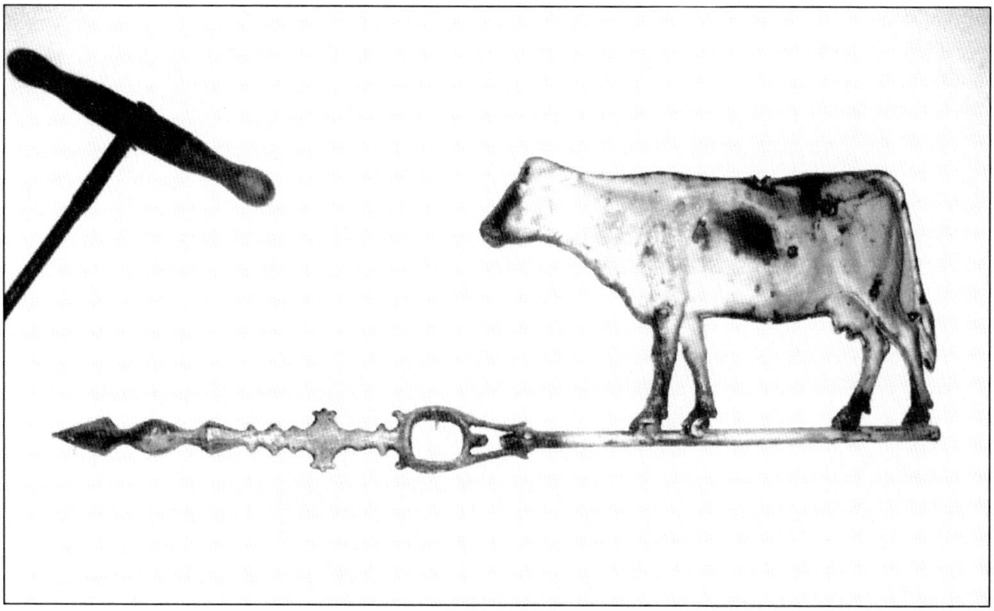

WEATHER VANE ON CARL BECK'S BARN. This weather vane was atop the barn (located behind the old firehouse) where Carl Beck used to make baskets for his floral business. The handle of an auger made its appearance in this photograph. (BVB.)

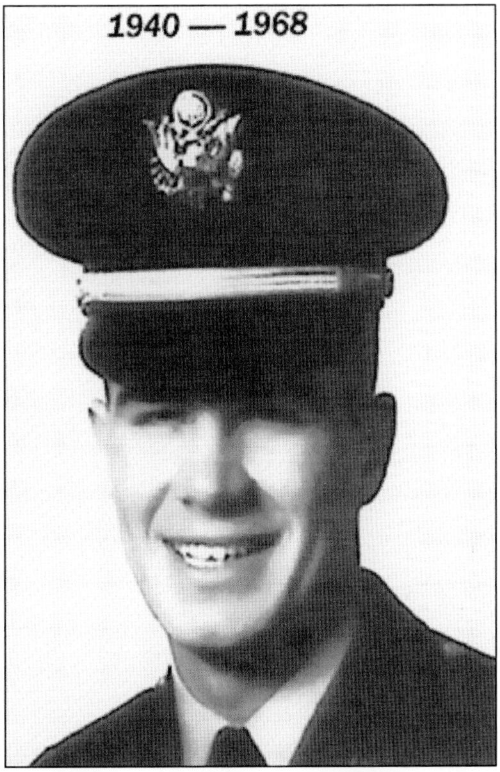

MAJ. GEORGE QUAMO. Public Law 109-311 was enacted on October 6, 2006, to honor Maj. George Quamo, a 1958 graduate of Averill Park High School. The law designated the United States Postal Service facility in Averill Park as the Major George Quamo Post Office. He was a member of the Special Forces Unit MACV SOG in the Vietnam War and was the recipient of at least 26 medals, including the Distinguished Service Cross. His actions saved the lives of 14 of his men. (ERC.)

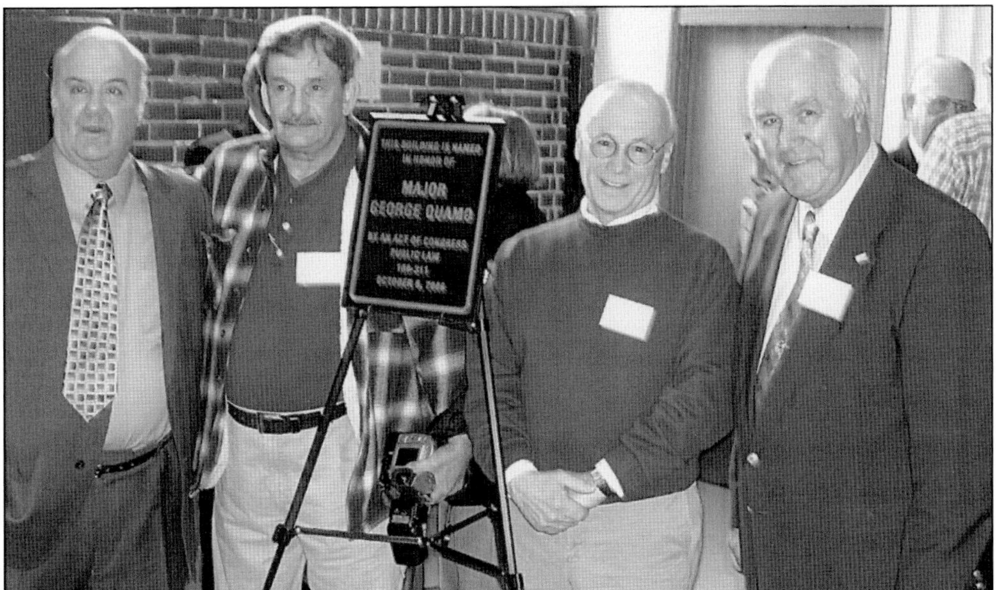

POST OFFICE PLAQUE FOR MAJ. GEORGE QUAMO. Seen here are, from left to right, James Quamo, Maj. George Quamo's brother, and members of the dedication committee, Fred Shoemaker, David Mardon, and E. Richard Castle, at the ceremony on April 14, 2007, designating the Averill Park Post Office in honor of Maj. George Quamo. Quamo was killed in a helicopter crash in 1968. At 27, he was the youngest major ever to have served in the Special Forces Unit. (SLHSC.)